Carni

MW01708630

November 23, 2016

I am honoured to be in your classes Veronica. Thank you for two great terms.

Deniz Başar

European University Studies
Europäische Hochschulschriften
Publications Universitaires Européennes

**Series XVIII**
**Comparative Literature**

Reihe XVIII Série XVIII
Vergleichende Literaturwissenschaft
Littérature comparée

**Vol./Bd. 133**

PETER LANG
Frankfurt am Main · Berlin · Bern · Bruxelles · New York · Oxford · Wien

Meltem Gürle

# Carnivalizing the Turkish novel

## Oğuz Atay's dialogue with the canon in *The Disconnected*

PETER LANG
Internationaler Verlag der Wissenschaften

**Bibliographic Information published by the Deutsche Nationalbibliothek**
The Deutsche Nationalbibliothek lists this publication in the Deutsche Nationalbibliografie; detailed bibliographic data is available in the internet at http://dnb.d-nb.de.

ISSN 0721-3425
ISBN 978-3-631-63459-2



www.peterlang.de

*to the loving memory of my mother…*

# CONTENTS

# INTRODUCTION

One of the reasons that make *The Disconnected*, Oğuz Atay's first and most influential novel, worth discussing is its vivid depiction of Turkey in the 70s. Atay's novel did what Tanpınar's *The Time Regulation Institute*[1] had done in the 1960s, and Uyurkulak's *Har*[2] was going to do in the 2000s: a tongue-in-cheek criticism of Turkey's project of modernization. However, when viewed from a broader perspective, it is also possible to place the novel in line with other modernist authors posing a question of cultural identity, a quality already observed by Ertuğrul: "As in the works of Joyce and Dostoyevsky, the question of cultural identity and cultural difference is brought about and marked by a certain relation of belatedness vis-á-vis Western modernity and opens up the question of the limits of the modern project as such" (629-30).

Turkey's modernization project is grounded in the bourgeois idea of modernity, which is characterized by a doctrine of progress based on the cult of reason, an ideal of freedom defined within the framework of an abstract humanism, and an orientation towards pragmatism (Calinescu 45). At the heart of this project also lies the twofold assumption that the country could become Western and national at the same time. Having its points of departure in rationality, the hallmark of the West, Turkey's modernization project envisions a unified nation on its way of gradual progress toward a better future.[3] It is in this homogenizing attitude that we find indications of the totalizing effect of this project. The problem with the modernist project in Turkey is that regulating rationality itself becomes a totality, and tends to "normalize" differences.

This is one of the reasons why *The Disconnected* lends itself to a Bakhtinian reading. Having witnessed the horrors of totalitarian regimes and two world wars, Bakhtin had no faith in the idea of progress within the modernist project. In *Rabelais and His World*—his doctoral dissertation, which he wrote in the 1930s but could not publish until 1965 because of the political climate in Russia under the Stalinist regime—Bakhtin states that under the influence of modernity

---

1 Ahmet Hamdi Tanpınar, *The Time Regulation Institute*, trans. Ender Gürol (Madison: Turko-Tatar Press, 2002).

2 Murat Uyurkulak, *Har*, 2 ed. (Istanbul: Metis, 2006). I have also written on the workings of carnivalesque in Uyurkulak's novel elsewhere. See Meltem Gurle. "'Cinema Grande'and the Rhetoric of Illusion in Uyurkulak's *Har,*" *New Perspectives on Turkey*, No. 36, Spring 2007, 125-144.

3 For a more thorough discussion of Turkey's project of modernization, see: Sibel Bozdoğan and Reşat Kasaba, eds., *Rethinking modernity and national identity in Turkey* (Seattle: University of Washington Press, 1997).

from the seventeenth century onwards, European history witnessed a fragmentation of the militantly anti-authoritarian attitude to life so characteristic of the carnivalesque Middle Ages. According to Bakhtin, the medieval aesthetic that celebrates the anarchic elements of popular culture was swallowed up by modernity (*Rabelais*, 72). The voice of the radically other, which Bakhtin characterizes as carnival laughter, was tamed or transformed.

Considering his emphasis on freedom, it is possible to read Bakhtin's work as a criticism of the totalizing attitude of modernist regimes in general, and a hidden polemic against Stalin's cultural politics in particular.[4] Similarly, Atay's novel emerges as a subtle criticism of the "cult of reason" that lies at the heart of the Turkish ideal of a unified nation, where unity implies uniformity because it can not stand the presence of the "other," fearing that it might challenge the validity of its own ground. Atay's book is distinctly unique, not only because it aims to uncover "the spirit of the Turks" while demonstrating the tension between the intellectual and the *rationale* behind the official version of "Turkishness," but also because it dares to express its conviction in the failure of the modernist project at a time when the country's cultural milieu was monopolized by the so-called "social realist" novels restoring faith in the idea of progress.[5] In short, *The Disconnected*, in which the echoes of carnival laughter are still heard, can be read as a manifesto against the idea of progress.

However historical this perspective may appear, the "national allegory" that Atay's novel offers will not be the only objective of this analysis. On the contrary, this reading of *The Disconnected* will hopefully prove Fredric Jameson wrong in condemning all "Third World" literature as "conventional and naïve." Relying on his sharp distinction of West European literature, and the texts pro-

---

4 Holquist mentions the book's cool official reception in the Soviet Union in the prologue to the 1984 edition of *Rabelais and His World*. For a detailed discussion, see: Katerina Clark and Michael Holquist, *Mikhail Bakhtin* (Cambridge: Harvard University Press, 1984).

5 When it appeared in 1970, Atay's first novel *The Disconnected* was not warmly received in literary circles. It was criticized for sacrificing unity for the sake of experimenting with different styles. One other reason that the novel did not become popular, especially among the left, was that it did not offer any ready-made solutions, or express faith in a better future as the so-called "village novels" did.
Before his death seven years after the publication of *Tutunamayanlar*, Atay finished another novel, *Tehlikeli Oyunlar* (*Dangerous Games*), a collection of short stories, *Korkuyu Beklerken* (*Waiting For Fear*), and a play, *Oyunlarla Yaşayanlar* (*Living With Games*), all of which had to wait until the 1980s to be appreciated by a larger group of readers. When he died in 1977, Atay was working on the sketches of a trilogy he tentatively called "The Spirit of Turkey." *See* Oğuz Atay, *Günlük* (İstanbul: İletişim, 1987), 234-44.

duced in the Third World, Jameson maintains that the social realistic third-world novel will always have a stale taste for the western reader, because like those countries themselves their literature also is underdeveloped and belated when modernity is concerned.

> The third-world novel will not offer the satisfactions of Proust or Joyce; what is more damaging than that, perhaps, is its tendency to remind us of outmoded stages of our own first-world cultural development and to cause us to conclude that "they are still writing novels like Dreiser or Sherwood Anderson." ("Third World," 65.)

In this study, especially in the third chapter, where there is a discussion of third world literature drawing upon Jameson's master-servant analogy, I argue that Atay's book is solid evidence that the third-world novel can offer the satisfactions of the great authors of the canon, and maybe even more. What makes Atay's novel a great book is not only that it provides a criticism of Turkey's project of modernization or modernity as a whole, but also that it is one of the best novels ever written in any language,

> [...] about the discomfort of appearing on the world scene (also the scene of world literature) in the role of a child, or a servant, and hence being belated; about the uneasiness of being always sketchy, unfinished, and forever a novice; about boredom, the agony of death, the feeling of guilt, and injustice; and above all, the desire of talking about these things mixed with the uncomfortable acknowledgement that it is kind of too late to do so. (Gürbilek, *Kör Ayna*, 188.

While analyzing the contribution of other literary texts to Atay's writing, this study takes into critical account Mikhail Bakhtin's theory of the novel as well as his key concepts dialogism and polyphony, which are closely related to heteroglossia and carnivalization. According to Bakhtin, the condition of our existence is heteroglossia, a conflicting multiplicity of languages; dialogism is the necessary mode of knowledge in such a world, a form of relationship between or among different languages.

Language for Bakhtin is a cockpit of warring forces, as each utterance finds itself occupied from within by alien significations. Every sign glances sideways at other signs, bears the traces of them within its body, and faces simultaneously towards speaker, object, context and addressee. Like human subjects, words are constituted by their relations to otherness, and language is always porous, hybrid and open-ended. There was never a first word, and there could never be a last one. The inherent incompleteness and unpredictability of language – the fact that I can never deduce from any two of your words what the third one is going to be – is a token of human freedom, and thus in a broad sense political. (Eagleton, "I Contain Multitudes.") [6]

Bakhtin describes three possible forms of dialogism in *Discourse in the Novel*: the dialogue between 1) the author and the protagonist, 2) the protagonist and other characters, and finally, 3) the language of the text and the language of other texts to which implicit or explicit allusion is made. This third type of dialogism, Atay's dialogue with other authors, will be the focus of this work in general, but there will be references to the other two types occasionally. *The Disconnected* will be approached as part of the tradition of what Bakhtin calls the heteroglot novel, the line of which runs from Rabelais to the picaresque novels and through virtually all the great novels of the modern period.

Correspondences between Bakhtin's thought and Atay's artistic practice become more understandable if we consider the fact that Bakhtin stresses that the formation of the self is a linguistic process; consciousness is a matter of self-articulation in an inner monologue that depends upon and responds to the surrounding environment of speech: an ideological communication. If we deprive consciousness of its ideological content, it would have absolutely nothing left. Atay's portrayal of consciousness in the inner monologues of *The Disconnected* is also language-dependent. Atay's characters exist in language – they speak themselves into existence. They are shaped by the languages around them. Hence, the double-voiced discourse, discourse oriented toward the discourse of another, takes several forms in Atay's novel: parody, stylization, irony, internal polemic, hidden dialogue etc.

Moreover, like Bakhtin suggests, Atay avoids all implications of origin, "presence," and authority in his characterization of voice. In his contempt for authority of all kinds, he forms an attachment to the "language of the misfit," the voice that sets itself in opposition to the dominant voice of the culture. In the analysis of the languages set against each other, be it Atay's dialogue with the canon, or with his characters, we will concentrate on this issue of the language of "the other."

What Bakhtin calls a dialogism, therefore, bears an affinity to Kristeva's notion of intertextuality, and especially when viewed from a Deridean perspective. It is impossible to conceive a *cogito* in the Cartesian sense that is self-sufficient and complete – stripped off of its relation with its 'other.' Derrida proposes that signifiers need not be given directly by the text, but may also be intrusions by intertexts that can be highly distanced, conscious or unconscious, since in the unending process of signification there is nothing outside the language, outside

6 This book report on *Mikhail Bakhtin: The Word in the World* (by Graham Pechey Routledge, 238 pp.) is also available at http://www.lrb.co.uk/v29/n12/eagl01_.html

the text.[7] Therefore, Bakhtin has, in a way, a kinship with postmodern authors, but there is this important difference that tells him apart: unlike the postmodernists, he allows for truth to exist. Unlike Lyotard, for instance, who refuses to accept the universal truth because it does injustice to other, separate and incommensurable truth claims, Bakhtin rejects it because of its internal structure, namely, that it speaks in a single voice, i.e., it is "monological." Despite some similarities, Bakhtin's concept of truth differs with Lyotard's because he allows for one absolute, which he calls dialogue.[8]

Does Derrida's "text" correspond to Bakhtin's "dialogue"? Although one can possibly claim that the two agree that there is no "outside" of the text/dialogue, we have to acknowledge that the meaning Bakhtin attributes to "dialogue" is different from Derrida's understanding of "text."[9] Like Bakhtin's understanding of discourse, Derrida's "text" is an ideological construct. However, as Bakhtin sees the world made up of a plurality of conflicting discourses, for Derrida, the world consists of a surplus of signification, an "overabundance of the signifier" that supplements its own "lack" (Derrida, "Structure," 92). According to Derrida, language encompasses all that can be known, and is at the same time able to expand, if necessary, to encompass still more. So, the text swallows all that there is. In the Derridean world, therefore, we find ourselves "inside" a vast social-historical-economic construct, where the possibility of the knowledge of the "outside" —of the truly "other"— always gets postponed.

7 Derrida comes up with his famous remark on the text in *Of Grammatology* "... it (reading) can not legitimately transgress the text toward something other than it, ... toward a signified object outside the text whose content could take place, could have taken place, outside language... There is nothing outside the text" (158). See Jaques Derrida. *Of Grammatology*, trans. Gayatri Chakravorty Spivak (Baltimore & London: Johns Hopkins University Press, 1976). For a further discussion related to semiosis also see Umberto Eco *The Limits of Interpretation* (Indianapolis: Indiana University Press, 1994) 35.

8 Dialogue, in Bakhtin's view, is not merely a form of communication, but the most fundamental human relation. "To be means to communicate dialogically. When dialogue ends, everything ends... All else is the means; dialogue is the end. A single voice ends nothing and resolves nothing. Two voices is the minimum for life, the minimum for existence." (Problems, 287) On one hand, no statement can claim truth without interaction with other, contradictory statements. On the other hand, no existing statement is refused to enter the big dialogue or the polyphonic truth. Yet for a statement to exist, it must be addressed to someone else. Statements and voices that do not posses this dialogic potential simply do not exist, or have no significance. This is the point that tells Bakhtin's dialogism apart from intertextuality in general.

9 One other reason that Bakhtin's dialogism does not correspond to poststructuralist intertextuality, because for Bakhtin the model language is spoken, rather than written.

The "other," being defined at the border of the text, constantly evades our grasp, never really comes to language. The "other" for Bakhtin, however, does not lie outside of language, as Derrida would have it. Bakhtin suggests a more hopeful operation, through which the "outside" does not prove to be "the inside" again and again the moment it comes to language. The "outside," though it may find expression in artistic construction, is in any case accessible through the anarchic element contained within the voice of the "other," which Bakhtin characterizes as carnival laughter (*Rabelais*, 72).

In short, while Derrida sees discourse as the free play of signifiers offering no promise of meaning at the end, Bakhtin regards these signifiers as being arranged in socially derived genres of speech set against each other in that they constitute the dialogue, which becomes meaning itself.

The dialogue that Atay establishes with the literary past will be the axis of this study. While dealing with the contribution of literary texts to *The Disconnected*, we will concentrate on how Atay draws upon the western canon and delivers it to the present in an enriched form by entering into a dialogue with the outstanding literary figures of the past. Atay, himself, is aware of the dialogue he established with his favorite authors, and he makes his protagonist Selim confess: "One day, I will write a novel putting them all in it, and I will make them pay for what they have done to me'. He is aware of the strain they put on him, "[...] the desire to be like all the authors he loved, to correspond to all of them at the same time was draining his energy" (358).

Yıldız Ecevit, in her biography of Atay, also points to the fact that Selim's obsession with books was a reflection of the author's awareness of his literary belatedness.

> *The Disconnected* was written by an author who, since childhood, felt more at home with books than the world itself. If the modernist novel of the 20$^{th}$ century is a journey in consciousness, as numerous literary critics agree upon, then it is natural that the milestones of Atay's own journey are other literary figures. The intertextual structure of his novel stems from not only the aesthetics of the 20$^{th}$ century novel, but also Atay's personality which is reflected in the passionate relationship of his character Selim with books in his early youth. (*Ben Buradayım*, 246.)

In fact, Atay points to all the authors (the ones he enters a dialogue with, some of whom constitute the basis of our analysis) one by one in a scene towards the end of the novel, where he portrays Turgut in a bookshop trying to choose some books for the road. After praising the bookshops in small towns for the possibilities they offer such as finding the copies of out of print books, he comes up with a list of authors:

> Here is Tolstoy: Let's take it. And now Dostoevsky. I wonder why these two never got along well. A genius like Tolstoy... Why couldn't he understand how precious Dostoevsky was? I understand them both. I think I do. [...] Let's get that Dickens, too. Rumor has it that he was one of the major influences on Dostoevsky. Part of the big chain of literary tittle-tattle, isn't it my dear Selim? We should also buy this Kafka, Olric: the novel of a hesitation. Wasn't there a novel with that name? One of ours.[10] [...] Can you leave Goethe on the shelf? No way. [...] And, it is very nice of you to remind me: Naturally, we should also get a copy of Don Quixote. He is a good old fellow. The journey of the mind! This is what counts, Olric. (530-532.)

As the novel unfolds, Turgut's spiritual journey provides us also with a map into Atay's literary journey in that it guides the author's dialogue with other authors and their styles. In addition to its focus on these canonical writers, and the impact of their major work on *The Disconnected*, this study is also interested in how Atay transforms these texts into the logic and language of modernity. The final chapter of this study, therefore, deals with two different but interrelated issues, 1) an approach to *The Disconnected* as a Turkish response to Joyce's *Ulysses*, i.e. Atay's dialogue with Joyce, and 2) a comparative analysis of Joyce's and Atay's poetics in communication with the literary past.

What both Joyce and Atay share as modernist authors is an ability to draw upon the literary past and deliver it to the present in an enriched form. Yet, each does it in a unique manner. When he writes, Joyce stands on his own ground, his feet deeply rooted in the language and tradition, of which he is, one way or the other, aware of being a part. Atay, however, is a total stranger in the sense that he is dealing with a material other than his own whenever he draws upon the western canon. So, when he writes, he finds himself face to face with his absolute other, i.e., the West.

The main objective of this final comparative chapter will be, therefore, to demonstrate that a dialogue between not only the present and the past, but also the East and the West, which renders Atay both similar to and different from his literary sibling Joyce, determines the journey in *The Disconnected.*

---

10 The novel Turgut refers to is *Bir Tereddüdün Romanı* (The Novel of a Hesitation) by Peyami Safa, journalist and novelist (1899-1961).

# FROM EPIC TO THE NOVEL: THE PROBLEM OF TOTALITY IN *THE DISCONNECTED*

Any review of *The Disconnected* begins with the humble acknowledgment of the novel's vast frame of reference, the great variety of voices and styles that it presents, and finally its resistance to being translated into another language. It is true that Atay stands out among his contemporaries in that he came up with a book that looks like a collection of speech genres representing several different layers of the society. *The Disconnected* is different from other Turkish novels of the time not only because it presents one of the earliest examples of a critical attitude toward the modernist project, but also because of the variety of colloquialisms, idiosyncrasies, verbal conventions, local jokes, and newspeak it employs in voicing this criticism. Hence, no one has dared so far to translate the book despite its unanimous recognition as one of the most important works of Turkish literature:

> Probably the most eminent novel of twentieth-century Turkish literature, a work that won high critical acclaim and popular following, *Tutunamayanlar* offers an endless series of tragicomic observations, an expansive and critical panorama of Turkish manners, attitudes and clichés through a profound sense of irony, parody, dark humor and existential questioning. Although it poses an earnest challenge to even the most skilled translator with its kaleidoscope of colloquialisms and sheer size (nearly 700 pages), it represents Turkish literature at its best.[11]

This variety of voices we encounter while reading *The Disconnected* make it clear that we are dealing with a multi-voiced and multi-styled novel. However, the dialogical nature of the novel does not only stem from the clash of these voices and styles, but also from the dialogue that the author establishes between his novel and other forms of literature, i.e., from the novelization of other genres.

The dialogue between the present chronotope, i.e., the novel, and earlier literary genres is one of the issues that Bakhtin brings forth as a problem that is specific to modernity, because of a dramatically increased consciousness about time. Modernity, as we will discuss in detail all through this chapter, endows the novel with the ability of coming up with the narrative of an open-ended present. The past, whatever is contained in the history of literature, is brought back to

11 This reference is due to a UNESCO survey on the following webpage: http://portal.unesco.org/culture/en/ev.php-URL_ID=19184&URL_DO=DO_TOPIC&URL_SECTION=201.html

life as a new form of representation, this time delivering a completely different meaning, and laden with new tasks. Bakhtin, therefore, values not the death but the rebirth of genres in the form of their "novelization," which suggests that literature always comes back to life.

In this chapter, I will focus on one these genres that the modernist novel borrows and makes part of its narrative structure. Drawing upon Bakhtin's theory of the novel, I will dwell on the various ways through which Atay communicates with the epic tradition by adopting epic conventions and employing them in a completely new context. While demonstrating the kinship between *The Disconnected* and encyclopedic narratives, such as *Gargantua* or *Tristram Shandy*, I will also show that Atay makes use of a narrative strategy that leads him to aesthetics of excess. In short, this chapter will focus on the logic of excess in *The Disconnected*, while referring to the narrative techniques that Atay employs to respond to the totality presented by the epic, including the use of several different styles and voices.

## Beyond the boundaries of the epic time

As Hegel announces in his *Aesthetics*, the objective mode of literature in the late romantic era passed from the grand verse epic to the novel, which is the appropriate form for the modern era. Among other reasons, the main cause for this transformation, according to Hegel, is that the novel becomes the narrative form of the rising bourgeoisie, a form that requires a more particularized mode of narration than we find in the traditional epic, which assumes the paradigmatic role as the representative collective myth of an entire culture.

> This novelistic is born when the knightly existence is again taken seriously, is filled out with real substance. The contingency of outward, actual existence has been transformed into the firm, secure order of bourgeois society and the state so that now the police, the law courts, the army occupy the position of those chimerical goals which the knight used to set himself. Thereby, the knightly character of those heroes whose deeds fill recent novels is transformed. They stand as individuals with their subjective goals of love, honor, ambition, or with their ideals of improving the world, over against the existing order and prose of reality, which from all sides places obstacles in their path. (Hegel, *Aesthetics*, 20)

Lukacs agrees with Hegel that epic is the mode of literature that represents the totality of the world in its immediacy, but also acknowledges that it is a form of the past now that this totality is lost: "The novel is the epic of an age in which the expressive totality of life is no longer directly given, in which the immanence of meaning in life has become a problem, yet which still thinks in terms of totality" (*Theory of Novel*, 56). With the advent of modernity, the historical evolution has brought the age of capitalism putting an end to the age of heroes.[12] The transcendental shelteredness of the Homeric epic gave way to the novel, the epic "of a world abandoned by god" (87). Since the totality of the epic world is lost with the advent of modernity, and can no longer be given to the forms of art, then "they [the forms of art] must either narrow down and volatilize whatever there has to be given form to the point where they can encompass it, or else they must show polemically the impossibility of achieving their necessary object and the inner nullity of their own means. And in this case they carry the fragmentary nature of the world's structure into the world of forms" (13).

For Bakhtin, like Lukacs, the epic cosmos relies on the comprehension of metaphysical time, as well as metaphysical space. In *The Dialogic Imagination*, he names three constitutive elements that characterize the epic, and one of these is "an absolute epic distance [that] separates the epic world from contemporary reality, that is, from the time in which the singer [the author and his audience] lives" (17). This distance is inseparable from the understanding of epic time. Bakhtin refers to Goethe's and Schiller's characterization of the epic past (*vollkommen vergangen*),[13] and defines the temporality of the epic as that of "absolute past," which indicates that the epic singer (author, audience) is at an infinite temporal distance from his subject matter, and that he sings about "utterly finished" events that belong to a reverently represented national past, in a language that is utterly different from contemporary discourse (*Dialogic,* 13-17). This is what gives the epic its universality. Since it is not situated within the present, it is not subjected to change. Being seen from a god-like point of view, the epic world is impersonal, timeless, and perfect.

However, when viewed from the perspective that Bakhtin offers, the epic is locked up in an already consumed past offering no chance of establishing contact with the "now," "here," and "this," i.e., the present. There is no possibility of "becoming" in the case of the epic. The novel, on the contrary, by eliminating the epic distance between the reader and the text "contemporizes" the epic world

12 In his *The Rise of the Novel*, though from a slightly different angle, Ian Watt also argues that the scientific, social and economic developments of this period began to have a greater impact on literature, and a more realistic, pragmatic understanding of life and human behavior, which recognized human individuality and conscious experience, began to emerge. According to Watt, therefore, what characterizes the novel is the individual's conscious experience. Its "primary criterion was truth to individual experience" (13). See Ian Watt, *The Rise of the Novel: Studies in Defoe, Richardson and Fielding*; University of California Press (June 4, 2001)

13 See J. W. von Goethe, "Ueber epische und dramatische Dichtung von Goethe und Schiller," in Saemtliche Werke, (Munich: Hanser, 1986), 126.

in diverse ways: through parodies and travesties, by turning it into an unfinished, still changing contemporary reality, and, above all, by overcoming the distance and making that world tangible (22-27). The novel, unlike the epic, offers "a realistic reflection of the socially varied and heteroglot world of contemporary life" (27). According to Bakhtin, therefore, the difference between epic and novel lies in the fact that the former is a finished form, whereas the latter is incomplete.

In fact, although Bakhtin's and Lukacs's theories develop in totally different directions, they take as their origin the very same idea that the novel is a genre which confronts the loss of immediate totality, and hence is characteristic of a world that speaks to us in many voices at once. Yet, as Lukacs grieves for the loss of transcendent meaning and the passing of epic timelessness in *The Theory of the Novel*, Bakhtin in "Epic and Novel" takes delight in overcoming the authoritative discourse of the epic through temporality. As Neubauer puts it, "here, as elsewhere, Bakhtin converts Lukacs's idealist melancholy into promise" (544).

Accordingly, the way Bakhtin understands novelistic irony also differs from that of Lukacs. Lukacs agrees with Hegel that irony is the product of the "paradoxical activity" of a constant assertion, negation, and self-correction.[14] In the world of Lukacs, irony emerges from the gap between the idealistic novelist's view of the world and the world as it really is being "embedded within the subjectivity of the author and the objectivity of lived experience which are in a rupture ever since the totality of the epic world was lost" (Parla, *Bildungsroman*, 23-24).

The same gap is also present in the relation between the author and his character. Once one assumes an idealist protagonist challenging the authority of his realist "maker," however, one can also plausibly argue that even the epic journey of Odysseus can be read —within the Lukacsian scheme— as a modern novel.[15] In fact, by treating Odysseus as "the great incarnation of Enlightenment," it is Adorno who opened the way to a criticism of Odyssey as a modern text centered on a modern hero. In the *Dialectic of Enlightenment*, Adorno maintains that the Homeric epic reveals the world "to be the work of ordering

14 See *Chapter 4* for the discussion of irony in relation to the narrative structure of *Bildungsroman*.

15 This is probably what inspired Joyce to borrow the structure of *Odyssey* and implement it in *Ulysses*, which is dominated by the loss of a transcendental "home." Interestingly enough, Thomas Mann also talks about the possibility of approaching Odyssey as a novel in his comparison of the novel with the epic. See Thomas Mann, "Die Kunst des Romans," in *Altes und Neues*: *Kleine Prosa aus fünf Jahrzehnten*, Frankfurt: Fischer Verlag, 1961 (363-377).

reason, which destroys myth precisely by means of the rational order in which it reflects myth." Its song of the deeds of Odysseus is a "nostalgic stylization of what may no longer be sung": the hero of the Odyssey is "the prototype of the bourgeois individual" and, hence, Homer's epic is already well on the way to becoming a novel (Horkheimer and Adorno, 36). For Hainsworth, on the other hand, *Odyssey* lacks the focused narrative structure of *Illiad* marking the end of the great epic tradition. After Homer, poets of genius turned to lyric; the poems of the epic cycle were "spasms of a dying tradition" whose attribution to Homer was "a grave injustice" (*The Idea of Epic*, 43-45). What Hainsworth calls lack of focus stems from the fact that the narrative of the *Odyssey* is centered on an individual rather than the community as a whole. There is an existentialist touch in Odysseus's journey. He is more like Gılgamesh than his Greek counterpart Achilles in that he seeks "home" rather than victory. In the *Odyssey* there seems to be a different notion of heroism. For Achilles in the *Iliad* it amounted to the honor accrued through success in battle, and preserving that honor in the name of his fellow men. For Odysseus, being a hero means something else: a journey back home. The way Odysseus takes an individualistic stance against the gods, and goes through a spiritual journey, makes him eligible for an analysis based on the dialectical understanding of irony that Lukacs proposes.

In the case of Bakhtin, on the other hand, irony spreads from the presence of several voices within the text as an alternative to the voice of the author. The fact that the author cannot know everything about the character (cannot possess the character in its totality) adds another level of irony and is responsible for creating the "dialogic" nature of the novel - the author has an opinion, but (as opposed to the Lukacsian all-knowing author) he can not claim to be in possession of the truth about his character. Similarly, in *The Disconnected*, Atay retains control of the work through the technique of employing a series of antagonistic discourses, but the novel does not become monological because his characters are still free, in the sense that their ideas are not shown to be wrong by some authorial voice within the text. On the contrary, what happens in *The Disconnected* is that all these voices are set against each other presenting a dialogic coexistence of dialects, jargons, social speech types, and professional discourses, and thereby demonstrating the ideological heteroglossia embedded in the novelistic discourse.

It is this heterogeneity that the novel offers what leads Bakhtin to conclude in "Epic and Novel," that it is the genre of the modern civilization. In the case of the epic, as opposed to the novel, there is no room for the heterogeneity that Bakhtin has in mind. The epic devours any diversity, and expresses it as part of a totalizing unity. According to Bakhtin, the novel as a genre is unique in that it is able to embrace, ingest, and incorporate other genres while still maintaining its status as a novel. Other genres, however, cannot emulate the novel without damaging their own distinct identity (*Dialogic,* 6). He repeats this view also in "From the Prehistory of Novelistic Discourse," and reveals how various different texts from the past have ultimately come together to form the modern novel (50).

Bakhtin maintains what gives the novel its characteristics (as the modern chronotope) is its capacity of representing the world in all its diversity, where diversity means difference in the true sense of the word. One has to note here that the epic also makes use of other genres, and employs them within its narrative structure, as Cowan argues: "What gives the epic its cultural priority, then, might be summed up as its function of *cosmopoesis*, its making of a cosmos wherein the other genres find their place and within which human life may be envisioned in its varied dimensions" (*The Epic Cosmos*, 5). The difference between the epic and the novel, however, arises from the fact that the novel displays an open-ended nature as opposed to the epic that presents a closed system, where meaning is finalized offering no possibility of change.

Bakhtin's assumption is not that the epic world is not interesting, but that as an idealized past it is completely exteriorized: like the characters it portrays, the epic world is always already complete. It is "a self-enclosed state of order" which posits an inherent meaning to all existence, whereas the world that the novel epitomizes is the place where such meaning can never be acquired. Hence, referring especially to nineteenth century Russian novel, Bakhtin suggests that the modern novel is essentially dialogical opening itself to diversity while taking a stance against the monological totality presented by the epic world. Moreover, since the dialogical language system of the novel is open-ended, the word here is never the last word, nor is the meaning the ultimate meaning.

Moretti, however, argues in *The Modern Epic*, that Bakhtin's notion of polyphony would apply to a new form of epic that emerges with the rise of modernity rather than the nineteenth century realist novel. What defines this new epic is the tension between the totality of the epic world, and the diversity of modernity. As Moretti convincingly argues, the drive, in works such as Joyce's *Ulysses*, is toward totalization, toward what Eliot called, in his famous essay on Joyce, the "mythical method," that is, "a way of controlling, of ordering, giving a shape and a significance to the immense panorama of futility and anarchy that is contemporary history." This probably also explains why Eliot calls *Ulysses* "a book" rather than a novel:

> Mr. Joyce's parallel use of the Odyssey has a great importance. It has the importance of a scientific discovery. No one else has built a novel on such a foundation before: it has never before been necessary. I am not begging the question in calling Ulysses a "novel"; and if you call it an epic it will not matter. If it is not a

> novel then that is simply because the novel is a form that will no longer serve; it is because the novel, instead of being a form which will no longer serve; it is because the novel, instead of being a form, was simply the expression of an age which had not sufficiently lost all form to feel the need of something stricter. (Eliot, 177)

*Ulysses* has often been called a modern epic –a diagnosis that obviously relies on the Homeric parallels that Joyce structured his novel upon. However, according to Moretti what distinguishes modern epic from other novels is a criterion unparalleled by any that has been named before: its unreadability. An unreadability that stems from the fact that the novel tries to embrace all that there is. This is a criterion that also applies to *The Disconnected.* Atay's book emerges as yet another example of the modern epic, which, as Marjorie Perloff maintains, "expresses an irresolvable tension between the remnant of individualism, as embodied in the stream of consciousness, and the 'encyclopedic' drive toward a larger totality that is no longer fully believed in, much less trusted."[16] Accordingly, the center of our discussion in the rest of this chapter will be based on the way Atay problematizes the worldview of the Epic, namely the economy of excess and the articulation of diversity.

## Encyclopedic narrative: the economy of excess

In the *Atlas of the European Novel*, Franco Moretti resumes his argument against Bakhtin's celebration of the novel's heterogeneity, which he has outlined in *The Modern Epic*, and maintains that the dialogical structure of the Russian novel in the nineteenth century is "the exception, not the rule, of novelistic evolution" (45). Moretti claims that the novel, being "the symbolic form of the nation state," became monological and homogenous in the nineteenth century. In fact, as Geoffrey Winthrop-Young argues, Moretti's nineteenth century turns out to be "one long campaign aimed at inverting Bakhtin's binary of open modern novels and closed ancient epics," where novels become monological (representing the nation-state), whereas polyphony (the overcoming of nations) is promoted by a new type of epic: "The strange hybrid contraption called modern epic appears necessary because there are more things in heaven and earth than are dreamed of in novels-but those dreams can be turned into texts only under the condition that they ironically lighten and debunk whatever unitary world view they may espouse" (23).

16 Marjorie Perloff, Rev. of Modern Epic: The World System from Goethe to Garcia Marquez, by Franco Moretti, ebr 4 (1997) available at http://www.altx.com/ebr/ebr4/perloff/ htm.

Edward Mendelson, on the other hand, introduces the term "encyclopedic narrative" to identify a genre that partly overlaps with Moretti's understanding of modern epic when one considers its characteristic desire to represent the world in its diversity. He refers to seven examples of the genre, namely Dante's *Commedia*, Rabelais' five books of *Gargantua* and *Pantagruel*, Cervantes' *Don Quixote*, Goethe's *Faust*, Melville's *Moby-Dick*, Joyce's *Ulysses*, and Pynchon's *Gravity's Rainbow.*[17] However, unlike Moretti, Mendelson suggests that encyclopedic narratives occupy a special and definable place in their national cultures:

> Each major national culture in the west, as it becomes aware of itself as a separate entity, produces an encyclopedic author, one whose work attends to the whole social and linguistic range of his nation, who makes use of all the literary styles and conventions known to his countrymen, whose dialect often becomes established as the national language, who takes his place as national poet or national classic, and who becomes the focus of a large and persistent exegetic and textual industry comparable to the industry founded upon the Bible. [...] For the most part, encyclopedic authors set out to imitate epics, but, unlike epic poets, they write about the ordinary present-day world around them instead of the heroic past. (Mendelson, 1267)

Mendelson's early analysis of the encyclopedic narrative is interesting, because it raises the question whether the novel can satisfy the encyclopedic ambitions for a totalizing representation of the world. Whether it is meant to be a "national allegory" or an effort to overcome the boundaries of the nation-state, the modern epic problematizes the representation of reality as a totality.[18] The aesthetics of excess in the modern epic is the outcome of this effort to represent all that there is in a world where reality is manifold.[19] Mendelson provides a set of criteria for

---

17 In fact, it was much earlier when Northrop Frye coined the term "encyclopedic form." Simply put, he means works that attempt to embody the entire life cycle and culture of a people, written by one or more scribes who presume to reach beyond the merely personal to a vision of the whole. In canonical literature, Frye alludes to the Bible, the eddas, the *Mahabharata*, the classical epics, the *Divine Comedy*, *Canterbury Tales*, *The Fairie Queene*, *Don Quixote*, *Paradise Lost*, *Pilgrim's Progress*, *Prometheus Unbound*, *Don Juan, Moby Dick, The Cantos, Ulysses, Finnegan's Wake, A la Recherche du Temps Perdu*. Like Mendelson, Fry also states that there is often a compilation of genres in encyclopedic works--a totality of form as well as of represented reality.
See Northrop Frye, *Anatomy of Criticism* (Princeton, 1957).

18 See *Chapter 2* for a thorough discussion of Jameson's concept of "national allegory."

19 One appreciates Mendelson for mapping out a schematic method in order to specify the structure of the modern epic. However, as he was busy trying to show the encyclopedic structure of the new genre, he seems to have overlooked that it is not the only feature characterizing the modern epic. Besides, the epic will be recycled, as Winthrop-Young

encyclopedic narratives which extends beyond their exceptional authors: 1) they all include an extensive account of at least one technology or science; 2) they are an encyclopedia of literary styles; 3) they all provide a history of language (are metalinguistic); 4) they all propose a theory of social organization.

Considering the criteria above, *The Disconnected* seems to have a well-deserved place in Mendelson's list of encyclopedic narratives. When the novel first appeared in 1971, Atay was severely criticized for mixing styles and including irrelevant detail, which made the book "practically unreadable," "full of redundant repetition," and even "a little boring" (319).[20] Even Berna Moran, who thinks highly of Atay, says in his account of the novel in *Türk Romanına Eleştirel Bir Bakış* (A Critical Review of Turkish Literature), that Oğuz Atay's experimental use of styles loaded the book "with a burden that it could not handle," and that Atay's novel is overloaded and "cramped" (289). As far as the 70's are concerned, the only voice that raises in favor of Atay's use of a variety of styles is that of Murat Belge, who stands up in his defense, and replies to the general criticism (that Atay wrote down anything that came to his mind) as follows: "This seemingly disorganized material is brought together as a result of a careful elimination, and is interwoven into the plotline not randomly, but in such a way that it constitutes a meaningful whole" (278).

In fact, the plotline of the novel is not that complex: Turgut, one of the double protagonists of the novel, leaves the comfort of his life, and following the footsteps of his friend Selim, tries to unfold the mystery behind his suicide. In a sense, the novel articulates a very similar situation to that of Nabokov's *The Real Life of Sebastian Knight*, in that it presents a fictitious biography, where the main character of the novel is tracking down the traces of his dead brother relying on the texts he left behind. *The Disconnected* as well, being a novel concerning the search for a dead character, sends both Turgut and the reader on a quest for the meaning of Selim's death. Like Nabokov, Atay makes use of letters, notes, journal entries, newspaper articles etc.

However, Atay and Nabokov have different agendas although they use the same raw material, the same plotline. "Remember that what you are told is really threefold: shaped by the teller, reshaped by the listener, concealed from both by the dead man of the tale," advises the narrator of *The Real Life of Sebastian*

---

says, but this time "under less hospitable post-epic conditions." (See Geoffrey Winthrop-Young, "How the Mule Got Its Tale.")
Since the "post-epic conditions" will constitute the background of the final chapter of this work, I will not delve into the matter more deeply here.

20 Ecevit is referring to several reviews here. See, Zühtü Bayar, *Barış Gazetesi* 9.8.1972; Abdullah Uçman, *Hareket Dergisi*, July 1973.; and Orhan Duru, *Radikal Gazetesi*, Kitap eki, 8.12.2001.

*Knight*, revealing the author's desire behind the formation of the novel. Nabokov expects his readers to actively engage in the construction of his novels. In *The Real Life Sebastian Knight*, he philosophizes on the relationship between the author/narrator/reader, and questions the limits of the reader's contribution to the formation of an artistic work. He also urges us to give considerable thought to the position of the author (in a sense Nabokov himself) who, being "the dead man of the tale," eludes the reader's desire to know.

What connects Atay to Nabokov is that they both like to play games. While approaching Nabokov, as well as Atay, one does not want to find oneself in the shoes of boring Mr. Goodman, or of the English businessman who "preferred books that made one think" (181). Neither Atay nor Nabokov is a satirist, who would look for an opportunity to teach one a lesson in the end. Instead, they make use of parody and the playful atmosphere that it creates. So, as a reader, one must be ready to play the game that the author has set up. The difference between these two authors, however, arises from the fact that Atay, unlike Nabokov, does not sacrifice his dialogue with the reader for the sake of the game.

Although it is unquestionably a remarkable intellectual achievement, one has to admit that Nabokov's text is dominated by pure *logos*. *The Real Life of Sebastian Knight*, the reader feels, is a carefully designed book contemplating about its own achievement. The intellectual pleasure that one derives from reading Nabokov's novel stems from the fact that the book is a puzzle about the nature of writing. Hence, it takes great pleasure of playing cat-and-mouse with the reader. One should always keep in mind that Nabokov establishes the terms for reading his novels, just as Sebastian "seemed . . . to be constantly playing some game of his own invention, without telling his partners its rules" (181). Atay, on the other hand, emerges as an author that stands at the crossroads where Nabokov meets Dostoevsky. The game is there, but the rules appeal to the spirit as well as the intellect. What penetrates to every single corner of Atay's novel is a *pathos* deriving from the fact that its characters cannot "hold on to the world." What defines them is their vulnerability. Yet, this is not meant to invoke pity in the reader. The disconnected carry their vulnerability like an invisible crown on their heads being aware that it is both a curse and a gift that enables them to see more than the others. Even in the most entertaining passages where Atay experiments with different styles and points of view, we feel the melancholy deriving from this simple fact.

The commentary to Selim's autobiographical poem, "Yesterday, Today, Tomorrow," for instance, is a compilation of a series of fake biographies, encyclopedic entries, and supposedly academic articles involving statistical data, which reminds us of a Nabokovian experiment with styles and language.[21] The passages here in this commentary, however, are not cut off from the sentiment emanating from the larger plot: humor and agony go hand in hand. We can never feel for Sebastian Knight, because of the distance created by Nabokov's cynical narrator V., but we feel for "the disconnected" despite the comical aspect of the commentary. One such passage saturated with humor is the one that describes "the disconnected" as a zoological family, and emerges as one of the best examples of how Atay's novel makes use of the encyclopedic language while also remaining true to the melancholic mood of the novel:

> From the Encyclopedia of Bizarre Animals: The Disconnectus Erectus: They are clumsy and cowardly animals. . . . At first sight they even look like humans. But their claws are very weak. They can't climb hills. When they have to descend, they let themselves slide down (they fall frequently). They don't have much body hair. Although their eyes are big, their sight is not well developed, that is why they can't detect danger from afar. Their males cry in sad tones when they are left alone. They call for mating in the same sad tones. Usually they live in other animals' shelters as long as the hosts can bear the situation. Sometimes they live in deserted shelters. They don't have any family order. After birth, mother, father, and children go their separate ways. They don't know how to live in a community, and they can't organize against an attack. They don't have regular feeding habits. When they live with others, they eat what the others bring in. When they are left alone, they forget to eat. Since all their behavior depends on imitation, if they don't see the others eating, they don't understand they are hungry. It is forbidden to hunt them in these periods of weakness. Their instincts are not well developed. They don't know how to protect themselves. And again, because of their imitative nature, they constantly enter into fights because they see other animals doing it. No disconnectus erectus has ever been recorded to win a fight. Nevertheless, since their memories are weak, they keep forgetting the old defeats and keep fighting. Although religious books forbid eating these animals, they are illegally hunted. It is very easy to hunt them. If you look at them with tenderness, they will approach you immediately. To kill them afterward is extremely easy. But since they carry some harmful bacteria, the state health administration bans their slaughtering. Feelings such as slight uneasiness, oppression, and a guilty conscience are thought to be caused by the consumption of the disconnectus. Animal trainers have worked hard to teach them some tricks and employ them in the circus, but because of their clumsiness, they were unable to learn any tricks. And some disconnectus that were brought to the stage made the audience quite sad rather than merry (people ran to the ticket office to get their money back). It is generally believed that the disconnectus have the strongest sense of religion after ele-

---

21 In fact, as Yıldız Ecevit also points out, this sends us back to another Nabokov novel, *Pale Fire,* which includes a foreword, a poem written by a professor, extensive commentary on the poem, and a table of contents. See Vladimir Nabokov. *Pale Fire.* (New York: Random House, Inc., 1962). See also Yıldız Ecevit, *"Ben Buradayım...,"* 242-244.

phants. Some writers have claimed that they go to heaven after they die. But this seems improbable since they create chaos wherever they gather. (128, trans. Ertuğrul)

In a humorous passage about the disconnected as a "type," Atay comes up with an unmistakably sad image of a group of primates. The disconnected, though they may be numerous, emerge as incurably solitary individuals, and there is no bonding between them or a relation that helps them to reintegrate to the society of what sounds like a group of monkeys here. Being misfits, they lack a sense of belonging, which would otherwise enable them to function properly within the system. And not being able to fit into the logic of the system, they end up as outcasts.

The question is, of course, why Atay adopts a mock-scientific discourse to tell us about the disconnected, unarguably the main motive of his novel. If this is the ultimate story that he wants to convey to the reader, then why does he resort to a form of parody that relies on an exaggeration that borders on absurdity? The mock-scientific discourse, the most common manifestation of encyclopedic narrative, supposedly displays scholarly "knowledge," and professes to have an access to truth. By making use of a pseudo-academic discourse, Atay not only tells us that such "truth" is far from being accessible, but also underlines the fact that the lives of the disconnected should not be taken too seriously. In Atay's text, any idea that claims priority over the others will be put into place. When language comes dangerously close to being "monological," it will be immediately counter-balanced with a discourse resistant to the one preceding it.

When Parla mentions the presence of *Meddah* humor in *The Disconnected*, she probably has this ambiguous quality of the text in mind. In the oral tradition of Turkish literature, the *Meddah*[22] duplicates the meaning of a word while sometimes emptying it of its content. As Parla argues, the voices of the double protagonists of Atay's novel overlap from time to time with that of the *Meddah* in that it creates an excess of words (*Don Kişot*, 211-12). Parla writes that "the *Meddah* humor" in Atay's text functions as a device of alienation detaching the reader from the topic at hand when it tends to get boring or dangerously emotional. Apart from relieving the tension, the *Meddah*'s language is rich in that it

22 *Meddah* was a one-man show (at the time of the Ottomans) that played in front of a small group of viewers like a coffeehouse audience. The play is generally about a single topic, and the *meddah* (the story teller) plays different personalities within the story. Depending on the person the *meddah* was impersonating in the story, he used an umbrella, or perhaps a handkerchief, to signal the change of personality. The control of voice was the most important skill in this type of show. What Parla refers to here is the *meddah*'s ability to play with language with the intention of entertaining and interacting with the audience.

is open to voices that carnivalize daily life. In addition to comic verbal compositions, and various genres of billingsgate[23] or abusive language, Atay also uses other techniques for parody like those we have mentioned above. All of these, which, according to Bakhtin, emerge as the indispensable elements of the carnival, are not alien to the skills of the *Meddah* —that in turn become the components of Atay's writing.

Likewise, it can be said that Atay employs several other voices in order to benefit from the rich eclectic structure of the Menippean satire[24], which deflates the monological seriousness of Turgut's journey. The way he repeatedly makes use of fake analyses, catalogues, statistical data, etc. can be regarded as part of this intention. The following example is taken from a passage, where Turgut discusses the relations with "the second sex" in a third world country that lives under authoritarian rule:

> According to the bulletin of the institute of healthy amorous advances, in the course of one year there have been registered cases of twelve-thousand-seven-hundred-sixteen dates at pastry shops, seven-thousand-eight at bus-stops (one-thousand-eight-hundred-twenty five of which never really took place), one-thousand-four-hundred-sixty-two in the open air (parks, fields, in the islands etc.) and only six-hundred-twelve in movie theatres. One should also add secret love affairs to these numbers (since there was no sign of Selim's name on the list, we assume his case belongs to this category) The rules of probability tell us that the number of secret love affairs should amount up to four-thousand-six-hundred. According to the records of the police department, there have been approximately one-hundred-twenty-six-thousand looking and sighing, forty-four-thousand slightly touching at the bus, four-thousand-two-hundred aimlessly stalking, eight-hundred-fifty following the girl until she gets home, and fifteen-thousand-seven-hundred intense infatuation with no possibility of being loved back. The number of hopelessly platonic lovers (and this number is precise) is eight-hundred-fourteen. (410)

In passages like these, Atay has two things in mind: 1) mocking the analytical attitude typical to the western mind, and showing that it can never grasp the

23 The raucous cries of the fish vendors in London's famous fish market with the same name gave rise to the use of "billingsgate" as a synonym for profanity or offensive language.

24 For Bakhtin, carnivalization has a long and rich historical foundation in the genre of the ancient Menippean satire. Bakhtin says that "menippea" or "the carnivalesque" enters into all kinds of relationships, transforms itself, and combines with other genres. He believes the "menippea lives in such dialogized and carnivalized medieval genres as 'arguments, debates', morality and miracle plays and later in the mystery and sotie." (See Bakhtin, Problems of Dostoevsky's Poetics, 182.) Bakhtin says "the Menippean satire has the capacity of insinuating itself into larger genres" (161) and that it "absorbed the diatribe, the soliloquy and the symposium" (160).

world as it is, 2) by making use of the contrast between constraint and excess, demonstrating the formation of a totality —which rests on the same analytical thinking. Therefore, despite the abundance of information, the employment of excess as a stylistic device in this passage gives the reader a claustrophobic feeling characteristic to the restrictions any totalitarian state imposes upon the individuals. The statistical data provided by "the institute of healthy amorous advances," —an image where Vonnegut meets Orwell— spreads a feeling of being watched all through the passage. An insatiable urge for organization, codification, and systematization dominates such passages in *The Disconnected.* We witness the same suffocating atmosphere elsewhere in the novel where this overambitious, detail-hungry, and meticulous voice appears.[25]

One of the formal manifestations of the encyclopedic narrative is the compulsion to make long catalogues —another aspect of the aesthetics of excess we mentioned above. Rabelais has an unquenchable appetite for such lists in *Gargantua.* Describing how there was great strife between the cake-bakers of Lerne, and those of Gargantua's country, he comes up with a long inventory of names that the two parties called each other:

> The bun-sellers or cake-makers were in nothing inclinable to their request; but, which was worse, did injure them most outrageously, calling them prattling gabblers, lickorous gluttons, freckled bittors, mangy rascals, shite-a-bed scoundrels, drunken roysters, sly knaves, drowsy loiterers, slapsauce fellows, slabberdegullion druggels, lubberly louts, cozening foxes, ruffian rogues, paltry customers, sycophant-varlets, drawlatch hoydens, flouting milksops, jeering companions, staring clowns, forlorn snakes, ninny lobcocks, scurvy sneaksbies, fondling fops, base loons, saucy coxcombs, idle lusks, scoffing braggarts, noddy meacocks, blockish grutnols, doddipol-joltheads, jobbernol goosecaps, foolish loggerheads, flutch calf-lollies, grouthead gnat-snappers, lob-dotterels, gaping changelings, codshead loobies, woodcock slangams, ninny-hammer flycatchers, noddypeak simpletons, turdy gut, shitten shepherds, and other suchlike defamatory epithets; saying further, that it was not for them to eat of these dainty cakes, but might very well content themselves with the coarse unranged bread, or to eat of the great brown household loaf. (Rabelais, Chapter 1. XXV.)

Following Rabelais, Atay makes his characters to resort to long lists in *The Disconnected.* However, while it is a part of folk humor in the case of Rabelais, a tool to deal with the high language of official authority, for Atay the use of catalogues emerges particularly as the representation of the bureaucratic political system in Turkey, which, according to Atay, is the outcome of the logic of mod-

25 Possibly the only exception to this "Big Brother effect" is Atay's parody of the novel of formation, where he mocks the idea of the all-knowing author. See *Chapter 4* for the relation between the obsessive narrative voice and authorial presence in *Bildungsroman.*

ernization. In a passage where he dreams of a utopic return to a more naïve state of consciousness, Turgut wages a war against modernism. Typically, he starts with Descartes, and imagines that his books "were piled up in public squares and burnt in fumes". But he cannot stop there, and in a Rabelaisian manner, he comes up with a list of various documents to be burnt so that the country finally cuts the ties with the analytical tradition of the West.

> Together with them [the works of Descartes] all the documents, certificates, vouchers, briefs, cards, deeds, archives, notes, records, land registers, bonds, bills, identity cards, court sentences, banknotes, bus passes, monthly tickets, reports, laws, rules, regulations, charters, codes, death certificates, love letters and all the other letters, labels, tags, permission notes, memoranda, discharge papers, tables of organization, decrees of appointment, resignation letters, boring reviews, membership cards, menus, poverty certificates, proxies, trust deeds, warrants, copies of all documents validated by the notary, school reports, notifications of evacuation, rental contracts, Carnegie's advice, newspapers, honor lists, electoral rolls, commission reports for the elected, tickets, marriage certificates, testaments and wills, uninteresting daily calendars, meaningless reminders like "I waited until twelve, and now I'm leaving" or "I'll drop by tomorrow afternoon" or "We'll be home tonight" or "Let's meet at the office on Saturday," posters, bills, placards, banners with the photos of famous singers, work permits of prostitutes, collected daily articles published as books, jokes, interviews, stamp collections hid in locked drawers, passports, signboards forbidding things, labels on shirts and underwear, licenses for guns, exam papers, New Year's cards, postcards for religious feasts, documents belonging to the state register of persons, all certified documents, punch cards, name cards, invitation cards, rosettes, all the strange badges and pins that the delegates are supposed to wear in congresses, lottery tickets, coupons for interest rates, playing cards, aprons for kids with the embroidered message "don't kiss me," reservation cards at restaurant tables, plates at the doors of meeting rooms that read "meeting inside," plates at the doors of shops that read "closed" or "lunch break," plates inside shops that read "we are here for the customer" or "customer is always right," plates that give a piece of advice like "never put off until tomorrow what you can do today" or "honesty is the best policy," notebooks with double lines, notebooks with single lines, ruled papers and plain papers were all burnt. (415-16)

Here in this passage, the apparently random listing of various "papers" turns out to be a metaphor of the relation of the individual to the State; a relation that is governed by a seemingly endless chain of bureaucracy. The mechanism of power has penetrated into the remotest corners of people's lives, and in order to be able to get rid of the whole web of relationships infiltrated with such bureaucracy one has to burn everything. The impossibility of reaching the core of this bureaucratic system is represented in the unthinkable project of burning all the documents governing the lives of individuals. As opposed to Rabelaisian festive excess, therefore, we have an almost Kafkaesque multiplication of signifiers through which meaning becomes completely inaccessible.[26]

## Speech genres and the articulation of diversity

As we have already mentioned, the epic absolutizes the world in a sealed past, that is fixed, frozen, unchanging and graspable. The modern epic, however, is based on a dilemma: on the one hand it expresses a desire to represent the world as totality like the epic, on the other hand, it has to acknowledge the loss of that totality when confronted with the variety and fragmentation of the modern world. In *The Disconnected* Atay problematizes this dichotomy mostly by employing parodic devices in order to demonstrate the impossibility of a full representation of the world as it is. The economy of excess, for instance, parodies the desire to capture all reality. The world is simply too big, too rich and too much to be represented by the Aristotelian classifications, categorizations that the mind is susceptible to make. The target of Atay's parody therefore is not only the epic but also the whole classical mind-set.

However, this is not the only method. Atay also resorts to other devices such as the employment of numerous speech genres to represent the variety and richness of the world. *The Disconnected* is open to all kinds of speech genres, such as letters, poems, journals, encyclopedic articles, pseudo-academic analyses etc.

---

26 I am using the term "Kafkaesque" also in reference to the telescopic space that Kafka creates in some of his parables, such as 'Before the Law' and 'An Imperial Messenger', the first also published as part of *The Trial*, the second also appearing as part of *The Great Wall of China*. In the first story, the protagonist spends a lifetime failing to get through a gate which he learns at the last was built only for him. In the second story the dying emperor's message cannot reach the ear of the subject for whom it is intended because it is impossible for the messenger to get out of the palace.
As in 'The Great Wall of China', so in this part of Atay's novel, details challenge the whole of the text producing an effect similar to that of an Escher picture. The picture which seems to fit together, collapses when the detail comes into the foreground. The part becomes larger than the whole, the inside bigger than the outside, hence giving rise to the formation of a telescopic space, where the image is inverted. Like the emperor's messenger who can never leave the palace because he can not cross the infinitesimal points in space (being locked up in Zeno's paradox of motion), Atay's singular text unfolds itself in such way that it contains an infinite number of details.
For a detailed description of the "telescopic space", see Christopher Kelen, "The Great Wall of China and Kafka's Limitless Tropology." *Queen: A Journal of Rhetoric and Power,* Vol. 2.1.
http://ars-rhetorica.net/Queen/Volume21/Articles/Kelen.htm

Parla objects to the idea that the voices in Atay's novel are capable of entering a dialogue, and calls *The Disconnected* "a pandemonium of discourses,"

> Nobody listens to anybody else, no discourse lends an ear to another discourse, no language is aware of the presence of another language. This cultural disorder that the intellectual swims —maybe we should rather say 'drowns'— in, does not possess any variety because it does not open itself to dialogue. In order to be able to talk about variety, one has to presume an environment where various languages and discourses lend an ear to each other. (*Don Kişot*, 213)

Parla maintains that this cacophony is the sound of the Turkish culture, where nobody has the tolerance or time to listen to another. In fact, any communication with the others emerges as a problematic issue in the case of the disconnected. In a very interesting article on the limits of polyphony in *The Disconnected*, Irzık, while admitting the carnivalesque quality of the novel, maintains that Turgut confiscates the voice of others killing the possibility of polyphony. Hence, the other is not represented in the novel as it is, but rather gets filtered through the consciousness of the main character ("Çokseslilik," 44-47).

Parla's argument is sound if one approaches it from the perspective of dialectics.[27] If one envisions the formation of a synthesis between conflicting discourses, as Parla does, then it is possible to say that the *telos* is missing in Atay's novel – which it is. From a Bakhtinian perspective, however, there can be no such thing as discourses existing by themselves, which is possibly what Parla has in mind when she says, "they do not lend an ear to each other." Dialogue is the natural form of human life as culture. It is the essence of our being here. It is also possible that Parla means the speech genres in the novel are monological in themselves, because they do not acknowledge the presence of one another. However, when viewed in the unity of the novel, we observe that they are not randomly scattered within the text. They are meaningful within the whole in that they cancel each other —though they offer no possibility of *Aufhebung*.[28] Therefore, it is impossible to grasp the meaning of one discourse

27 Bakhtin explicitly opposes any attempt to reduce dialogism to the Hegelian dialectical scheme, which he is always suspicious of, and refers to as "Hegel's monological dialectic." See Tzvetan Todorov, *Mikhail Bakhtin: The Dialogical Principle* (Minneapolis: University of Minnesota Press, 1998), 104.

28 *Aufhebung*, is the term that Hegel uses for negativity transcended and contained in a higher level of truth, which in German has three main senses: 1) 'to raise, to hold, to lift up', 2) 'to annul, abolish, destroy, cancel, suspend', 3) 'to keep, save, preserve'. When I use the term here, I have all of these senses in mind. For Parla obviously, a dialogue between discourses is possible only in that they enter in to an antithetical relationship through which one would be aware that one's error gives rise to the formation of another

without the presence of the other. In short, as Eagleton says, dialogism "does not mean bending a courteous ear to others [...] it means that every word or utterance is refracted through a host of other, perhaps antagonistic idioms, through which alone its meaning can be grasped" ("I Contain Multitudes").

As a result, what Atay deals with in *The Disconnected* is parody, as Jameson understands the term. If we were to agree with Parla that the discourses Atay presents are deaf and dumb to each other, we would have to admit the presence of pastiche rather than parody, because the former does not offer a possibility of dialogue. Jameson's diagnosis that the end of the modern period brought with itself also an end to the uniqueness of literary production – as of anything else – is justified in his argument of pastiche, which emerges as an empty imitation, a copy that is evacuated of its meaning. What also signifies this dramatic change, according to Jameson, is a turn "to the past: the imitation of dead styles, speech through all the masks and voices stored up in the imaginary museum of a now global culture." This situation inevitably gives rise to what Jameson calls "the random cannibalization of all the styles of the past, the play of random stylistic allusion," in that pastiche does not presume a certain pattern that can be acted upon, or a meaning that can be derived from that pattern ("Cultural Logic," 202).

Once we give in to the allegation that there is no possibility of communication between the speech genres in *The Disconnected*, we evacuate the meaning from these passages reducing them to pastiche, that is, "speech in a dead language" or "blank parody, a statue with blind eyeballs" (Jameson, "Cultural Logic," 202). It is very hard to claim that this is the case for Atay's novel. In *The Disconnected*, every discourse is situated against what lies before itself, which justifies the presence of the former and endows it with meaning. The existence of "original meaning" or a "final signified" might be highly questionable, but the dialogue itself is meaningful, as Bakhtin would have it.

Let us consider for instance, the passages in the commentary concerning language reform. Obviously Atay is mocking the efforts on the side of the young Republic to purify Turkish language. The insistence of the government in the implementation of what is called "pure Turkish" as opposed to "Ottoman Turkish" constitutes one of the issues that Atay problematizes in *The Disconnected*. Therefore, there are several parodies of the language reform and its political connotations. An interesting point is that Atay not only underlines the impossibility of forming a pure language, but also makes fun of the artificiality of the overly stylish and ridiculously rhetorical Ottoman discourse. These two dis-

---

truth. Thus the perceived error necessarily implies another truth of a higher level pushing the process forward – necessarily towards a *telos*.

courses are in a dialogue although they do not borrow "expressions" from each other, or "hear" each other's thoughts. These two parodies, which are set against each other, turn out to be meaningful in that they are placed one after the other in the commentary following Selim's poem "Yesterday, Today, Tomorrow." Atay obviously despises both parties equally, and believes that they are both artificially constructed. Neither the old and conservative generation that clings stubbornly to a dying language, nor the young nationalist generation that talks in a stillborn language satisfies the author of *The Disconnected.* However, he uses these voices in his novel. When asked about the language of his novel, Atay says in an interview, "There is a part in the novel written completely in pure Turkish, and another part that is written in Ottoman. If you read, you'll see that I can write in both languages with equal ease. And, of course, I also have my own language" (261). [29]

*The Disconnected*, among many other things, is also a novel that is about language, as Ecevit says in her biography of Atay (262-63). The novel is full of parodies about language, one of which is the following passage from the commentary, commenting —this time from the point of view of a young Republican linguist— on the nature of Turkish language:

> Before they migrated from Central Asia to the motherland, the life of the Turks was entirely tribal. The social order in the Turkic tribes rested on the requirements of tent civilization. We can prove how far we have moved from that tribal life by taking a look at some words, which were completely unknown and alien to the language of those tribes (namely pure Turkish), but we cannot do without in today's daily life, such as, glass, straw, necktie, rent, cherry, lighthearted, table, plate, coffin, music, education, bed frame, word, and sentence. The fact that these words did not exist in pure Turkish, which is an archaic branch of modern Turkish, might give us an idea about the lives of these tribal people:
>
> Turks did not use to look out of the window.
>
> Turks did not use to sit on straw mats, and did not shovel issues under the straw. This habit started with the Ottomans.
>
> Turks did not use to wear neckties.
>
> Turks did not like lightheartedness. They were sober people.
>
> Turks did not use to pay rents. The habit of paying rents started when Turks moved from a period of primitive communism to that of landed bourgeoisie.
>
> Turks did not eat cherries at all.
>
> Turks did not have supper at table, and did not use any plates whatsoever. They ate from the pot in the middle.
>
> When Turks died, they were not put into coffins and buried. The old Turks did not have such customs.

---

29 Ecevit refers to a Doğan Hızlan interview published in *Yeni Gazete*, in March 16, 1971.

> Turks did not use to listen to music.
> Turks did not go to school.
> Turks did not express themselves with linguistic devices like words and sentences". (117)

In addition to such fake academic articles, we also read examples from several other genres, such as drama, poetry, fables, etc. Probably the most interesting among these are the sham biographies that the novel is crowded with. Atay keeps inventing characters, and never tires of introducing them to the reader. Again in the commentary, written in pedagogical style borrowed from history books, we read about the background of the great Jewish mathematician and philosopher Shlomoh Spear, a pseudonym that Selim cooks up for his close friend Süleyman Kargı. The story flows with references to imaginary books in English and German, such as, 'Trivial Aspects of Great Mathematicians', 'Die Geist der Mesopotamia' etc. Finally, Shlomoh gives up mathematics, starts writing poems, and ends up in Antiochia, where he becomes a controversial figure. He gets into serious trouble, and finally has to flee to Cyprus. At this point we are presented with one of Shlomoh's poems that bothers the Antiochian authorities, and the commentary that follows:

> Like as the impossibility of drawing a perfect circle
> So can mind and experience never govern human soul.
> It is not always God who shapes our fortune.
> It is not clear where one should draw the line between matter and soul.
> Betrayals follow you wherever you go
> Even if you run away from great turmoil.
>
> I think this poem is as stale as horse biscuit. They say it sounds much better in Hebrew. I have no intention to find out whether this is true. Content-wise it is even worse. I doubt that Shlomoh was well schooled in philosophy. The way he tries to use mathematical principles as a key to philosophical understanding shows that he does not quite grasp the human aspect of philosophy. (121)

The artist's conflict with authority is there, the criticism of the Enlightenment is there. These are themes we will be returning to again and again in reading *The Disconnected.* However, what is more interesting here is that at this point of the novel the text gets so complicated and puzzle-like that we, the readers, start to feel as if we were walking down a spiral. The sphere within the sphere within the sphere is where we are. We are reading the commentary on a poem that is within the commentary on another poem that is in a biographical text, which, we are told in the preface to the novel, is an anonymous manuscript sent to the publisher. The mirror images of the text we are holding stretch within the novel *ad infinitum*, which is again, a manifestation of excess. Atay likes to play games. And this is no secret.[30]

Nurdan Gürbilek writes in "*Oyun ve Adalet*" (Game and Justice), one of her several articles on Atay, that there is always "an excess of words in Atay's novels," which is part of the games he plays: "The noise that soars from Atay's novels stems from the commingling and clashing of all these discourses that we mentioned before. It sounds like the noise that little kids make when they change roles while playing a game. It is a noise that sounds like gibberish to an outsider" (*Ev Ödevi*, 13). When she talks about the excess, Gürbilek seems to be in agreement with Eagleton, who writes that the excess of meaning, in general, is the outcome of dialogism: "Signs are never self-identical, and always mean more than they say (a surplus that includes what they don't say)" (Eagleton. "I Contain Multitudes"). She observes that Atay's world is a place where words keep growing uncontrollably, where anybody who talks feels obliged to produce more and more words until the moment he loses all meaning —hence, running the risk of demagoguery.

This emphasis on "demagoguery" takes us to another biography that we come across in this part of the novel: the story of Ziya Özdevrimsel,[31] who campaigns with zest and vigor for a series of reforms brought by the revolutionary spirit of the republic, and looks as if he has popped out of Tanpınar's *Time Regulation Institute*.[32] He is presented as a great revolutionist who not only complied with the reforms, but also introduced new ones. He is so devoted to the revolution that "nobody has seen him without a hat after the proclamation of the Hat Reform (rumor has it that he had a soft hat with a short brim for indoor use), without any clothes after the Apparel Reform, writing in Arabic letters after the Alphabet Reform, or eating using his hands after the Knife-and-Fork Reform." How he benefits greatly from his trips to Europe and America constitutes the backbone of the biography, and it is emphasized that he owes his cultural formation to the research he carries out in the West. We are assured that the story of each reform is worth telling, but the most interesting among all is the incident that gave rise to the "Baby Swaddling Reform." What is interesting about this

---

30 In *Tehlikeli Oyunlar* (Dangerous Games), Atay's playfulness becomes even more obvious as Gürbilek discusses in her brilliant article "Oyun ve Adalet" (Game and Justice). See Nurdan Gürbilek, *Ev Ödevi*. Istanbul: Metis, 2005.

31 "*Özdevrimsel*," which means "true revolutionary," is the surname that Ziya takes during the Reform of Family Names.

32 The absurdity of Ziya Özdevrimsel's loyalty to reforms reminds us of Halit Ayarcı's (Halit the Regulator's) project of *The Time Regulation Institute*, an institution which becomes the landmark of the Turkish Republic's "insatiable desire and unique capacity for modernization." (Irzık "Allegorical" 558).

story is that Ziya Bey hardly gets to the hospital where he is inspired to propose the reform that is practically the implementation of the western style of baby wrapping. Up to this point we are told several other stories about the things that happen to him on the way:

> One day, as he was idly walking in the streets of Childharoldshire (a campus town), Ziya Özdevrimsel comes to an intersection. (When he returned to Turkey, he had the exact replica of this intersection built in Ankara, on the road to Dışkapı. In addition to simply ignoring the difficulty of building three roads at that intersection, he even insisted on the construction of a fourth road opposite to the Ministry of Finance – much to the dismay of visitors from abroad because it looks perfectly out of place at the first sight – so that it looks exactly the same with the original.) As he was approaching the crossroads where the traffic lights are (these traffic lights were the ones that brought him the title of the creator of the Reform of Traffic Signals), he did not notice that the light was "red", because he was preoccupied. His mind was busy with possible reforms to come. Well, in fact, Ziya Bey could not understand the meaning of the "red light." ("Understanding the meaning of something" was one of the idioms that Ziya Tahiri incorporated into the Turkish language during the Language Reform. He was so dedicated to the Language Reform that he wanted to change his name to "Işık," but he gave up the idea - and was content with the change in his family name - when Kamil Bey, the Minister of Health, told him: "My dear Ziya, we can not change the name of everything. Do you think I should also drop my name and be called "Olgun"?) (141)

Digression is another form of excess. *Tristram Shandy*, for example, which begins with its hero about to be born, becomes so sidetracked by digressions that the story ends shortly after his birth. Similarly, this small story does not really talk about Baby Swaddling Reform. Even after Ziya Bey gets hospitalized due to a traffic accident, we see that we cannot really return to the main story line. An unmistakable detour keeps postponing the object of the story. Each time we think that we are about to pick up the thread of the main storyline, the text suddenly veers off in yet another direction – that is one way or the other related to the story. Is this because *how* the story is told is more important for Atay than *what* the story is about? [33] It is true that Atay has a kinship with Sterne in that his narrative is based on endless free play and a performative style. There are moments when Atay's text comes close to that of Sterne in that it displays Tristram Shandy's logic of digression: "Remember the characters in Alice's Wonderland: they have this habit of moving to another subject when they get stuck in an argument. Let us do the same, Olric" (536). When he says this, Turgut seems

33 This brings us back to the distinction made by the Russian Formalist critics between the *fabula* (the chronological series of events that are represented or implied in a fiction) and the *sjuzet* or *syuzhet* (the order, manner and techniques of their presentation in the narrative).

to agree with Shandy, that "digressions, incontestably, are the sunshine;--they are the life, the soul of reading;--take them out of this book for instance,--you might as well take the book along with them; [...] restore them to the writer;--he steps forth like a bridegroom,--bids All hail; brings in variety, and forbids appetite to fail" (*Tristram Shandy*, 95).

However, what makes this affinity important for us is the acknowledgment of the impossibility of closure.[34] In referring to the open-endedness of the novel, Bakhtin suggests that the new genre is too large and too rich for the monological uniformity of the epic, which, in its completeness, presents an "autarchic" unity. The novel, on the other hand, requires a completely new approach of narrative, which liberates it from ideological readings, and gives the text back its privilege of being an "anarchic" device favoring diversity over totality. Accordingly, in welcoming a dialogical open-endedness and acknowledging the impossibility of closure, Bakhtin also "rejects dialectical forms of thinking, which always move toward a higher unity of synthesis" (Morris, *Bakhtin Reader*, 15).

Jale Parla discusses the open-ended nature of the novel in relation to what she calls the "missing text." In her article "The Object of Comparison," she refers to the contribution of the technique of missing text to the rise of the novel in Turkey. She writes that the technique first employed by Ahmet Mithat became a marker in the development of the Turkish novel and adds that this motif of "the promised but never told or partly told tale" is used not only to whet the appetite of the reader, but also "to keep the vistas of fabulation open (for the writer as well as the reader), to expand the horizon of narrative freedom, and to provide immediacy for author-reader dialogue" ("The Object," 123).

Parla views the presence of a missing text in a literary work as the problematization of representation. According to Parla, each and every author writes with the intention of representation, but not all authors make the problem of representation the axis of their work. No wonder that this technique keeps emerging in the history of Turkish novel "every time a novelist attempts to take a new step to break from the tradition, or to give expression to a mimetic crisis that s/he

34 I am using the term "closure" in the particular sense Derrida attributes to word —not in the general meaning as the "ending" of a text. Deconstruction emphasizes the lack of totality and closure in any form. However, Derrida insists on the distinction between "closure" and "end." In a 1967 interview, he states that the term "closure" indicates a *spatial* domain that is finite but unbounded (however fissured and ruptured), as opposed the "end" that suggests a *temporality,* in which change can occur. According to Derrida, beginnings and ends occur only within a closure; and a closure is that for which there can be no beyond. See Jaques Derrida *Positions*. Trans. Alan Bass. (Chicago UP, 1981).

feels needs a solution" (123). Being inspired by psychoanalytical criticism,[35] Parla focuses on the idea of the loss of the object, and asks what these lost texts stand for in novels such as *Don Quixote* or *The Disconnected*:

> Being a form of narrative metonymy, the missing texts are junctures that tell us the contract between the author and the reader can be abolished any moment; they are the lapses in the text where the impossibility of such an imaginary contract is represented. They remind the reader of the following: What you are holding in your hands is just a narrative. A narrative written by this author. However, there are innumerable other narratives that have been or will be written. And the book you are holding now is impregnated with the possibility of change in the light of all these narratives in the past and the future. As this book is not the last one on earth, no reading is the final reading of a text. (Don Kişot, 62)

Parla's "missing text," owes to Bakhtin —as well as to Derrida and Lacan— and leads us back to a reconsideration of the openended text. The numerous styles and genres that we come across in *The Disconnected* indicate the unclosed, uncompleted structure of the novel. These textual encounters, which Atay successfully incorporates in his work, become the collective language of the novel, an open-ended flux where there is and will be place for each and every discourse. Each of these reveals the "salient features of novelization" as Bakhtin describes them in "Epic and Novel": "they become... free and flexible, their language renews itself by incorporating extraliterary heteroglossia..., they become dialogized, permeated with laughter, irony, humor, elements of self-parody and finally--this is the most important thing--...an indeterminacy, a certain semantic open-endedness, a living contact with unfinished, still-evolving contemporary reality (the open-ended present)." (*Dialogic*, 6-7)

One cannot help but agree with Parla, who, in her analysis of Atay's novel, maintains that the disconnected cannot hold onto anything "save other texts"

---

35 Especially Lacan, who goes through the Freudian idea of lost object, defines the loss of object as a three level operation: Real, Symbolic and Imaginary that requires subject, object and the Other.
In order to be able to understand the core idea of Parla's missing text, one should bear in mind the status of *objet a* in Lacan. The essence of *objet a,* and our confrontation with it, is constituted in its very loss.
Although in both cases, the link between object and loss is crucial, in the case of *objet a,* as the object of desire, we have an object which is originally lost, whereas in the case of Parla's missing text we are faced with a problem of representation, an object the complete representation of which is impossible. (This problem of representation may also be approached in relation to Lacan's analysis of the Real, which he also calls the "impossible" because of the same reason: the problem of representation.) See Lacan, J. (1957), Le seminaire IV: *La relation d'objet* [Seminar IV: Object relations]. Paris: Seuil, 1994. Lacan, J. (1966), Écrits. Paris: Seuil.

(*Don Kişot*, 224). Atay's texts feed on other texts rather than life itself. And texts… there are great numbers of them. Parla argues that Turgut gradually goes mad, as he discovers he cannot put all the texts together and come up with a reasonable explanation for Selim's suicide. The acknowledgment of the impossibility of putting all the texts together is also the understanding that finally dawns on Turgut that he cannot attribute a meaning to his loss. This is the end of his search within the limits of rationality, and the end of the yearning for the long lost totality of the Epic.

# THE NIGHTMARE OF HISTORY: LIMITS OF "NATIONAL ALLEGORY"

History is a nightmare from which I am trying to awake.
– *Stephen Dedalus*

History becomes a central —and personal— issue in *The Disconnected*, especially after Turgut discovers the manuscript Selim wrote years before his suicide in an attempt to entertain his good old friend Süleyman Kargı. In the commentary attached to the manuscript, a mock-autobiography called "Yesterday, Today, Tomorrow," we read that the problem about history is that it had been "stowing away all the documents it did not like from Selim and his lot," and Selim's account of his own history promises to shed some light on facts that have been covered up. This is the first thing we read in the commentary supposedly written in the sensible voice of Suleyman:

> The urge to create a consistent philosophy of history resulted in the deliberate concealment of numerous facts. It could not have been otherwise, something had to be done. Nobody had the right of detaching Selim from his past and future. Somebody had to pay the price, and somebody would. Yesterday, today and tomorrow were his, and had to become one and the same with his life. [...] This is what the song derives its name from. What exactly had happened yesterday? One had to dig into the past and look for yesterday, because it was the sole ground upon which today and tomorrow rest. This is what Selim did, because only then could he walk around naked in his second coming—as he says in line 237. (115)

From then on, we are provided with clues that Selim's personal history will be our beacon light in understanding the country's history, and vice versa. The fact that the protagonist's private history becomes a key in grasping what is happening in the public sphere does not mean that the two overlap. On the contrary, as we read from Selim's account of his own history, we see that it usually crosscuts the country's evolution. The song "Yesterday, Today, Tomorrow" displays several voices parodying Turkey's official history. Atay's attitude in *The Disconnected*, reflected in the development of his double protagonists Selim and Turgut, is one that challenges the totalizing attitude of authority, an authority which through the use of rhetoric fabricates its own truth—that is, the illusion that the country is on its way towards a more western and modern state or, in other words, the *Occidentalist fantasy*.[36]

---

36 Ahıska develops the concept of Occidentalism and elaborates on the Occidentalist fantasy in Turkey, which nurtures an ideal and static truth, a "timeless modality of being

The desire to become western and to remain national at the same time emerges as one of the main issues parodied in the novel, such as in the passages of the biographical poem "Yesterday, Today, Tomorrow" constituting Selim's memories of childhood. Selim's voice imitating that of a confused high school kid, asks, "Cranium fibula radius / Sacrum patella carpus / How am I going to learn by heart / The Latin names of bones / of a man, who prays in Arabic to his God?" (106) Elsewhere in the interpretation of the song, he sarcastically comments on how the Turkish bourgeois entertains the idea of being modernized if they can utter a few words in French. Picking on his provincial father, who would adopt the language but not the culture (the politeness of the French being the point here), Selim comes up with the following passage:

> As for the issue of French, the whole country was made up of *francophones* those days. Languages like Armenian or Greek spoken by the provincial minorities or taught at *mektep*s – before the Republic – were no more considered as foreign languages. Even Numan Bey, who had a vague acquaintance with the languages of minorities, would scold his wife in French when he thought there was not enough salt in his supper (he always found some fault with supper). '*Donnez-moi un peu de sel*!' he would say. (Numan Bey thought politeness was waste of time, and hence he would not add '*Si'l vous plait*'.) (151-152)

However, in the last analysis, it is of little importance whether Selim's private history crosscuts or overlaps with Turkey's development. What matters is that there is enough evidence to claim that the narrative structure of *The Disconnected* reveals strong ties between the two realms: the public and the private. Selim's song is dominated by the desire to be "freed from the illusion of history" (115). It is an illusion, a "truth" fabricated by political authority, or rather a dream as he later admits in the following exposition of line 509 of the poem: "History is nothing but a misrepresentation. History is a dream that stretches from the past into the future, and that we are having today. Like all dreams, it can be interpreted, but not while you are living in it (202-3). As if to support Selim's sense of entrapment, the historical dreams in *The Disconnected* have a suffocating and nightmarish quality reflecting a deep sense of anxiety, as Irzık notes in her article called "Allegorical Lives: The Public and the Private in the Modern Turkish Novel" (556). In reference to the reappearance of Atatürk as the father of the nation in the dreams of the protagonists of *The Disconnected* and Adalet Ağaoğlu's *Lying Down to Die*, Irzık contends that "the dreamer, an isolated individual on the verge of suicide and struggling to wake up from 'the nightmare of history,' must stand for the whole Turkish nation" (553).

---

Western and national at the same time." See Meltem Ahıska, "Occidentalism: The Historical Fantasy of the Modern," *South Atlantic Quarterly* 102, no. 2/3 (2003).

But does this condemn a novel like *The Disconnected* to be read only as a "national allegory," as Jameson suggests? In his much-debated essay "Third-World Literature in the Era of Multinational Capitalism," Jameson labels all third-world texts as 'national allegories,' and adds that this is especially true for the novel, which is one of the "predominantly western machineries of representation."

> Third-world texts, even those which are seemingly private and invested with a properly libidinal dynamic, necessarily project a political dimension in the form of national allegory: the story of the private individual destiny is always an allegory of the embattled situation of the public third-world culture and society. ("Third World," 65)

Irzık acknowledges that Fredric Jameson's definition of Third World literature in terms of the relationship between the public and the private is "a very important insight," but goes on further saying that it is "too simplistic to see this relationship as simply a lack of differentiation" ("Allegorical Lives," 564). Drawing upon Neil Larsen's observation of certain Latin American novels,[37] she argues that one can hardly talk about the type of allegory that Jameson has in mind when one considers Turkish novels written in the second half of the twentieth century, because they are far from exhibiting highbrow viewpoints when it comes to the representation of such political consciousness. In fact, there is "a certain repressive conflation of the public and the private that the political allegories in several Turkish novels parody and resist even as they self-consciously reproduce it." The employment of reversal and irony —basically Bakhtinian gestures— is a way of going beyond the limits of national allegory, as Irzık demonstrates in the case of *The Disconnected*:

> *The Disconnected* is an even more radical refusal to construct a life story that could be appropriated and articulated into a national narrative. This refusal takes the form of taking the allegorical impulse to a parodic extreme. Selim's supposedly autobiographical poem, "Yesterday, Today, Tomorrow," for instance, is surrounded with a mock commentary consisting of a perverse proliferation of ridiculous life stories inserted into ridiculous historical narratives. The absurd abundance of biographies, identities, and histories creates a constant background noise which interferes with even the most serious attempt to find the essence, the proper meaning of an individual life, as in Turgut's search for the truth Selim's life and death are supposed to represent. Oğuz Atay's characters are dispossessed not only of possessions and status,

37 As Irzik points out, according to Larsen, Latin American novels observe "An almost conscious decision to create only characters whose national-allegorical representativity is so complicated and ironized as to be made virtually impossible." (564) See Neil Larsen, "Imperialism, Colonialism, Postcolonialism," in *A Companion to Postcolonial Studies*, ed. Henry Schwartz and Sangeeta Ray (Oxford: Blackwell, 2000), 38–39.

> but also of allegorizable lives. They are disconnected not only from the comforts of bourgeois existence, but also from the "grand narratives" of the nation. ("Allegorical Lives," 562)

One of these "grand narratives" of the nation, for instance, is reflected in the relatively optimistic social climate of the 1970s, when the growing rate of poverty had not yet resulted in wearing out the belief in a better future. Being a modernist state, Turkey believed in the unified effort of its people in carrying the "belated" motherland to the level of developed countries. Despite the lack of political stability and a series of economic crises, people had not abandoned their faith in the values of the Republic: work hard and build the nation. Here is how Turgut perceives the motto of the young Turkish Republic:

> [...] When does the Turk come to his senses? He passed the Monument of Confidence. He stopped and walked back. He entered the park. No kids: time for siesta. The little villains are sleeping now. He looked at the statues of the monument. They did not look like Turks. He remembered what Kenan used to say: he smiled. They look like the German-Japanese. One is proud, the other one is confident, and the third one works hard. (280)

Be proud, work hard, and have confidence (in the State)! The high expectations of the Republic from its citizens, are reflected in the appearance of the statues that look like western people: well organized, successful, and satisfied with their lives. The joke about the Germans and the Japanese is very apt for the period, because Turgut, like most Turks, both despises and envies these nations for the hard work they put into the reconstruction of their countries after having lost the Second World War. The Turks are not hard working. That is why, they should be told at every single opportunity that they are capable of building a nation. Elsewhere in the novel as in this particular example, by positioning himself in opposition to the core ideology of the Republic —and the official history that this ideology generates— Atay justifies Irzık in her assessment that the disconnected can not be evaluated within the framework of the narratives of the nation.

In addition to Irzık's insightful analysis, one feels obliged to note that the protagonists of Atay's novel are disconnected not only from the "grand narratives" of the nation, but also from those of the West, such as the dialectic of the master and the servant. Jameson's dramatization of the relationship between West European literature and Third World texts as "lordship and bondage" is part of a "grand narrative" of the West, namely the dichotomy of the subject and the object, which provides the basis for both Hegel's idealism and Marx's materialism. [38]

---

38 The main problem for Hegel, as it had been for his predecessors, was to overcome the dichotomy of the subject and the object, the knower and the known. The subject-object

As traditional philosophy views it, the knowledge that consciousness possesses is always the knowledge of an object. Then, we should expect Hegel to consider knowledge as a movement from concept to object, for concept is the subjective side of knowledge, and object is the objective one. However, Hegel reverses this order in the *Phenomenology*, and he starts with the objective, the immediate, the in-itself. The discrepancy that consciousness discovers between the object (the object for consciousness), and the concept (the knowledge of itself), moves it to the attainment of their identity. At the level of sense-certainty, we see an empirical "I" cut off from its concept, the knowledge of itself as itself. In Hegelian terms, its concept lies outside itself. As Hegel would put it, it should enter into "the play of forces," and be transcended to a higher level of consciousness by being negated by its "other," since "that which is confined to a life of nature is unable of itself to go beyond its immediate existence; but by something other than itself it is forced beyond that" (Hyppolyte, 17).

Jameson's analysis of the distinction between the cultural logics of Western Europe and the Third World is based on this play-of-forces which constitutes Hegel's dialectic of recognition. According to Hegel, the master is the abstract consciousness, in the sense that it alienates itself from the objects that surround him, and the servant is the dynamic principle, because it possesses the potential of becoming a real/objective self-consciousness through the master he fears and the objects he works upon. The master's situation in this context appears to be a conflict, since self-consciousness can only be gained through recognition of another self-consciousness. That is to say, the master, in order to exist as a subject, has to recognize the servant also as a subject, which is obviously impossible, because if he does this, he can no more remain as the master. The servant, on the other hand, recognizes the master, as a subject from the very beginning, and dialectically establishes his own subjecthood/self-consciousness through the master and his direct relation to the material world. The master, therefore, is condemned to idealism as opposed to the servant, who represents materialism. That is why, Jameson, in his analysis, denies idealism to texts of the Third World, while furnishing it with the collectivity that the West European literature lacks:

> It strikes me that we Americans, we masters of the world, are in something of that very same position.... All of this is denied to third-world culture, which must be situational and materialist despite itself. And it is this, finally, which must account for the allegorical nature of third-world culture, where the telling of the individual story

---

dichotomy is the outcome of the dichotomy of knowledge and reality. This is why, the relation between the master and the servant is a "a play of forces", a "life-and-death struggle". (232) For the subjective certainty to become objective truth one has to risk his life in the struggle. See Hegel, *The Phenomenology of Mind*.

> and the individual experience cannot but ultimately involve the whole laborious telling of the experience of the collectivity itself. ("Third World," 72)

In fact, the collectivity that Jameson attributes to the Third World is essential to Hegel's understanding of Spirit. Hegel's *Phenomenology* is based on a twofold assumption: the attainment of philosophical knowledge through the development of empirical knowledge, and the emergence of individual consciousness from its seemingly isolated position to universal consciousness. Although these two tasks that *Phenomenology* sets itself are not separable from each other, the first one can be viewed as an epistemological and the second as an ontological approach. While raising natural consciousness from an abstractly specific 'I' to the universal 'I' that embraces, or contains within itself the whole spirit of its time, Hegel also makes it possible for consciousness to attain absolute knowledge, since this knowledge is nothing but the awareness of itself as itself, i.e., the consciousness of Spirit. Thus Hegel's primary task is to show that individual consciousness should be aware of its ontological relation to other individual consciousnesses, and this is at the very heart of its being. Therefore, Spirit for Hegel is the experience of a subject that is plural rather than singular, or as Hegel puts it is an "Ego that is 'we', a plurality of Egos, and 'we' that is a single Ego." (Hegel, *Phenomenology*, 227).

> Spirit is a 'we': we must begin not with the cogito but with the cogitamus. Spirit is history: it becomes what it is only through a historical development because each of its moments, in making itself essence, must realize itself as an original world, and because its being is not distinct from the action through which it poses itself. Spirit is knowledge of itself in its history: it is a return to itself through, and by means of that history, a return such that nothing alien subsists in or for spirit, and such that spirit knows itself as what it is and is what it knows itself to be (this being of spirit is nothing but its very action) (Hyppolite, 322-23).

In fact, by denying the West this collectivity and the realm of the public sphere, Jameson not only detaches West European literature from its ties with history, but also condemns it to an abstraction that is cut off from life itself —which in Bakhtinian terms, is a situation which destroys the organic unity between life and art.

In what is to come, we will take a closer look at this detachment and evaluate it from a Bakhtinian perspective. But before doing that we will argue that Jameson's analogy based on the rigid opposition of the abstract idealism of the master and the down-to-earth materialism of the servant fails to account for the presence of a novel like *The Disconnected*, where there is no process bridging the gap between the knower and the known, or achieving the identity of subject and object. In order to do this one should assert the possibility of knowing the truth about all reality. Atay's novel, however, does not hold onto any truth. In fact, by denying the possibility of attaining absolute knowledge, it also refrains from designating an absolute knower.

Therefore, it makes much more sense to approach Atay's novel from the perspective of Bakhtin's theory, which attributes an ambivalent nature to reality rather than limiting it to an understanding based on rigid binaries, such as the subject and the object. Bakhtin suggests that the author confronts the monological voice of unchallenged ideology by answering with a plurality of voices, which constitutes the carnivalesque spirit that reduces the ordered and hierarchical world to a theater without footlights, a world where all of us are participants and none of us are commentators. Thus, a "grand narrative" is effectively subverted —as the novel presents a continuous reversal of binary oppositions including that of the master and the servant. What is at work in *The Disconnected*, therefore, is a constant degradation, which is, whether it is expressed as parody or in any other form, the essential principle of grotesque realism that removes the boundaries between the ideal and the material, the upper and the lower, the mental and the bodily (Bakhtin, *Rabelais*, 19).

## The knight of the "playful" countenance": The Quixote of the third world

According to Bakhtin, the sharp distinction of the ideal and the material, as Jameson reproduces it in the relationship between the west and the third world, is characteristic of modernity. And this split finds its initial but best expression in Cervantes's novel *Don Quixote*, which, Bakhtin maintains, introduces a double existence instead of a unified whole: Quixote and Sancho.[39] While referring to the Janus-faced quality of the Fool in *Rabelais and his World*, Bakhtin argues that the bourgeois conception of the grotesque gave rise to the splitting of the mental/bodily, spiritual/material principles of being, which was once united in the ambivalent images of medieval figures. The sharp splitting of idealism and materialism —in Bakhtinian terms, of the upper and lower strata— , is reflected in the emergence of Don Quixote and Sancho Panza, where these two principles

39 As Walter L. Reed humorously notes, "the problem of Cervantes in Bakhtin's poetics is initially a simple one: his inconspicuousness." Neither Cervantes nor his novel Don Quixote figure at all prominently in Bakhtin's voluminous theorizing about the novel as a literary form. In the roughly 1200 pages of Bakhtin's major writings on the novel currently available in English, there are some twelve pages worth of discussion of Cervantes' masterpiece. See Walter L. Reed, "The Problem of Cervantes in Bakhtin's Poetics," *Cervantes: Bulletin of the Cervantes Society of America* 7.2 (1987): 29-37.

are not intermingled, but represented in two isolated individuals: "Sancho's materialism, his potbelly, his appetite, his abundant defecation are on the absolute lower level of grotesque realism of the gay bodily grave (belly, bowels, earth) which has been dug for Don Quixote's abstract deadened idealism" (22). Hence the splitting of the public from the private. As the servant represents the materialistic, the collective, the multi-voiced objectivity, the master stands for the idealistic, the individual, and one-sided subjectivity. As the servant points to the realm of the public referring back to the collectivity bondage, the master is isolated from this collectivity in that he is locked up in his private reality.

What makes Atay's novel interesting is that we can hardly tell apart what stands for the consciousness of the master from that of the servant. While reading *The Disconnected*, we constantly feel this twofold presence: No matter how quixotic Atay's double protagonists appear, the "Sancho" within them always leaks out through the surface. Or whenever we tend to believe what dominates the text is the language and imagery of the lower stratum (Sancho's world), the text is interrupted with an intellectual or artistic gesture that reminds us of Quixote's romantic idealism. In short, at times *The Disconnected* takes us back to medieval aesthetics where the split between the mental and the bodily had not occurred yet; a time when the bourgeois ego had not established itself as the sole truth, and the connection between the particular existence of man and the rest of the universe was not disturbed.

In Atay's novel, there are moments when we sense that the private is not cut off from the public, or the self is not truly disconnected from its other, and the link that the characters establish with life is not broken. But this has nothing to do with the materialism that the servant represents if we have to go back to Jameson's analogy. On the contrary, the characters of Atay's novel (Selim and Turgut), while being disconnected from the materialism of the western world, are deeply connected to others on a gut level – a connectedness, which Bakhtin would probably attribute to the medieval times, that is, before the onset of modernity. As Aijaz Ahmad argues, Jameson does not quite say whether what he means by the third world is a pre- or non-capitalist state (13), but he may be implying both in the following formulation:

> [. . .] one of the determinants of capitalist culture, that is, the culture of the western realist and modernist novel, is a radical split between the private and the public, between the poetic and the political, between what we have come to think of as the domain of sexuality and the unconscious and that of the public world of classes, of the economic, and of secular political power: in other words, Freud versus Marx [. . .] (Third World," 66)

Like Ahmad, I will argue that, even if we may accept Jameson's categories of the private and the public, "the relations between them are wholly different in third-world culture," the western eye, the self-designated knower, fails to notice that "the radical split between the private and the public," located in the capitalist mode, does not apply to the third world that is defined by the "absence of this split" and has an "immediate meaning" (Ahmad, 14).

In other words, Freud meets Marx in the third world. This becomes especially obvious in *The Disconnected* when Atay comes up with the parody of a group of young revolutionaries depicted as an ancient Turkic tribe in Central Asia. All the talk of "the struggle" and "the revolutionary process" immediately strikes the reader (familiar with the terminology of the leftist organizations of the 70s) as a travesty of Marxist agitprop — combined with a tremendous amount of sexual energy:

> Orkan, who did not want to lose the attention, quickly ended his monologue with these words: "… I'd like to finish now since we will go back to these issues again in the last analysis. So, let me hear your constructive criticism now."
>
> Kutbay grumbled: "Do you think we would let you talk for so long if we were able to come up with constructive criticism?" He threw the bowl of *kimiz* and broke it to pieces. "This doofus is gonna be our leader. Why do you think? Because none of us can afford a pissing contest with this windbag. We have to live with it." Gökçin bent towards him, "Go for leadership if you like. I'll back you up."
>
> "No, I can't. The girl is waiting for me in the tent. Do you think I would volunteer for such burden? If I do, you would jump at me shouting 'the cause, but the cause' while I'm on top of her. […] I'm just doing my job. During daytime I'm raising her consciousness and in the night I'm raising her skirt." (170)

Elsewhere in the novel, Atay's acute sense of being belated or underdeveloped is almost always merged with an instantaneous reference to the private, personal, and unofficial.

> Nowhere in the world can you see such scandal. As the country of underdeveloped love affairs we occupy the top of the list of world states. According to statistical data provided by the United Nations, it is only Nigeria and Gana that are less developed when it comes to love. The percentage of people really falling in love is forty-two in a hundred thousand. If the five-year plan is actualized with a hundred percent success, this percentage will increase up to eighty-six in a hundred thousand in the year 1980. The number will still be too small. Nobody really cares about this issue in the State Institute of Statistics, because everybody is married there. Since the implementation of the five-year plan, it was only Güner – a classmate of mine – who fell in love, but the girl was a singer in a bar. And because it was carnal love, it did not count. (409-10)

Apart from these humorous passages, which may still be regarded within the limits of Jameson's definition of "national allegory," one should also mention the sentiment that dominates Atay's novel in relation to the discussion of third world literature. When viewed from that perspective, what unites the public and the private in the East is not the materialism of the servant, as Jameson suggests, but the immediate unity of the spiritual and the material as symbolized by Selim, the combined image of Quixote and Sancho. In fact, there are moments in the Atay's novel, when the disconnected acknowledge the other as no different from the self without being confined into the power struggle Jameson envisions. In the following passage we see one such moment, where the tensions of modern culture such as class difference or intellectual snobbery are transcended—at least, momentarily:

> Rainer Maria Rilke would never get drunk with a shoe salesman, almost illiterate and a complete stranger, and have a heart to heart chat with a sergeant at the stairs of the tram on the way back home.
>
> And he would not regret it (with the same sincerity) five years after the event.
>
> He would not wonder whether he deceived himself or the shoe salesman, and suffer for not being able to tell. (604)

What Atay talks about here is something truly eastern —which cannot be articulated within the boundaries of the grand narratives of the West, be it Freud or Marx. The interconnectedness between the self and the other that Selim mentions here, cannot be observed in the divided, atomized, individualized texts of the West. By portraying how people from completely different backgrounds can connect easily and simply, Selim refers to the lack of distance that one can have in the eastern world, and the regret that follows because of the acknowledgment of a limited personal space. This is all familiar to the eastern reader — especially the regret— while at the same time it is alien to the West. Modern European literature is crowded with works on the impossibility of connecting to the other – with the only exception of Dostoevsky, who probably should be regarded as an eastern author in the first place, especially when one considers his heartfelt contempt for the highly institutionalized and individualized West.

As in the world of Dostoevsky, nothing lasts for a long time in Atay's novel: every sentiment is coupled with its opposite, every move is reversed, every endeavor fails. In this sense, he reminds us also of another Russian, Anton Chekhov who announces that "Russian excitability has one specific characteristic: it is quickly followed by exhaustion" (*Letters*), when he condemns his "dear Selim" to a similar defeat in the eyes of the West: "Selim, as in all his endeavors, began to write these songs like a Turk, but despite his good will and effort, he could not finish them like an Englishman" (134).

Why this bitter sense of defeat? If eastern sentiment is loaded with a sensitivity and warmth that is alien to the West, then why the feeling of being left out of the game? The following part of this chapter will aim at shedding light on these issues.

## History a la Sancho Panza

> Sancho Panza, who by the way never thought much of this, succeeded in the course of years, through the supply of a number of knight and robbers tales in the evening and night hours, to distract his devil, whom he later gave the name Don Quixote, in such a manner that the latter, without restraint, carried out the craziest deeds, but which, due to a lack of a predestined target, which should have been Sancho Panza himself, did not harm anyone. Sancho Panza, a free man, voluntarily followed Don Quixote on his quests, maybe out of a sense of responsibility, and obtained from this a great and useful entertainment until the end of his life.[40]
>
> *The Truth about Sancho Panza* – Franz Kafka

What dominates Atay's novel, as well as the rest of Turkish literature, according to Gürbilek, is a feeling of literary belatedness. In her latest book, *Kör Ayna, Kayıp Şark* (Blind Mirror, Lost Orient), she expresses her conviction that the evolution of the novel in Turkey should be viewed in the light of "what Gregory Jusdanis calls 'belated modernity,' what Tanpınar describes in *Peace of Mind* as 'stepping into the river as a late-comer,' Cemil Meriç in *Jurnal* as 'entering a play in the middle of the fifth act,' Atay in *The Disconnected* as '*appearing on stage playing the part of a servant*'" (182).

Gürbilek argues that the anxiety of failing to be original is not limited to the discovery of a national literary belatedness despite being largely related to it. She refers to the recurrent criticism blaming Turkish novelists for lacking original characters and genuine voices, and maintains that originality has been the central problem of all characters since the rise of the novel:

> The irony is that the history of the novel since Don Quixote is full of characters living in the world of borrowed ideals and bookish aspirations, characters that thereby fail in evaluating the real world. It is no coincidence that novelistic characters are condemned to an ordinary fate to the extent that they long for something exceptional: a genuine voice of their own. In *Crime and Punishment* Raskolnikov sheds blood because he wants to differentiate himself from the ordinary masses, taking great pains to be like Napoléon, just to see in the end that his bloody act is nothing but an ordinary judicial case, himself nothing but a "pale copy of characters from a foreign novel." The underground man curses the common laws just to see in the end that the curse itself is just as borrowed and bookish as the thing he curses. Kirilov of *The Possessed* prefers death in order to challenge God with the "courage to desire noth-

---

40 trans. by Muhittin Mungan.

> ingness," but his death itself will merely be an imitation of Christ's death. The Turkish scene is no different. ("Dandies and Originals," 602)

In reference to Turkish novels, Gürbilek also mentions *The Disconnected*, and draws attention to the fact that Selim's problem is no different from the other characters in terms of belatedness in that he fails to grow up "because he confuses what is bookish with what is real, perishing early in life because of the desire to be a Dostoyevsky, a Gorky, and an Oscar Wilde, all at the same time"(602). Selim is aware of his own situation, as he tells Esat in the following passage:

> What all these plays, novels, stories mean to me is completely different from how other people perceive them. The story of all life, of the entire humanity is told and completed in these books. For me, each new book is a new experience of life. I breathe through these books and their authors. I live with prefaces. No author is capable of surprising me, because I know his or her life from the beginning till the end. I know them by heart. What you call real life is different, though. You can never know what people are going to do next. They confuse me. They baffle me every day. It is much easier to live with my authors. He was born in the town N. in 1886. His father, his mother, his siblings, the milieu he lived in, the pain and suffering he went through unbeknownst to his friends and foes, his obsessions, the real reason why he broke up with his friends… All of these are between the lines. When I first start reading a new book, I wonder about the author. The things I do not know about him. But I relax, because I know that I soon will learn everything.' (334)

When he is a teenager, Selim devours books, and as he calls it, "kills" one author after another. First he is an admirer of Oscar Wilde. Then he denounces him for snobbery and starts worshipping what might be considered Wilde's antithesis: Gorky. He talks about how he comes to know all those authors through the prefaces of their books, how he becomes like a member of their families, how sad he feels when one goes through the first sorrowful experiences of early youth, how he is filled with joy when another gets published, and how he memorizes all the love affairs they ever had.

> 'Life and Works. I will never tire of reading these over and over again. There is always this preface at the beginning of each book telling me about Life and Works. I read it again and again.' […] In the end, he would go completely out of his mind and say that he would become an author of prefaces. He would say this would bring him worldwide fame, because it never occurred to anybody that one could write only prefaces and nothing else. Why hadn't he thought about that before? It was highly possible that there were thousands of hundreds of people out there dying to read prefaces. If the demands of these people were properly met, one could even make a fortune. (356-7)

Selim calls himself "an ideal reader", a reader that the novelists have been waiting for. When talking to Esat, he insists that he is a 'first class reader, no, even better than that: a stateroom reader." Referring to his beloved authors, he says that they would be overjoyed if they knew how much Selim appreciates their works. If they had the chance of watching Selim read their books, they would be so moved that "they would never be able to stop writing; they could never die" (360).

In addition to his incurable bookishness, with his faith and saintly persistence on one hand, and his tragic isolation on the other, it is obvious that Selim is yet another Quixote on the stage of world literature. Like Dostoevsky's kind Prince, he is too good for this world.[41] Yet, the quixotic existence that determines Selim's nature does not equip him with a sugary optimism. Selim, unlike Myshkin, is a Quixote aware of his own otherworldliness, and brings it down to earth through this recognition:

> You would call me a bookworm. Someone who pursues empty dreams. The pale shadow of life. You might think I am no different from Don Quixote, who loses his wits from reading too many tales of chivalry and comes to believe that he is a knight. Yet, there is a difference. I think I am Don Quixote.' (334)

Without Sancho, the outside observer, it is impossible to see Quixote as he is. In other words, Selim is not only the Quixote of his own story, the messianic dreamer, but also Sancho in that he sees himself from outside with the eyes of the realistic observer. Atay's Quixotic Selim is his own Sancho. He is the one who carnivalizes his own idealism by pointing at its abstract quality, i.e., Sancho's function in *Don Quixote.* As regards the disconnected, the characteristics that Sancho shares with the double protagonists of Atay's novel is a parodic power that feeds on the grotesque and demystifies the idealism of the master while opening the way to the exploration of the whole story under a different light.

An example of how grotesque realism functions within Cervantes's novel is when the Don writes a love letter for Sancho to convey to Dulcinea and then reveals Dulcinea's identity to him. Sancho is shocked, since he knows her to be a coarse peasant, but he promises to take the letter, which is written observing the conventions of the romances of the day. On the way, however, having met the curate and the barber Sancho discovers that he has lost the notebook that contains the letter to Dulcinea. He says the loss of the letter does not trouble him much, "for he had it almost by heart, and it could be taken down from him wherever and whenever they liked." As the barber urges him to repeat it, so that they can write it down, Sancho comes up with the following:

---

41 See *Chapter 5*, for reflections of Prince Myshkin of *The Idiot* in *The Disconnected.*

> Sancho Panza stopped to scratch his head to bring back the letter to his memory, and balanced himself now on one foot, now the other, one moment staring at the ground, the next at the sky, and after having half gnawed off the end of a finger and kept them in suspense waiting for him to begin, he said, after a long pause, "By God, senor licentiate, devil a thing can I recollect of the letter; but it said at the beginning, 'Exalted and scrubbing Lady.'"
>
> "It cannot have said 'scrubbing,'" said the barber, "but 'superhuman' or 'sovereign.'"
>
> "That is it," said Sancho; "then, as well as I remember, it went on,
>
> 'The wounded, and wanting of sleep, and the pierced, kisses your worship's hands, ungrateful and very unrecognized fair one; and it said something or other about health and sickness that he was sending her; and from that it went tailing off until it ended with
>
> 'Yours till death, the Knight of the Rueful Countenance."
>
> (Chapter XXVI – Part 1)

When Sancho introduces the image of a woman scrubbing the floor, instead of Quixote's dignified phrase "sovereign and exalted Lady," he puts everything in perspective. As he testifies in the very same chapter, the woman that the Don takes to be Dulcinea, is actually a base woman called Aldonza Lorenzo. In fact, she is "the lustiest lad in all the town… the whoreson wench, what sting she has and what a voice!" Similarly, the presence of Sancho in Selim's language is what gives a solid presence to the abstract idealism of his quixotic discourse, and makes it tangible. In the letter he writes to Jesus, we see this quality of bringing down the ideal, or the profanation of the sacred:

> Dear Jesus,
>
> I'm sorry for all that has happened. *Mea culpa*. I've been thinking of you all these days. I cannot take my hands off of your book. You are right about every single issue. Everything would have been completely different the day when we met if I had known the things that I am thinking about now. But you will see, I'll be a transformed man next time we meet – if we ever meet again. I have changed so much that you won't be able to recognize me. My parents will not be at home on Wednesday. Why don't you come? We could talk without being disturbed. (132)

Returning to Jameson's analogy of the master and the servant, one should also consider the fact that the idealism which Jameson attributes to the West is something that is partly fabricated by the third world, especially in the East in the form of Occidentalism,[42] which reminds one of Kafka's reading of the relation-

42 I am using the term 'Occidentalism' referring to the meaning that Ahıska attributes to it. Ahıska, while discussing the portrayal of 'the West' produced by non-Westerners, introduces a concept of Occidentalism, which "is different from an idea of internalized

ship between Sancho and Quixote. In *Die Wahrheit über Sancho Pansa* ["The Truth about Sancho Panza"], Kafka transcends the dualism personified in the characters of Sancho and Don Quixote, and their particular relationship that involves the problem of self-consciousness in the Hegelian (or Jamesonian) terms of the servant or the master (or the third-world and first world).

In his own version of Cervantes's story of the Don and his servant, Kafka imagines a reversal of roles, in which Sancho becomes the creator and Don Quixote, rather than an author of adventures, turns out to be a demon cast out by Sancho. Kafka's reading of the relationship is very interesting in that it chooses to represent the idealistic Don as a thought entity, and an evil one too. The parable imagines that Don Quixote is actually an aspect of Sancho Panza that has been projected into the real world. Kafka's Sancho attributes all his desire for a better life, honor, and status to his imaginary character called Quixote, who is the outcome of this literary projection. So, what Sancho creates in the form of the Don is a fabrication, a narrative, a story – very much like the image of the West in the 'non-West.' Sancho, paradoxically, is capable of seeing through this situation, that is to say, he is fully aware of Quixote's being an abstraction, and enjoys it unreservedly. While turning the master-servant relationship to, what Bakhtin might call, the "dialogized interiority" of one character, Kafka's parable also problematizes the subject/object dichotomy, and the binary oppositions that follow, i.e., idealism/materialism, madness/rationality, or art/life.

As his protagonist Selim does, Atay lives under the shadow of the narrative of the West, which is partly his own construct. Like Sancho, who "philosophically followed Don Quixote on his crusades," Atay follows the path of the great authors of the West "and had of them a great and edifying entertainment to the end of his days." But they also torture him, because he feels he is being watched by figures of the Western canon that he idealized and mystified. He lives under the terror of his own construct: "Even books don't take me seriously. They despise me as whores would look down upon merchants too generous with their money.' (335) He is angry with the authors he likes; he says they haunt him: "They are all killjoys. They ruin everything, and turn my life into hell" (358).

In his diary where he constantly talks about the impossibility of representing himself as he is, Selim refers to the western world as "they." In a desperate moment, he says: "They always have a better version of me – whatever has become

---

Orientalism or a defensive reaction against the West." She rather uses it to describe "the set of practices and arrangements justified in and against the *imagined* idea of 'the West' in the 'non-West'" (emphasis mine). See Meltem Ahıska, "Occidentalism: The Historical Fantasy of the Modern," *The South Atlantic Quarterly* 102.2/3 (2003) 351-379.

of me – which they pull of out of their portfolio and thrust into my face." (604) He is equally scared of being understood and not being understood by the West. He seriously contemplates about the possibility of being understood: "What if they understand me in the end?" he asks, and answers his own question saying, "It would be even worse, much worse." (604) Worse than the present situation when the world does not have an idea who Selim/Atay is. If they were capable of understanding him, this would not mean that he would be recognized as the "other." On the contrary, it would indicate that the West has transformed him into the material it is made of.

Therefore, it would not be wrong to say that Selim lives in the shadow of what Jameson calls West European literature. His relation to the masters of the canon is not a simple one, as Esat later tells Turgut: "He used to respect the authors he liked. A respect intermingled with fear." But the Sanchoesque quality of Atay's protagonist always interferes with his sober reverence, and provides him with the power of challenging the authority of even those he truly admires: "[…] he could not resist the temptation of imagining them [the authors he liked] as ordinary people involved in petty details of daily life, and laughing at them. Putting them into ridiculous situations would save them from being conceited and arrogant, he would say" (358).

Selim's way of facing his belatedness is putting his favorite authors in ridiculous situations, and thereby opening a new crevice where he can operate as the author of his own story. However, we come to understand that it is more than a game that Selim plays. This also what Atay does in *The Disconnected*, which renders him unique in the cultural climate that surrounded him, because he was able to resist the urge of yielding to the western canon despite his respect/fear for it. Instead of blindly imitating the subjectivity of the master, Atay resorts to the liberating power of laughter knowing that this is the only way out of bondage – even if we think within the limits of the Hegelian dialectic of recognition, where the power of the master comes to an end when the servant stops recognizing him as the master.

In Kafka's brilliant parable too, the authentic object of the Don's quest is Sancho Panza himself, who fails to offer him recognition granting the truth-value of his adventures. One such instance is when he refuses to believe Don Quixote's account of the cave as the knight tells Sancho and Basilio's cousin, and how he saw Dulcinea in her enchanted form there. Sancho, who knows the truth about Dulcinea's enchantment, thinks Don Quixote is crazy.

"And do the enchanted eat?" said the cousin.

"They neither eat," said Don Quixote; "nor are they subject to the greater excrements, though it is thought that their nails, beards, and hair grow."

"And do the enchanted sleep, now, senor?" asked Sancho.

"Certainly not," replied Don Quixote; "at least, during those three days I was with them not one of them closed an eye, nor did I either."

"The proverb, 'Tell me what company thou keepest and I'll tell thee what thou art,' is to the point here," said Sancho; "your worship keeps company with enchanted people that are always fasting and watching; what wonder is it, then, that you neither eat nor sleep while you are with them? But forgive me, senor, if I say that of all this you have told us now, may God take me- I was just going to say the devil- if I believe a single particle."

(Chapter XXIII – Part 2)

As Kafka suggests, without Sancho, without the element of laughter he introduces into the picture, Quixote loses his point of reference. He turns into absolute abstraction. Laughter, on the other hand, is the realm of the servant. It is the material, tangible, dynamic principle that urges the master to reconsider the ontological question he has been posing since the time of Plato: How can I know the truth about being?

The problem with this question is that it presumes that the fundamental way of being rests on the relationship between the knower/subject and the known/object. Hence, it is entirely based on an epistemological consciousness.[43] The subject of knowledge is a self-referential subject. It is the subject who projects his or her own world and attributes a meaning to the other from the project of the self. The western philosophy from Plato on, therefore, is reflected in the consciousness of Quixote, who projects his interiority to the outside world, and regardless of the "other," constitutes his own reality and lives upon it. In other words, the Don's consciousness stands for the subjective certainty of the master that claims to be the absolute.

This is the way Don Quixote attributes "meaning" to the objects and people around himself, as in the case of the windmills, the helmet, and the sheep. In his book *Deceit, Desire, and the Novel*, Rene Girard talks about this aspect of Cer-

---

43 According to Levinas, this is the biggest error of Western philosophic tradition, which has made one particular relationship to reality an exclusive relationship: the relationship of knowledge. Philosophy has become a reflection on knowledge. When it speaks about the subject, it only speaks about the subject of knowledge: in other words, about the epistemological consciousness. See Emmanuel Levinas. *Totality and Infinity: An Essay on Exteriority*. Translated by Alphonso Lingis. Pittsburgh: Duquesne University Press, 1969.

vantes's novel, and calls Don Quixote's madness an "ontological sickness" that he can pass to others, at least momentarily. Referring to specific instances in the novel where Quixote's friends try to cure him pretending to be as mad as he is, Girard writes: "Don Quixote spreads the ontological sickness to those around him. The contagion, which is obvious in the case of Sancho, affects everyone in contact with the hero, and *especially those who are shocked or roused to indignation by his madness.*" (97)

Don Quixote, a self-certainty that claims to be the absolute, sees what his mind and imagination create, a reeking inn becomes a gorgeous castle, the wench Aldonza is turned to the maidenly beauty of Dulcinea, his one true love, who he swears by in his battles and contemplates when he is idle. But I will concentrate on the instance of the windmills because that is the clearest example: Quixote sees "'thirty monstrous giants... with... long arms... the length of two leagues.'" (Part 1, Chapter VIII) Such is the demented mind of the master. Sancho tries to tell Quixote that the giants were only windmills, but he does not listen.

Apparently one can argue, as many critics did, that what Cervantes employs here, is a simple "perspectivism": "the inescapable fact that each individual necessarily confronts life from a unique vantage point, peculiar to himself." This would account for "Don Quijote's and Sancho's varying reactions to the same signifier with greater precision than heretofore possible. We know now how it is that Don Quijote can read "giants" and Sancho "windmills" in the same text."[44] However, the problem is that of a subjectivity which loses its perspective completely because it loses its point of reference. As the public sphere represented by Sancho is justified in its judgment through the collectivity it represents, the perspective of a private and isolated subjectivity is doomed to be abstract and empty.

What happens next in the story of the windmills is even more interesting. Sancho, not being able to persuade the Don, plays along with the master, and displays some of the madness of the knight, or adopts some of his lunacy only to make his life easier: "Be that as God will," says Sancho, "I believe it all as your worship says it," and offers him his assistance. Obviously, the "ontological sickness," Quixote's self-referential subjectivity, also takes hold of Sancho, and drags him from one place to another at times. Despite his disbelief in the master's narrative, Sancho follows his master into madness either out of a sense of duty, or – as it is the case most of the time – because he hopes some gain out of

44 For a detailed discussion of "perspectivism" in *Don Quixote*, see Carroll B. Johnson, "Beyond Metaphysics: Semiotics and Character in *Don Quijote*, I" *Cervantes: Bulletin of the Cervantes Society of America* 5.1 (1985): 3-17.

it.[45] When Quixote asks him to take the letter to Dulcinea, he is not convinced. But he takes it anyway, because the Don promises him an award. Sancho even tells the priest and the barber that Don Quixote has promised to give him a governorship and a beautiful wife when Don Quixote himself becomes an emperor. The priest and the barber conclude that Sancho has gone mad and promise him in jest that Don Quixote will certainly become an emperor or at least an archbishop. This last point troubles Sancho because he fears that an archbishop would not provide him with adequate rewards.

> To which Sancho made answer, "If fortune, sirs, should bring things about in such a way that my master should have a mind, instead of being an emperor, to be an archbishop, I should like to know what archbishops-errant commonly give their squires?"
>
> "They commonly give them," said the curate, some simple benefice or cure, or some place as sacristan which brings them a good fixed income, not counting the altar fees, which may be reckoned at as much more."
>
> "But for that," said Sancho, "the squire must be unmarried, and must know, at any rate, how to help at mass, and if that be so, woe is me, for I am married already and I don't know the first letter of the A B C. What will become of me if my master takes a fancy to be an archbishop and not an emperor, as is usual and customary with knights-errant?" (Chapter XXVI – Part 1)

The type of practicality that Sancho displays in the above passage is what Atay notices about Turkey's relationship with the West. The relation of Sancho to Quixote is that of imitation and utility. As we have mentioned above, the servant goes with the master and pretends to take part in his "ontological sickness" only to compromise temporarily —not because he really believes that he can partake in the madness of the master. Like Sancho, who occasionally laughs at Quixote, the third world is also aware of the master's madness, but follows the first world anyway, either because it is easier to do so, or because it looks promising and beneficial. So, what connects the servant to the master is not fear, but convenience. The master sets the example and the servant mimics him.

This mechanical quality of westernization is one of the characteristics of Turkey's project of modernization. And it is what both Turgut and Selim are

45 Is it not exactly what happens today, when Americans, "masters of the world," one feels obliged to quote Jameson, decide to attack some make-believe enemy, windmills if you like, and drag along third world countries (the unwilling servants) despite their lack of faith in the cause? Can we say that casus belli announced by the USA in the case of Vietnam, the Gulf War, and the last invasion of Iraq was convincing for the third world? Hardly. But the master sees what he sees, and he pulls the servant with himself. The difference is, however, when you live in the third world, you can not help but notice that the guns and the death toll are not make-believe.

allergic to. Even from his childhood on, we hear Turgut complaining about the modes of existence being imposed upon him. His first year at school is traumatic, because he does not recognize himself in the books he reads. His impression of his first reading book at primary school also indicates the beginning of Turgut's identity crisis:

> In this weird book, kids, who were not exactly dressed like us, kept throwing balls at each other. These guys, who did not seem to belong to any of the neighborhoods I know, would keep their savings in their piggy banks —we had no moneyboxes at our place—, and their fathers, who were surprisingly young men with no mustache like our brother Ahmet, would buy them little toy boats called 'felucca.' And there was this thing called the fatherland, which was supposed to be guarded very well. Every morning we would gather in the school garden, and shout our lungs out reciting in unison the vow that we love our fatherland more than our souls. (58)

Work hard, obey the rules, and believe in the progress you can make. Who knows, maybe one day you can become someone like those boys in the reading book. This is the way Turgut feels. Being a child in the early years of the Republic, Turgut's life is cracked open and divided into two as he meets for the first time the official ideology of the state. On one hand, there is the traditional undercurrent in his life represented by his comparatively conservative father, on the other hand, there is the counter influence provided by the enlightened teacher.

> The disputes between my father and my teacher constituted the loveliest memories of my first encounters with what is called 'culture.' I remember deriving a secret pleasure out of the communication between these two parties, who were talking through me, and did not even know that they were arguing. The first day of school, I remember rushing back home and informing my father about my first discovery: 'Father, you were wrong. I am not going to *mektep*, but to school.'[46] My father lifted his face from the newspaper he had been reading and gazed at me with tired and indifferent eyes: 'Let things stand for now,' he said. As I later found out, this phrase was the summary of my father's personality. 'Let things stand for now' he would say, and having said this he would not only make himself stop, but also bring a halt to everything. He would curb my speed and my mother's heedless temper with this incessant phrase of his: 'Let things stand for now.' If my father's philosophy, 'letthingsstandfornowism,' does not take the place it deserves in the history of thought, this will be truly unfair." (59)

At a time when everything moves with great speed towards a better future, and when all the citizens of the country were called to take part in the progress, no

46 The Turkish word for school, *okul* sounds more like the French *école*, which helps to emphasize the contradiction between two cultures here.

wonder that Turgut's father did not have a chance to spread his philosophy of 'letthingsstandfornowism.'

Therefore, the atmosphere created by Turkey's ambitious project of modernization, the history that Selim wants to rewrite, cannot be thought separately from the idea of westernization. All through the novel we hear both characters not being able to deal with the deep impact of the education system they have been through. Being part of the process of westernization, the education reform, especially the uniformity that it imposes on the lives of its citizens, resurfaces in Turgut's consciousness towards the end of the novel, when he finds himself in a small coffee house in the middle of nowhere:

> He stood up after reading for a while. He walked towards one of the coffee houses on the square. He walked in. He enjoyed the soothing coolness of the coffee house. A shadowy and relaxing coolness. A cup of coffee with medium sugar. A medium for the gentleman! Economy of words. They save seven thousand six hundred twelve words on coffee with sugar every day. He liked the coffee cup. Like a stone. With no handle. Looks like *Keloğlan*.[47] The radio is airing a program on education. The shopkeeper and the waiter are all ears. They learn how many sides a triangle has. The boy in the radio learns about mathematics with great surprise in his unbearably shrill voice. A man with a deep voice pretends to be teaching the boy about triangles. He makes the boy repeat. Music in between. Pedagogical. The boy talks in a way that makes him stretch every word he says. So does the man. They pound on the words and extend them as long as possible so as to make them more understandable: And whaaaaat have weeeeee just leeeeeeeearned, a triangle haaaaaaaaaas threeeeeeeeee sideeeeeeeeees... All these grownups, they have bent over the radio letting themselves be taught by a nerve-cracking wiseacre: they are listening to the talk about triangles. They are staging a play on mathematics, Olric. The father appreciates his son for having come up with correct answers. 'Bravo', he says from time to time. The shopkeeper smiles proudly as if he were the one who knew the answer. [...] Why don't parallel lines ever cross each other? Daddy, let me answer this one! Yes, Serap it's your turn. Paaaaaaaarallel liiiiiiiiines... Are these stretched words also part of the pedagogical method? Now, repeat after me, children! The choir of mathematics. Singing the choral symphony of parallel lines. (539)

Turgut's private —and if one considers the ending of the novel, unquestionably existential— moment in the coffee house is obviously interrupted and interwoven with the public, i.e., the observation of what is part of the indoctrination of the Republic: the education system. The parody of the education system, which requires absolute submission to authority, is based on a metaphor of a tautology:

---

47 Keloğlan, meaning 'the baldy boy,' is a beloved hero of Turkish folk tales. Being a peasant boy, Keloğlan represents innocence and simplicity coupled with one of the most cherished eastern virtues: modesty. This is probably why Atay calls this simple coffee cup 'Keloğlan'.

the triangle having three sides, a truth that is hardly questionable. By demonstrating how this self-evident truth is presented as a novelty, and received with excitement by the simple inhabitants of that provincial coffee house, Atay draws attention to the mediocre uniformity that authority propagates, which is exactly what Turgut runs away from – passage, like many others in the novel, where the public merges with the private.

All the same, as we have tried to argue in this chapter, the combined presence of the public and the private goes far beyond the representation of national question. As Ertuğrul puts it in a nutshell, while acknowledging the criticism that the novel offers of the progressive modernist state in parodying official history, one has to grant Atay the credit that he deserves in that he demonstrates the inseparable connection between the individual's sense of defeat and the failure of the project of modernity.

> The "Song of the Disconnected" parodies official history in its desire to create an origin by appropriating the traditional elements into a narrative of modern progress that will guarantee an identity. According to this official version of history, modernity is not a sundering of the traditional but is embedded in tradition itself as a seed; thus, what is happening today is the dialectical progress of that which has been at the origin all along. Cultural schizophrenia is produced and kept in place by this effort to weave the traditional and the modern into a narrative fabric. What the "Song of the Disconnected" reveals by parodying these narratives is the failure of the project of modernity, its inability to build an identity on the exhausted forces of a defeated culture, and the confusion created by the legends of past victories and the reality of the sad and failed present. Thus, "The Song of the Disconnected" is also a legend of exhaustion, fatigue, and death at the cultural/historical level. ("Belated Modernity," 640)

This is what grants *The Disconnected* universality, and places Selim and Turgut next to other great characters of modern literature, such as Dostoevsky's Ivan Karamasov, or Joyce's Stephen Dedalus. The cultural question behind their identity, that is to say, their approach to the problem of Turkishness as being "disconnected" not only from their own culture but also from the West, is no different from the meanderings of Ivan about Russian melancholy, or Stephen's account of Irish frustration. Selim and Turgut are not local heroes taking part in a "national allegory." On the contrary, in their own way, they try to find an answer to the existential question introduced by the modernity: what happens to the individual who experiences the loss of origin that gives meaning to his existence?

This chapter has been centered around not only an elaboration of Atay's dialogue with Cervantes, but also a discussion of where *The Disconnected* stands with respect to Jameson's thesis concerning third world literature, which he simply reduces to "national allegories." Considering the fact that Jameson's analysis of the distinction between the cultural logic of Western Europe and the Third Word is based Hegel's dialectic of the master and the servant, we have tried to show two things.

In the first place, even if we accept Jameson's analogy and approach the third world texts from the perspective of the dialectic of recognition, the dynamic principle in the master-servant dialectics is the servant, and thus if the servant stops recognizing the master as master, the master is doomed to an idealism which is completely cut-off from reality. This effectively reduces the West European literature to an abstraction lacking content, which is probably the conclusion that Jameson wants to reach, but does not prove to be satisfactory in shedding a light on western literature in general.

Secondly, by drawing upon the figures of Quixote and Sancho as archetypes of the master-servant relation, representing idealism and materialism respectively, we have pointed out that once the self is cut-off from its "other," it loses its perspective completely, becoming a Don Quixote chasing wind-mills. This split is the outcome of the advent of modernity in the West, characterized by a sharp distinction between materialism and idealism, as well as that between the self and the other.

Evidently, when Jameson talks about the idealism of the West, he relies heavily on this sharp split and projects it to the rest of the world. Drawing upon his master-servant analogy, we assumed that western idealism finds its best expression in the archetypal character of Don Quixote. The idealism of Quixote, however, is completely cut off from the public sphere. Like Hegel's "beautiful soul,"[48] Don Quixote discovers within himself a divine voice, and while contemplating himself, he enjoys the divine within himself. However, he refuses anything that is "earthly," and, therefore, is doomed to be detached from reality, separated from the world. It is true that his subjectivity is raised to the level of universality, but being incapable of interacting with the rest of the world, he fails to transform his thought into being, and pays the price for mere contemplation with his very existence. By contemplating, it wills himself out of existence, and fails to represent the universality he claims to bear within himself.

---

48 The beautiful soul is what Hegel discusses in relation to morality and the route that acting consciousness follows. According to Hegel, the beautiful soul (*die schöne Seele*) is the natural good, which easily reconciles duty with freedom. It naturally acts in accordance with duty; it is the pure good will in Kantian terms. But in the case of the beautiful soul, moral consciousness loses its concreteness, and tends to be contemplative rather than active. The irony about the beautiful soul is that the more it isolates itself from actuality, the more is it detached from the universal. While it takes itself to be the identity of the universal and the individual, what it really does is reducing both to an empty abstraction.

The West's failure to acknowledge the presence of the other, therefore, results in an abstract idealism which manifests itself either in the loss of self, as in the case of the beautiful soul, or as in the case of the master, which in turn becomes the rigid and hard-headed judging consciousness, convinced of possessing the knowledge about all that there is. We have argued that no comparable process has taken place in the East. What is at work in the East is a constant reversal of the binaries of the material and the ideal. When viewed from this perspective, what dominates the East is not the materialism of the servant, as Jameson suggests, but the immediate unity of the spiritual and the material, as symbolized by Selim Işık, the eastern visionary, who is the combined image of Quixote and Sancho.

This double presence is constantly felt in Atay's novel: no matter how quixotic its protagonists appear, the Sancho within leaks to the surface and vice versa. It is precisely that interplay between the idealistic and materialistic that gives content to the characters and the novel itself. Thus the double-protagonists of *The Disconnected*, Selim and Turgut, are not simply local heroes partaking in a "national allegory." They rather emerge as modern characters trying to find in their own way an answer to one of the main existential questions introduced by modernity, namely what happens to an individual experiencing the loss of what gave meaning to his existence.

# THE PRINCE AS JESTER: THE "HAMLETIZATION" OF THE TURKISH INTELLECTUAL IN *THE DISCONNECTED*

In *Problems of Dostoevsky's Poetics*, Bakhtin observes that Dostoevsky was the first artist to break free of the monologic tradition that dominated Western thought since Plato. However, he also admits the presence of polyphonic elements in other artists, such as Shakespeare and Balzac (33). In *Rabelais and His World*, he mentions Shakespearean tragedy as the most significant example where the rigid boundaries of the genre are overcome by carnival ambiguity:

> In world literature there are certain works in which the two aspects, seriousness and laughter, coexist and reflect each other, and are indeed whole aspects, not separate serious and comic images as in the usual modern drama [...] the most important works in this category are, of course, Shakespeare's tragedies. (122)

As Bakhtin himself opened the way for a reading of Shakespeare's tragedies in the light of his notion of the carnivalesque,[49] following the publication of Bakhtin's book in English in 1968, many critics worked on the plays accepting the invitation. Therefore, any study on Shakespeare and the carnival is indebted to several authors, such as Michael Bristol, Manfred Pfister, and Michael Gardiner, as Knowles reminds the reader in the introduction to his *Shakespeare and Carnival*. Unsurprisingly, there are also numerous studies focusing on the employment of the carnivalesque in *Hamlet*, Shakespeare's most popular tragedy.

One such study is Bristol's essay called "Funeral bak'd meals," which views Bakhtin's principles of the carnival under the light of the Marxist theory, and contends that both Claudius and Hamlet camouflage themselves with carnivalesque masks, but it is Hamlet who has an advantageous "understanding of the corrosive and clarifying power of laughter" (350). While mainly drawing on the relationship between Claudius, as the usurper of the crown, and Hamlet, as the one that challenges authority, Bristol also refers to Hamlet's interaction with "actual representatives of the unprivileged: " the Gravediggers, completes Hamlet's training in carnivalism (359). Aside from the "clear and explicit critique of the

49 While he establishes his key notion of 'carnivalesque' in *Rabelais and His World*, Bakhtin specifically refers to the varied popular festive life of the Middle Ages, but he also admits the possibility of observing traces of carnival spirit in the literature that follows. The carnival spirit survives in carnivalized writing, which, in its own practice, makes use of the characteristic inversions, parodies, crownings, and uncrownings of carnival. When it enters writing, carnival spirit offers a liberation from "all that is humdrum and universally accepted" (*Rabelais*, 34).

basis for social hierarchy", this scene shows Hamlet reflecting on death, body identity, community, and laughter. He confronts Yorick's skull but learns that "the power of laughter is indestructible: Even a dead jester can make us laugh" (360-61).

Another essay that draws attention to the trickster theme in *Hamlet* is Burnett's "Hamlet as Trickster", which concentrates on the traditional and Elizabethan figures of tricksters and views the play as a set of relationships "between those who trick and those who are tricked" (43). In Burnett's analysis, the focus is primarily on "Hamlet's own tricksy practices", and the Prince is portrayed as the one who "follows in the path of the trickster in choosing words and theatre as the weapons with which he will secure his role as revenger" (34-37). Like Bristol, who underlines the Prince's carnivalesque ability of turning political structures upside down, Burnett points to the anarchic quality contained in the nature of the trickster displayed by Hamlet. He points to the fact that Hamlet raises concerns about religion, succession, and gender, comparable to the "unprecedented social forms and new ideological configurations" experienced while Elizabeth I reigned as monarch. In a carnivalesque style, *Hamlet* affords Elizabethans "a release of tensions" and a means of "social protest" through its trickster(s) (49-50).

Gorfain approaches the issue from another, arguably more traditional, angle and claims that the use of laughter in *Hamlet* increases the play's tragic effect.[50] The "carnivalesque in Hamlet intensifies its complex tragic mode," as the "irreversible and vertical movement of tragic form joins to the reversible and horizontal continuum of carnival in *Hamlet* to produce the double vision" (27-28). She especially concentrates on the repetitive presentation of Old Hamlet's murder, through narrative, mime, and performance, which demonstrates how the "self-reflexive play with the boundaries between event and representation, past and present, subjunctive and actual, audience and performers defines and dissolves the differences between the world of the play and the world of the theater" (29). In reference to Bakhtin's observation of carnival knowing no footlights, Gorfain reminds us that "carnival obscures the differences between per-

---

50 Probably the among the first critics to mention the importance of comic scenes in that they add to the tension in Shakespeare's tragedies was Thomas De Quincey. In his well-known article, "On the Knocking at the Gate in *Macbeth*," Quincey discusses the dramatic effect of a seemingly unnecessary scene when a drunkard starts knocking at the gate in Macbeth at a time when everybody in the castle sleeps unaware of the fact that the king is murdered. Like Gorfain, Quincey argues in favour of laughter in tragedies claiming that they act as a counterpoint on the main event making it more effective. http://www.4literature.net/Thomas_De_Quincey/On_the_Knocking_at_the_Gate_in_Macbeth/

formers and audience, blending us all in a comedic vision of performance culture, so Hamlet uses its reflexive ending to make us observers of our own observing, objects of our own subjective knowledge, inheritors of the playful knowledge paradox" (43).

As it is generally agreed, the clowning scenes used in *Hamlet* and *Macbeth* are some of the finest examples of how "the carnival Fool" enters tragedy providing an alternate viewpoint by interrupting the main action of the play. As Culwell maintains, the clowns used the oral/ physical tradition to create diversity and to provide a more complete understanding of the theme by employing a "mingle mangle" of their own.[51] This popular technique of mixing comedy with tragedy, which was alien to other European plays of the time, was an indispensable characteristic of the Shakespearean drama.[52] Shakespeare himself makes fun of the critics of tragicomedy —probably the French— through Polonius, another clown-like character in *Hamlet*, who observes upon the arrival of the players in Hamlet, that the actors are well prepared to suit the demands of the audience:

> the best actors in the world, either for tragedy,
> comedy, history, pastoral, pastoral-comical,
> historical-pastoral, tragical-historical, tragical-
> historical-comical-pastoral, scene individable...
>
> (Hamlet, II,ii,392-397)

The clowning scenes, such as the Porter scene in *Macbeth*, and the Gravedigger scene in *Hamlet*, or the scene of murderers preceding the killing of Clarence in *Richard III* can be said to be instances of, what Bakhtin calls, "heteroglossia," introducing a variety of voices into the discourse of the play. And as Quincey and Gorfain claim, the placement of the clowning scenes is extremely important: they are usually introduced just before a tragic moment. The clowning scenes "give spectators a chance to catch their breath and mentally prepare themselves for what follows" (Epstein, 306). The synthesis of conflicting voices, however, provides the audience with a better understanding of the play.

In the Gravedigger scene, for instance, we are about to witness Ophelia's burial, one of the most touching moments of the play, and contrary to our expectation, we are presented two clowns busily engaged in what they take to be a philosophical discussion about life and death and insanity and what not. In this discussion, there is a lot to make the Elizabethan audience smile such as the re-

---

51 Lori M Culwell's "The Role of the Clown in Shakespeare's Theatre" is available at http://extra.shu.ac.uk/emls/iemls/shaksper/files/ROLE%20CLOWN.txt.

52 Even Samuel Johnson, a genuine neoclassicist who had faith in three unities of place action and time, excused Shakespeare for mixing tragedy and comedy acknowledging that real life is a mixture.

mark on Hamlet's insanity: "...[insanity] will not be seen in [Hamlet] there [in England]; there the men are as mad as he" (V, i, 18-19). The seemingly intelligent conversation that they carry is also loaded with elements of mockery that cancel the seriousness of both the gravediggers and the philosophical schools they refer to, such as the Latin speaking humanists of the time. The first clown, when speaking on the nature of Ophelia's death, describes it as "in self defense," then proceeds to misquote the Latin in labeling it "se offendendo" (self offense), then changing the word "ergo" into "argal". The clowns also try their chances in Aristotelian logic, saying that "...if I drown myself wittingly it argues an act, and an act hath three branches: it is, to act, to do, to perform..." (V, i, 10-11). Obviously, the argument is irrelevant, and proves nothing. However, the scene is funny as a whole because of the way that the two clowns take themselves dead serious, and continue the conversation confidently.[53] By allowing folk humor — here personified as the gravediggers— into tragedy, the highest form of literature, Shakespeare seems to be lifting "the walls between official and non-official literature," which are inevitably to crumble, because "the adoption of the vernacular by literature and by certain ideological spheres was to sweep away or at least weaken these boundaries" (Bakhtin, *Rabelais*, 72).

It is a good idea to place the clowning scenes at the center of any study of the carnivalesque in Shakespeare's tragedies, but when talking about *Hamlet*, one also has to pay special attention to the Prince's pretended madness: his *antic disposition*, which focuses on the quality of the clown within the Prince himself. One such study is Robert Barrie's essay called "Telmahs: Carnival Laughter in Hamlet," which regards Hamlet as "his own Fool," who reduces the whole idea of tragedy to laughter. While arguing that the Elizabethan audiences were encouraged to participate in the downfall of the Fool, Barrie claims that the carnivalesque uncrowning enters the scene in *Hamlet*, where the Prince emerges as a

53 In a sense, the two clowns of the Gravedigger scene also resemble Rosencrantz and Guildenstern, because Shakespeare seems to have divided one character into two in both of the cases to keep the conversation going. Mina Urgan, in her book on Hamlet, indicates that Rosencrantz and Guildenstern are so similar that it is hard to distinguish who is talking, and that is the reason they have come to be called 'the knife and the fork' by Shakespeare players. Drawing on the same idea, Tom Stoppard, in his play *Rosencrantz and Guildenstern are Dead*, makes the two characters get confused about their own identities. This is also true for the Gravediggers who complete each other's sentences while arguing about Ophelia's suicide. One could still claim that one is more intelligent that the other —and so is Rosencrantz who seems to be slightly brighter than Guildenstern— but they have the same function in that they can easily shift into each other's discourse, and fill each other's place until the end of the scene. *See* Mina Urgan. *Shakespeare ve Hamlet*, (Istanbul: Altın Kitaplar, 1984), 418.

character that challenges official culture. Hamlet, being transformed into the ambivalent figure of the carnival Fool, "appears to erase itself not merely through metadrama or other linguistics-based critical theory, but through the laughter of Death, which is not satirical laughter but the inclusive, absolute, all-affirming, feasting, social laughter of the folk (all the people), the laughter of carnival" (97).

Barrie's analysis is interesting in that it views the Prince's madness from a completely different angle than that of more orthodox critics of Shakespeare, such as Levin, who repeatedly underlines what he takes to be an indisputable fact: the source of the Prince's *antic disposition* is a humanism typical of Erasmus. Therefore, Hamlet's madness, like the foolishness of Erasmus's Folly, is the manifestation of a criticism of the world – a satire, if you please. [54]

> Hamlet is re-enacting the classical *eiron*, the Socratic ironist who practices wisdom by disclaiming it. More immediately, Shakespeare was dramatizing the humanistic critique of the intellect, as it had been genially propounded by Erasmus, to whom life itself was a kind of comedy [...] (Levin, 124-5)

Such a reading of Hamlet's gesture would fail to satisfy any Bakhtinian purpose, because it remains within the realm of the Platonic presenting a world of rigid binary oppositions of appearance and reality. [55] Hence, it reinstates the belief in a universal and unchanging truth that has to be taken as the central point according to which everything is situated. [56] This understanding of irony is rather a tame version in that it cancels all the anarchic elements in the Prince's madness reducing him to a social critic and a humanist. [57] Barrie also refers to Levin's in-

---

54 For a further discussion of the Fool as an Erasmian concept, see William Willeford, *The Fool and His Scepter: A Study in Clowns and Jesters and Their* Audience. (Northwestern University Press, 1969), 25-26.

55 The term irony has its roots in the Greek comic character *Eiron*, a clever underdog who by his wit repeatedly triumphs over the boastful character Alazon. The Socratic irony of the Platonic dialogues derives from this comic origin. The Greek word *eiron* also means to "separate" indicating always a gap between appearance and reality, between what 'seems' and what 'is.'

56 Socratic irony does not even lend itself to dialectics, as Hegel sees it, let alone to Bakhtin's dialogism. According to Hegel, it was "only a manner of talking against people." By questioning the Sophists, what Socrates aimed at was to show the falsity and incoherence of their doctrines, and thereby, find enlightenment for himself. Thus, for Hegel, Socratic irony is a dialectical method of inquiry leading towards the truth. The problem is that the truth itself remains "outside" this method. It stands apart as an unmoved, eternal object, as Plato conceives it (*Philosophy of Right* 101).

57 In his essay called "Hamlet and Counter-Humanism," Knowles concentrates on the Renaissance values in *Hamlet* and works on the significance of the commonplace in humanist rhetoric and dialectic, by which Stoic and Christian thought depreciates passion.

terpretation of Hamlet's madness, and admits that "such a Hamlet, while critical of official corruption, poses no real threat to official values" (84).

*Hamlet* is not a pedagogical play. It is not a satire meant to topple the authority only to replace it with its like. And Prince Hamlet is no social critic. Neither is he a moralist with a story to tell in order to teach us a lesson. He rather acts like the carnival fool capable of turning his own tragedy topsy-turvy, as Barrie demonstrates in his analysis of the Mousetrap scene (86-87). The irony in Shakespeare's play, therefore, is different from what Levin calls the Socratic irony, in that it goes beyond the binary oppositions and opens itself to ambiguity and double meaning.

This is exactly what Gürbilek talks about when she discusses the function of irony in *The Disconnected.* In her analysis of Atay's text, Gürbilek draws attention to the difference between irony and satire. She reminds the reader that irony, unlike satire, does not presume the presence of an objective and unchanging reality, which can be pinpointed and acted upon. Irony begins at the point, where the border between truth and falsehood becomes blurred. The subject of irony accepts from the very beginning, the role of the carnival Fool, who stands at the borderline between reality and illusion (*Yer Değiştiren Gölge*, 29). Gürbilek employs a Bakhtinian understanding of the Fool here, which also applies to the disconnected, who is not simply an actor playing his parts, but always remains a fool wherever he surfaces in the novel. Because of their ability of challenging the world outside, i.e., the society in general, Turgut and all the disconnected represent a certain form of life, which is real and ideal at the same time, and stand "on the borderline between life and art, in a peculiar mid zone" (Bakhtin, *Rabelais*, 8).

In this chapter we are going to argue, in the light of this approach, that Turgut, like his literary kin Hamlet, emerges as a reincarnation of the medieval jester, who, taking liberty of his madness, uncrowns the king, and shows us that authority is not as sacred and untouchable as it seems. Yet, when the jester puts the crown on his own head, he does not take himself seriously as the king does. He knows that every crowning will be followed by an uncrowning, and this is the only reality to be discovered behind all the illusion (*Rabelais*, 370). That is why, Atay, like Shakespeare, prefers the mock-serious tone of irony to the monolithically serious tone of satire that pretends to offer a cure for social tensions. The

---

In his anguish and grief Hamlet's subjectivity is realized in a consciousness that rejects the wisdom of tradition for the unique selfhood of the individual, which according to Knowles, is "not an anachronism retroactively conferred by the culture of bourgeois individualism, the essentialism of liberal humanism." (1066) See Ronald Knowles, "Hamlet and Counter-Humanism," *Renaissance Quarterly*, Vol. 52, No. 4. (Winter, 1999), pp. 1046-1069.

life of the disconnected does not emerge as an alternative to authority; it rather functions as a device that lifts the veil of what claims to be the truth, i.e., it allows us to glimpse through the "truth" fabricated by authority. Therefore, it can be said that rather than assuming a truth that can be annihilated and replaced by another form of truth, which would be equally vulnerable to criticism, Atay sides with artistic illusion, which emerges as the expression of a "free and critical *historical* consciousness" (73, emphasis original).

## "Fathers of the text" and sons of the republic

In reference to the strong authorial presence observed in the novels written during the Reformation period (*Tanzimat*),[58] Jale Parla employs the term "fathers of the text," indicating the authors' totalizing attitude towards the text and characters (*Babalar ve Oğullar*, 43). According to Parla, in some cases such as Namık Kemal's *Intibah*,[59] we can even talk about an author that indulges in becoming an "informer," because Kemal exceeds the conventional degree of intervention provoking the reader against the character. The other authors of the Reformation are no different, because they feel obliged to inform the reader of the truth, which, in their way of conceiving the world, is fixed and unchanging. Parla draws attention to an allegory of truth that lies at the heart of early Ottoman novel:

> This allegory, which constitutes the ground for the Ottoman reformists to write novels, should be read as follows: Truth is universal: it is naked, absolute, singular and unchanging. It is the same for everybody and should be regarded that way. However, sometimes it is hard to understand it, and sometimes it is hard to accept it. Therefore, it has to be decorated with elements of fairy tales. This is what the novelist

58 The *Tanzimat*, meaning reorganization of the Ottoman Empire, was a period of reformation that began in 1839 and ended with the First Constitutional Era in 1876. The modernization process of the Ottoman Empire was effectively associated with the *Tanzimat* reforms. The reforms aimed to encourage Ottomanism among the many ethnic groups that had secessionist goals and stop the rise of nationalist movements within the Ottoman Empire. The reforms tried, but failed, to integrate non–Muslims and non–Turks more thoroughly into the Ottoman society through civil liberties and regulations.

59 Namık Kemal wrote Intibah (Awakening) in 1879. The novel portrays a young man torn between the values of traditional family life and his desire for a prostitute. It constitutes, as Ahmet Evin points out "the first attempt in Turkish fiction to achieve a type of psychological dimension observed in European novels within a thematic framework based on Turkish life." See Ahmet O. Evin, *Origins and Development of the Turkish Novel*, 68.

> does. He is the one who both interprets and adorns truth; he is the sage of truth who embellishes it with story telling elements. This is how the stories that are meant to convey the unquestionable and absolute truth become inescapably allegorical; and allegory becomes the axis that our novel, at least at the beginning, is built upon. (52)

According to Parla, the allegory that dominates early Turkish novel is that of an orphan (17). The central argument of Parla's analysis in *Babalar ve Oğullar* (Fathers and Sons) is the claim that Turkish novel is born into a "fatherless" home, where the son feels the urge prematurely growing and taking the responsibilities of the father. The allegory of the fatherless child, obviously, has its roots in the disintegration of the Ottoman Empire, and the threat coming from the West, which, according to Parla, was usually depicted in early novels as an irresistible woman representing sensual love. So, the picture is complete: the Turkish intellectual gets stuck between the dying father and the she-devil that is to replace him. Parla warns us against the Freudian connotations of this allegory:

> What determines the Reformation thought is not the desire to kill the father, but rather the effort to resurrect the dying father. [...] The father-son relationship in the Reformation is not that of a confrontation but one that is based on continuity. Our first novelists are the offspring of this conservative relationship and they are all authoritarian children who had to become their own fathers in search of the long lost fathers of their own. (18)

"A dead father is a good father," says Bülent Somay in a subtle reference to Parla's thesis and with, what I like to think, a sarcastic smile (50). One cannot help but agree with him when one considers the political climate of the 1970s, when the problem was not "fatherlessness," but a father that was rather "too much." The authority of the young republic extended its dominion to every single corner of human relations exercising a total control over its people. The fatherless sons of the Ottoman Empire became very rigid fathers themselves in order to create a nation out of the remains of the dying monarchy. In fact, the Turkish Republic was established by the "fathers of the text" who have always expressed a firm belief in an absolute truth and never suspected that it might be their own fabrication. The metaphor, therefore, takes the form of an authoritarian father representing the modernist state. A hundred years after *Tanzimat*, which, according to Parla, was a period "when the absolute authority weakened but continued to hold an absolutist worldview," there comes a time for the sons to question the authority of the father. And Atay was among the first to do this.

Although we can still hear the echoes of what we may call "the spirit of Reformation" in the 1970s, what determines "Turkishness" is no more a desire to return to the traditional values of the East, but a revolutionary attitude at the service of a progressive cause —the making of modern Turkey— which overlapped with the sentiment of the leftist youth voicing the belief in a great worldwide revolution against the last vestiges of imperialism. In the 1970s the enemy is still the West, but it is no longer portrayed as a *mademoiselle* seducing the shy Ottoman gentleman, but rather as a wicked old man pointing his bony finger at you in the posters of Uncle Sam —or, more vividly, as the solid presence of American battleships appearing on the Bosphorus.

In short, Turkey was under the influence of what is called "the leftist winds of change" blowing all over Europe and Latin America owing to the "Spirit of '68." Governed by the desire of creating a better world, Turkish youth sought freedom and equality like their peers all over the world. What is surprising in the history of Turkish left is that their search seems to have coincided with the rather authoritarian Kemalist ideology that was being followed in the making of modern Turkey. To a great extent, revolutionaries saw no conflict with the ultimate aim of their progressive cause and the totalizing attitude of the modernist state. Their problem was not with the State, but with the government, which, they believed, had become the mouthpiece of imperialism and capitalism originating from the West.

Bülent Somay writes one of the most interesting analyses shedding light on the spirit of the 70s in Turkey. The essay, which Somay, very aptly, calls "The Hamlet Generation," draws on the allegory of "fathers and sons" introduced by Parla, and, getting engaged in a psychoanalytical reading of the period, goes further by claiming that the revolutionary youth of the 70s was living under the shadow of the ghost of their father (Mustafa Kemal) who charges them with the duty of saving the mother (the Republic) from the hands of the usurpers of power (the rightist government that follows the footsteps of the capitalist West) (50-51).

The Hamlet metaphor offering the image of youth burdened with the duty of saving the mother/land under the guidance of a dead father/leader perfectly overlaps with the sentiment of the manic and turbulent 70s. What renders Atay indisputably unique among all the authors of the time is that he was the only one to see through the mechanisms of power at work in the Hamlet metaphor. Atay grasped this manic atmosphere characteristic to the 70s, and used it to question the totalitarian nature of all progressive causes, be it the revolution or the making of a new nation. Upon a background of the so-called "village novels" of the time, a sub-genre that reflected the ideology of left-wing Kemalism being dominated by a patriotic sentiment usually embodied in the portrayal of an idealist hero who, undertaking the duty of guarding the Republic, goes to Anatolia and serves people, *The Disconnected* emerges as a peculiar moment in the history of

Turkish literature, where such patriotism comes under scrutiny.[60] If we agree that the whole history of "Turkishness" boils down to an allegory of "fathers and sons," as Parla suggests, then we have to admit that Atay, with the help of his allusions to Hamlet, attributes a completely different meaning to the analogy in that he portrays an anti-hero in the person of his protagonist, and presents Turgut not only as the "savior," but as the jester as well: the Fool/King of the carnival.

## The problem of patriarchal authority: the Hamlet metaphor in *The Disconnected*

Keeping Somay's analogy in mind, we can opt for a reading of *Hamlet* as a play mainly concerned with patriarchal authority, and approach Atay's novel from a similar angle, while maintaining that the father's authority in the case of the latter overlaps with that of the State. Like Hamlet, who finds himself trapped within a country where power fell into the hands of people that wronged the rightful, Turgut has to face the power of a political authority that clamps down upon every single individual that dares to question the system. The totalitarian nature of the State becomes more and more obvious as we delve into the lives of ordinary people who have internalized the order of things as given. In fact, Turgut gradually comes to realize his anachronistic position at a time when all the questions have already been answered leaving no place for doubt.

This is the way that leads both Hamlet and Turgut to the position of the carnival Fool. Hamlet's *antic disposition* is an attitude that mimics the court jester —Yorick if you like— who feels completely free to mock the absolute authority while others tremble with fear. The *antic disposition*, in this sense, is not an element but rather the essence of the play, something that provides the text with an attitude towards the rest of the world that is "out of joint." Both Turgut and Hamlet make clear to the reader that there is no way out of the *rationale* of absolute authority other than the festive madness of the Fool. Therefore, arguing that a reconfigured carnival spirit finds its way into *The Disconnected*, we will

60 In a recent article, Parla maintains that the "village novels" in question, such as Mahmut Makal's *Bizim Köy* (Our Village, 1950), Talip Apaydın's *Sarı Traktör* (The Yellow Tractor, 1958), Yaşar Kemal's *Teneke* (Tin, 1955), and Fakir Baykurt's *Kaplumbağalar* (The Turtles, 1967), are the product of a "paternalistic nationalism" which found its best expression in the ideology of the time "a synthesis of Kemalism, nationalism, socialism, and communism – quite an incongruous mix." (18)
See Jale Parla, "From Allegory to Parable: Inscriptions of Anatolia in the Turkish novel," *New Perspectives on Turkey*, no. 36 (Spring 2007).

explore the ways in which Atay offers a modern version of the popular festive elements, especially the clown or the 'Fool,' who signifies the symbolic destruction of authority and a resistance to the mechanisms of power. The heart of this analysis will be the claim that, owing to the dialogue he carries on with Shakespeare, Atay presents Turgut's attitude towards the world as an "*antic disposition*" in its own right.

The allusions to Hamlet in *The Disconnected* take new meaning in that they become a key in understanding the carnivalesque quality of both texts. Whenever he draws on *Hamlet*, Atay almost always points to the Jester-quality of the Prince, and uncovers the grotesque in Turgut's discourse. One such example is when he places his Hamlet next to Christ – as if responding to Graves's suggestion[61] – and engages them in an imaginary dialogue in Turgut's mind. In this scene, where Hamlet meets Christ, Turgut constantly interferes and reminds the reader that both characters fall short to fulfill their tasks of setting things right. This is a picture, in which, both characters get mocked, humanized, and decrowned in the Bakhtinian sense of the word:

> I am Hamlet, Prince of Denmark. And who are thou? Well said, my boy Hamlet! Keep up the good work. He is from the nobility, you know, he will look down upon the other. The other is wrapped up in his white robe in such a way that one can see only his face. In what language are these two going to talk? One doesn't speak Danish – no, there is no way that he speaks Danish. Hamlet has no beard or mustache. Does he speak Hebrew? The other, as if to spite Hamlet, wears both a beard and a mustache. Poor guy, he doesn't speak anything other than his native language. Most probably, he has never had a haircut, either. Do these two guys have anything in common? But, of course! They both fight for their fathers. Whoever pleaseth me, he also pleaseth my Father in Heaven. Hamlet, I am thy father's spirit. Oh, poor soul! Yet, they can not agree on the matter of taking revenge." (255)

Atay later extends the metaphor of Christ and uses it not only to reveal the personality of his protagonist Selim, but also to describe the position that the leftist youth found itself in the 70's. He may be attributing a revolutionary quality to Christ, or a messianic role to the leftist radicals hoping to save the world. What if Jesus had already visited Turkey in his Second Coming, he asks, and tells us what would have happened making allusions to the totalitarian government of

61 While Levin compares Hamlet to Quixote and Myshkin, Graves compares him to the archetypal figure that lies behind these two characters: Christ himself. While claiming that Hamlet in his madness resembles the 'antic' picture of Death depicted as the joking skeleton, Graves points out to the Christian connotations of this figure. In fact, he claims that Hamlet's "resemblances to Christ… grow more noticeable as the play nears its end." *See* Michael Graves, "Hamlet as Fool," *Hamlet Studies*, 4 (1982), 72-88.

the time with its defining traits of obsessive record keeping, strong secret service, and an unmistakable paranoia.

> From the official records: The Jesus Christ ID card
>
> NAME: Jesus SURNAME: Christ MOTHER'S NAME: Mary FATHER'S NAME: God Almighty PLACE OF BIRTH: Nazareth DATE OF BIRTH: Jan 1, 0000 MARITAL STATUS: Single NATIONALITY: Roman Empire PROVINCE: Israel DISTRICT: Betlehem STREET or VILLAGE: Nazareth CHAPTER 34 VOLUME 2
>
> Special note: Draft-evader. (605)

And a few lines later:

> He [Jesus] has been seen with thieves and prostitutes. Has been forced to visit the Prosecutor's Office because of charges concerning religious propaganda. Released each time due to lack of evidence. [...] They call him The King of Jews. Rumor has it that he is a harmless lunatic. No charges have been pressed about lunacy, though. It has been claimed that he performed some miracles during indoor meetings with his followers. Police raided and searched the place, but found no trace of the so-called "miracles." The crowd, which later dispersed peacefully, was only carrying a heated discussion about a book. [...] We placed one of our men among them: Judas. He keeps informing us about the developments. We can get hold of him any moment if necessary. It is all a matter of informing the military that he is a draft-evader. (605-7)

This kind of transformation is the result of parody, in the Bakhtinian sense of the word, where it means not simply mocking a text, but reshaping it in the form of an "internalized, dialogized hybrid," within which languages and styles mutually illuminate each other. In the above passage, not only does Christ get humanized, but also the political situation in Turkey in the 70's is mocked and made tangible. Or elsewhere, in Hamlet/Turgut equation for instance, we find a completely new reading of the Prince's hesitation, which sheds light on to the defining quality of Turkish intelligentsia, which suffered from political messianism and intellectual elitism that resulted in a political paralysis failing to take action.

Echoing Hamlet's regret of "O cursed spite, that ever I was born to set it right!" (I, v), Turgut believes that he is not fit for the task of understanding Selim and making him understood by other people. While Selim gets more and more associated with Christ as the book unfolds, we find that Turgut becomes a Hamlet in his soliloquies reflecting the Prince's meanderings:

> You killed him once. I'm not going to let you do it again. I will clean him up from his first death and open the way for his Second Coming. I wish it weren't me. I wish it were somebody else to fulfill this task. Someone more able than I am. Can a coward and a weakling like me handle such a difficult situation? (378)

One can hear the voice of the angst-ridden and soul-searching Hamlet in Turgut's interior monologues: "Am I a coward?" asks the Prince. But although he curses his fate of having to "set things right," Hamlet surely acknowledges the necessity to do so: there is "something rotten in the state of Denmark," and one has to do something. This feeling of "having to do something" is reflected both in Selim and Turgut, who from time to time act as each other's alter egos. For instance, though he fails to actualize it, Selim believes in his own utopia that has Christian undertones of "let thy kingdom come."[62] As we stated above, the allusions to Hamlet go hand in hand with references to Christ, and Gürbilek, makes a nice point in drawing attention to Atay's messianism, and sends us back to the chapter called "The Judgment Day":

> There [in that chapter] you will see that there is a time when class distinctions are abolished; when the peasants do not sit under the sun wearing their thickest clothes waiting at the gates of state offices; when aspiring artists do not end up as advertisers, or authors as engineers, architects as economists, bartenders as lawyers, lawyers as shop assistants, free man as servants; there is a time when people who want a decent life do not get disgraced; when kids are not threatened with scary tales or the wrath of God; when the provincials are not looked down upon by those who have no quality other than being born in the city; when the pain in our chest and the ache in our heads are lifted; when the privilege of reason is denied to the West; and when the mad are released from loony bins on bail. (*Ev Ödevi*, 30)

Before assessing the value of madness in the eyes of Bakhtin, and in this text, it is worth mentioning an additional theoretical resource here in literary theory that is struggling with the same totalitarian aspect of the cult of reason. Like Bakhtin, Foucault also takes discourse seriously, and studies the way it constitutes 'regimes of truth' that rules out alternative accounts, which connects with some of the concerns we find in Bakhtin's work. Foucault highlights the role of the mad as the slave in reproducing master-slave relationships, and the capillary action of power as it circulates upward as well as downward, holding oppressor and oppressed in its systematic grip. In the world of Bakhtin, however, there is not much place for such binary oppositions, as the mad can break lose from the loony bin and become the wisest man, the sane can always turn to be half-witted.[63] Hence, the image of the Fool that we will trace in *The Disconnected* will bear the ambivalence, or as Bakhtin calls it, the "gay relativity" of the car-

62 Though he comes to realize that his utopia is doomed to fail. *See Chapter 5.*

63 For a detailed discussion of the mad as the oppressed see the account that Foucault provides in his history of madness: Foucault, *Madness and Civilization* (London: Tavistock. 1961).

nival in that it exhibits no certain character that can be pinpointed as the absolute.

Once one notices that the two main characters of *The Disconnected* can be regarded as each other's alter egos, the text opens itself up for other potential readings — some of them also related to Atay's allusions to Shakespeare's play. Although it is perfectly possible to view Turgut's search for his dead friend in line with Hamlet's effort to be the voice of his father's ghost in this world, one can also successfully argue that Turgut sounds more like Horatio, at times, burdened with the task of telling Hamlet/Selim's story to the world. At times, he feels as if Selim left a word behind, a cause that has to be reported "aright to the unsatisfied." It is as if he said to Turgut, "I am dead, thou livest." Therefore, Selim's death clings like Hamlet's last words to Turgut's ear:

> As thou'rt a man,
> Give me the cup: let go; by heaven, I'll have't.
> O good Horatio, what a wounded name,
> Things standing thus unknown, shall live behind me!
> If thou didst ever hold me in thy heart
> Absent thee from felicity awhile,
> And in this harsh world draw thy breath in pain,
> To tell my story. (V, ii)

This is what Turgut feels the urge to do. In order to be able to tell his friend's story, Turgut knows that he has to fully understand him. And in his journey, as he comes to understand Selim, he detaches himself from the rest of the world and becomes what Selim always has been: a disconnected. *The Disconnected*, therefore, can be read as the story of an Horatio that is gradually becoming a Hamlet, that is to say, a Hamlet in his *antic disposition*. The urge to tell the world about Selim requires passing through the same processes and becoming Selim.

> Selim lived differently; that is, he could not live, he died. Maybe this task is given to you Milord. Selim was just giving us the light? Maybe, Milord. I wished he taught me how to think before he died. I wish he did not hide. I don't think he was hiding, Milord. I know, I learned a lot, Olric; but death, he is hiding the death. You will live, Milord. I want to live with the knowledge of death, Olric. (314) [64]

Turgut is aware of this transformation at the time when he starts to talk with his imaginary sidekick, Olric:

---

64 Translated by Ertuğrul.

> I am not Selim, Olric. I'm afraid I will become another Don Quixote reading Selim-novels and yearning for Being-Selim. Don Quixote was a great man of nobility, Milord. I have a deep respect for him. I'd be honored to serve him. (379)

The reference to *Don Quixote* is not a coincidence: Turgut debases the ideals of the modernist state, as Don Quixote degrades the medieval ideals of chivalry and ceremonial. But there is more to it. As we have argued in the previous chapter, the reference to Quixote also implies the presence of Sancho, which brings us to the representation of the Fool as a divided self; *ergo* Olric's emergence within Turgut's internal monologue. Turgut's monologue gets dialogized/ carnivalized with Olric's appearance on the scene. When Olric is introduced into the picture, it becomes clear that Turgut, like Hamlet, has been gradually losing control over his madness, which he thought he might contain. In other words, Olric is the way that leads to Turgut's madness. One could argue whether it is absolutely necessary to introduce a secondary character into the protagonist's monologue to provide actual conversation, and a dialogization of the discourse. In fact, Bakhtin's idea of dialogue has nothing to do with actual conversation. The voice of the other is always contained in one's discourse. In "Discourse on the Novel," Bakhtin says, what matters is to grasp the idea that "to be" means "to communicate dialogically" and that a text would be lifeless if it fails to notice this:

> If the novelist loses touch with this linguistic ground of prose style, if he is unable to attain the heights of a relativized, Galilean linguistic consciousness, if he is deaf to organic double-voicedness and to the internal dialogization of living and evolving discourse, then he will never comprehend, or even realize, the actual possibilities and tasks of the novel as a genre. He may, of course, create an artistic work that compositionally and thematically will be similar to a novel, will be 'made' exactly as a novel is made, but he will not thereby have created a novel. The style will give him away. We will recognize the naively self-confident or obtusely stubborn unity of a smooth, pure single-voiced language (perhaps accompanied by a primitive, artificial, worked-up double-voicedness). We quickly sense that such an author finds it easy to purge his work of speech diversity. (*Dialogic*, 327)

So, you can equip your text with actual conversation but end up with the Platonic dialogue, where one of the characters always affirms the other, and the body of the text remains monological. Bakhtin is not saying that the internal dialogue can not be expressed in conversation, but that it can not be "exhausted" in conversational form: "Double-voicedness is never exhausted in these dialogues, it cannot be extracted fully from the discourse--not by a rational, logical counting of the individual parts" (330); "these potential responses can never be fully actualized, can never be fused into finished utterances, but their insufficiently developed forms are nevertheless acutely felt in the syntactic construction of the double-voiced hybrid" (361).

Olric dialogizes Turgut's discourse not only because he offers a possibility of conversation, but also because he performs the function of all sidekicks: that is, playing against the hero, or asking the questions the reader would ask. Turgut's imaginary sidekick also opens a way for the free play of words: "The radio said it would be partly cloudy. This means there will be a part that is not cloudy, Milord" (521). Turgut's keen self-consciousness, which is there from the very beginning of the novel, becomes so solid that it gives rise to the creation of an imaginary character —another alter ego if you like. As the main character approaches the limits of reason, he wants to posit all reality to another character that can stay calm and rational under any circumstance. This is why, as Turgut gets gradually detached from life, Olric voices a more down-to-earth viewpoint representing a commonsensical attitude, like that of Sancho.

> I want people of this country to reclaim the trust deed they have invested to the intellectuals, Olric. This has been said before, Milord. I'm not talking about words, I'm talking about deeds, Olric. I think you would be bored if you were accompanied by any of these people now. And I want them to get bored of themselves: this is what I want. I want them pull down the walls between us. If they ever manage to pull down the walls, then they can find a way of not being boring, Olric. (536)

The name Olric seems to be borrowed from *Hamlet*. It sounds like an amalgam of Yorick, the court jester, and Osric, one of the attendant lords. Turgut's imaginary manservant sounds like both: he provides a counterpoint to Turgut's line of thinking and puts him into place, as a court jester would do and, and sometimes he agrees with "the master," as Osric does in *Hamlet*. But in the last analysis, Olric is rather an imaginary Sancho, an inner voice that tells us Turgut is no longer his old self, that he is not in peace with the outside reality now. We hear about Olric in the first page of the book —"In those days there was no sign of Olric."—, but he does not appear until the brothel scene, when Turgut puts on his *antic disposition*.

## The brothel scene: Turgut's antic disposition

Ankara, Ankara
Ye kind-hearted step mama.[65]

The brothel scene has a well-earned reputation for being the most memorable episode of the whole book. Halfway through the novel, Turgut goes to Ankara for a business trip, and visits a series of public offices. But his main mission turns out to be finding Selim's old friends one by one and talking to them about the possible reason of his suicide. With this motivation, he meets several people including Metin, one of Selim's friends from childhood, who seems to be the accumulation of everything that Turgut feels contempt for: he is a master of platitudes, an admirer of the gaudy sentimentality of Turkish tangos, and a person who lives his life strictly in accordance with the plotline of the cheap novels he reads. What is more, he is shallow, conceited, and ignorant. In contrast to Turgut, Metin is miles away from soliciting any form of self-exploration. In fact, he is one of those who ponder nothing deeper than their evening meal. In short, Metin is the Polonius of *The Disconnected.* When we listen to Turgut talking to Metin, we can hear echoes of Hamlet's dialogue with the "tedious old fool." Like Hamlet, who tries to understand how Polonius has once been a loyal servant of his father, Turgut finds it hard to grasp what kind of a bond connected an intelligent and sensitive person like Selim to this idiot. As he does very often in this chapter, we hear Turgut using to separate voices, one outer and one inner, in his conversation with Metin. His voice is easily discernible from Metin's dull and monotonous utterance:

> "Have you ever read Burhan Cahit, Turgut?" Well, this is where you end up, Turgut. You asked for this. Now you have to play along. "Not really." How can you "not really" read someone? Forget it, he does not care. "If you knew what a great pen he was." Well, I can't know everything, can I? "There is this novel which talks about one of those devilish women seducing a young man." Let me tell you, in this setup I am definitely taking side with the woman. "The man is a rich contractor. He spends all his money just to keep this blond bitch happy." Turgut smiled at the blond woman sitting next to them. I said I am on the side of women. (228)

And later about Turkish tangos:

> "Waiter, we would like to ask a favor from the orchestra." Oh God, please forgive me my sins. "Which tango was it that you said, Metin?" "I like the one that goes like 'Watching the stars falling into the night, I secretly prayed to God,' " I hope the whole sky collapses on your head. (231)

---

65 "Ankara Ankara, ey iyi kalpli üvey ana" from *Oteller Hanlar Hamamlar için Sürekli Şiir* (Continuous Poetry for Hotels Inns and Baths) by Cemal Süreya.

The phoniness and banality of Turkish tangos makes Turgut almost physically ill. They radiate a sentimentality similar to that of Hamlet's sham love letter to Ophelia, and the small poem contained in it: "Doubt thou the stars are fire; Doubt that the sun doth move; Doubt truth to be a liar; But never doubt I love." (II, ii) This is the language and sentimentality of Polonius rather than Hamlet's. It is obvious that Hamlet wrote the letter knowing that it will end up in the hands of Polonius. And envisioning the moment of Polonius reading his letter, he resorts to the most overworked, stale and flat form of romanticism that would fit the letter's intended owner.

Like Hamlet, who when in the company of Polonius, acts like a trickster, Turgut takes great delight in mocking Metin, whom he sincerely despises. In the brothel scene, when Turgut cleverly avoids talking sense, Metin gets confused and does not take anything that Turgut says seriously. This enables Turgut to let out some of his feelings disguised as the babbling of a madman. He employs the language of the jester and with clever use of puns turns the world inside out: mixtures of praise and abuse, the praise of folly, images of things upside down, inside out, bottoms up. There are times when he reminds us Hamlet's talk about the 'fishmonger'[66], or his last remark in the scene with Ophelia urging her to "go to a nunnery." [67]

---

66 When he calls Polonius a 'fishmonger', Hamlet could be merely picking out a simple profession to debase the position of the Lord Chamberlain. However, it could also mean a prostitute's pimp, and Hamlet could be making a comment about Polonius' interference with Ophelia's private life. "Fishmonger" is Elizabethan cant for "fleshmonger"–a pimp, procurer, or bawd. In Hamlet's view, Polonius treats Ophelia as so much flesh for barter–and rightly so, given Polonius' "I'll loose my daughter to him" (II.ii.175).
Later, in the scene when the players arrive, Hamlet confounds Polonius with his ramblings on Jephthah: (II, ii.285) Hamlet's reference is to a story in Judges 11 (in the Geneva Bible version). Jephthah promised the Lord that if he would give Jephthah victory over the Ammonites, Jephthah would offer up the first person to come out his front door as a burnt offering. His daughter and only child is the lucky winner. Before she's sacrificed, though, she begs leave for, and receives, permission to spend two months in the mountains with her "companions" to bewail her eternal virginity. She gets herself to a nunnery. Then Jephthah "did with her according to his vow which he had vowed: and she had known no man."
Hamlet is chiding Polonius for similarly sacrificing his own virgin daughter–barring her marriage and procreation (and ultimately sacrificing her life). And he is also jabbing an insult at Polonius (and commenting slantingly on his own situation): Jephthah was "the son of a harlot." …

67 In the space of thirty lines, Hamlet tells Ophelia five times to go to a nunnery, in slightly different forms. It makes perfect sense, under the circumstances, for Hamlet to be telling Ophelia to go to a convent and remove herself from the fleshly world, but it is also possible to assume that Hamlet is referring to a brothel. "Nunnery" had two very dif-

Hamlet, in this remark, summarizes the whole situation, reveals Polonius's political greed toppling his authority, and switches the image of a lady with that of a prostitute. Similarly, the removal of the boundaries between binary oppositions plays an important role in *The Disconnected.* When saying "nunnery" Hamlet might have meant a convent, but obviously Atay takes the metaphor seriously, and sends his Hamlet to a brothel. Turgut and Metin, after spending the whole night hopping from one bar to another, finally end up in a whorehouse. The ambivalence of the carnivalesque enters the picture also in *The Disconnected*, but the equivalence of ladies and whores in *Hamlet* is approached from the other way round. As opposed to Hamlet, who is disgusted by the behavior of his mother, and takes his hostility out on innocent Ophelia calling her a whore several times in the play, Turgut treats the prostitutes like ladies and calls the proprietor of the house 'Mother':

> "It's very cozy here. Bring my slippers. Bring my nightgown. Bring my good old self with it". The proprietor of the house approached him and whispered, "Don't make a scene or I'll call the cops". Turgut stood up. A woman walked down the stairs and gave a signal to one of the men waiting in the room. They left together. "Investment and consumption. Come on Mother, have I ever been bad?", Turgut said. Then he looked at the woman sitting on the couch: "We love each other and we want to get married." (236)

The brothel scene is the outcome of a typical carnivalistic gesture of turning things 'upside down', a continuous reversal of the spiritual and the material (the upper and the lower) levels, which is an essential quality of grotesque realism. Turgut is fed up with the cheapness of life; he is tired of the world like Hamlet was: "O God, God, how weary, stale, flat, and unprofitable seem to me all the uses of this world!" (I, ii) But Turgut's contempt for the mediocrity of the life around himself —represented by Metin in this episode— is not an abstract idea. Neither is his disdain for the capital that symbolizes the father's authority. It is transferred to the lower stratum of the body, and thereby, is given a presence. References to food, drink and the bodily image of the prostitutes are all grotesque in their nature bearing "a deeply positive character" (Bakhtin, *Rabelais*, 62). Though he is being half-ironic when he announces the climax of the long night in Ankara, Turgut seems to be aware of this positive character of the body:

> "We are going to the origin of things, Metin!" "What do you mean origin of things? Where are we..." Turgut stood up. He was swinging bravely. "We are going to the

---

ferent meanings in Tudor England: it did mean both a convent and a brothel in Shakespeare's day. Its meaning as a "brothel" was colloquial even in Tudor England, but Shakespeare is known for employing low literature interchangeably with the high, which would please Bakhtin.

> bottom of everything. To the origin of things." He leaned on the table. He grinded his teeth. "We are going to the *lombelico del mondo*, to the bellybutton of life, Metin." "But where?" "TO THE WHOREHOUSE!" Everybody stopped talking. Turgut shouted, "Bill. Overcoat. Car." He rushed to the door. He yelled at the driver. "Go!" "Where to?" "TO THE WHOREHOUSE!" (235)

They enter the brothel behaving like an official delegation trying to contain themselves, but Turgut in his drunken frenzy announces: "Hey, we will buck up this place. With the torch in our hands we will fight against darkness." Then he approaches the proprietor of the place and says: "Grand Mama, we came here to die in the arms of Venus." "No girl with that name here" (235). "The torch breaking the darkness" is the most popular metaphor of Turkish notion of enlightenment. Having its roots in the cult of reason, Turkey's project of modernization envisioned a youth that would struggle against ignorance, illiteracy, and religious fundamentalism. It is worth noting that Turgut borrows this image, which is part and parcel of official language, and charges it with a new meaning, that is to say, the sexual connotations of penetration. The metaphor of the torch, in Turgut's discourse, becomes a phallic symbol penetrating into the unknown, "the darkness," obviously a reference to the brothel as a whole, which serves an image that turns the enlightenment ideal topsy-turvy. The power of the carnivalesque becomes obvious here in that it is capable of destroying "the hegemony of any ideology that seeks to have the final word about the world, and also to renew, to shed light upon life, the meanings it harbors, to elucidate potentials; projecting, as it does an alternate conceptualization of reality" (Bakhtin, *Rabelais*, 9).

As a grotesque figure in this scene, Turgut is the reincarnation of the market place fools being truly ambivalent in his nature, i.e., containing both folly and wisdom in his attitude, and praise and abuse in his language. The medieval fool/jester and the modern grotesque clown, are part of a continuing evolution, and are best explained when viewed as belonging to the literary tradition of Menippean satire,[68] as described by Bakhtin. The fool is not a comic actor playing its part on the stage; he is rather the incarnation of carnival spirit that transfers anything that is regarded as absolute, stable or mythical into the gay level of popular festive degradation.[69] The fool is definitely at work in the brothel scene,

---

68 See *Chapter 1*, §n. 31.

69 Kinser, however, argues that there is a limit to what Bakhtin calls Rabelais's "carnivalesque" view of the world —"Rabelais's worldview, elite and popular by turns, is always nonofficial and hence frequently subversive, inversive, and carnivalesque. The links between the parts of Rabelais's text that are inversive and subversive and those parts that, even when supporting king and church, do so nonofficially (humorously, humanistically, fabulously), might be more accurately characterized as organicist and

which reaches its climax at the moment when Turgut announces the identification of his situation with that of Hamlet:

> All of a sudden, he made a dash toward the middle of the room. His throat was throbbing with swollen blue veins, his face had turned crimson. "I seek refuge in your country," he said. "I, Turgut Ozben, son of the King of Denmark, heir to the Ottoman land, I am addressing you from the pulpit of history." (236)

Like Hamlet, Turgut in his *antic disposition* is indebted to his medieval counterparts, such as those of the Feast of Fools, and turns every quality upside down bringing out the most in every single character he meets in the novel. He is one of the all time great jesters taking the carnival spirit with him wherever he goes. One cannot help but notice the theatricality of Turgut's discourse, which is typical to the Fool.[70] What might be called "gallows humor" up to that point in the novel, assumes a grotesque quality in the brothel scene challenging all forms of authority – even that of the reader. We cannot help being intrigued by the power of this bizarre scene, because it offers a joyful alternative to the tedious monotony of the description of the bourgeois in the novel. In this chapter, it becomes more than obvious that Turgut is meant to be an anti-hero, who surprises and entertains us equally. Unlike the other characters he discovers the power of laughter that is capable of creating a new world, and acts accordingly:

> "Metin!" he yelled. Metin was dozing in an armchair. He raised his head. Puzzled, he looked around. "Are we leaving? " he asked. "No. We have just arrived. We are guests of this country. We are among friends. These good people, God bless their soul, have bestowed upon us the honor and pleasure of ruling their country tonight. Metin! You will be my grand vizier. And I will be the minister of finance. I am waiting up the stream and making money by the bucket. All the world is a whorehouse: every newcomer has gone all the way with us and then gone away. Grand Mama, shut the curtains! And you, sweetheart, turn the lights off! Just leave that red light over there on the counter." (237)

Turgut meets Shakespeare's "All the world is a stage" with his "All the world is a whorehouse," which sounds more like a statement of fact rather than a complaint. One cannot help but wonder whether the "topos" (in this case the brothel) that Atay chooses for this statement overlaps with the territory designated as

---

spiritualist than as popular and carnivalesque." *See* Kinser, Samuel. *Rabelais's Carnival: Text, Context, Metatext* (Berkeley: University of California Press, 1990) http://ark.cdlib.org/ark:/13030/ft596nb3q0/

70 Like that of Hamlet, the language Turgut employs has a theatrical quality in the sense it sounds a bit "practiced". Holderness talks about theatricality in Hamlet in a chapter called "Madness and Metadrama" in his book *Hamlet*. See Graham Holderness, *Hamlet* (Philadelphia: Open University Press, 1987), 57-81.

motherland. Is Ankara, the heart of Anatolia and the embodiment of the sacred ideals of the Republic, depicted as a whorehouse? If so then one should pay homage to Franco Moretti, who has recently come up with the idea of the novel as the chronotope of nation-state in *Atlas of the European Novel,* where Moretti announces himself to be a literary cartographer involved in "the study of space in literature" while mapping the settings of novels, locations of plot events, and movements of characters (3). Referring to the English countryside as it appears in Austen's novels, Moretti says that the plots of her novels "take the strange, harsh novelty of the modern state and turn it into a large exquisite home" (20). In a sense, Atay has also undertaken the mission of transforming the nation-state in to a familiar "home" – though, obviously, not in the vein of Ms. Austen.

The picture of the mother/land trusted in the hands of youth by the ghost of the dead father/founder being replaced with the image of a whore results in the "Hamletization" of the novel in this scene. Here, in what might be called the "bedroom scene" of *The Disconnected,* Turgut transfers the image of progress from the high mythical level (upper strata) to the gay level of popular festive degradation (lower strata). This gay swing, which replaces (not only the motherland but also) the capital city, the symbol of official authority, with the brothel, is the outcome of a continuous reversal of the sacred and the profane (the upper and the lower) levels, which is an essential quality of grotesque realism. The contempt of the disconnected for the authority of the State is not an abstract idea. Once it is replaced with the bodily image of the prostitutes, it can no longer remain in the world of ideas. It is transferred to the lower stratum of the body, and thereby is given a presence, a fullness. By bringing down to earth and familiarizing the unfamiliar, this reversal annihilates the fear that political authority has been inducing into the lives of the disconnected. The typically grotesque image of the brothel: the bodily fluids, the stains on the sheet etc. are all related to the bodily lower stratum. As cosmic matter that can be interpreted bodily, they provide the reversal of the spiritual with the material, humanizing and transforming that which claims to be the Absolute. Therefore, it does not surprise us when the image of Christ —this time being materialized as Selim— is reintroduced, because this image, like everything else, is supposed to be subjected to the downward movement:

> [...] My friend, who would honor us with his presence, is the real owner of this country. In his second coming, he will be seen among us riding on a white horse. In his early youth, he spent most of his time strolling through these streets, but never being able to gather his courage to enter one of those rooms, he felt defeated each time. Sometimes, for hours and hours he would sit in a waiting room, just like this one, and wait for a sensitive soul who would understand how he felt. In his second coming, this street will be covered with triumphal arches. All the gates will be deco-

rated with laurels. That day will be announced as national holiday, and the girls here will not accept any customers. Instead, they will be waiting for him to come waving their flags at the windows. The cops will wear their best uniforms and make sure that nothing unpleasant happens that day. Because it will be so jam-packed that you will not be able to find empty seats even if you try to book them three days ago. However, street vendors will not be tolerated. Because he would have wanted it that way. All the streets will be swept clean, and the street sweepers will wait for him with their brooms on their shoulders standing to attention. Even Safter will be different. For that day only, he will get rid of his flip-flops and wear shoes. And all the customers will stand outside the gate holding hands and in their Sunday best.'

One of the girls started sobbing. A customer asked his friend "What holiday?" Metin looked puzzled. Turgut continued:

'It is the brothel scene of the Liberation Day". (239-40)

All the details concerning Turgut's night at the brothel present the character of a popular festive performance: they are part of a gay and free play, but they are also full of deep meaning (Bakhtin, *Rabelais*, 207). Turgut degrades the whole culture behind the idea of progress when he turns the liberation day celebrations into a gay parade. The official celebrations of the liberation day are the reconfirmation of the existing hierarchy, the norms and values of the establishment. Like the official feasts of the Middle Ages they asserted "all that was stable, unchanging, perennial" being "the triumph of a truth already established, the predominant truth that was put forward as eternal and indisputable" (9). By introducing the anarchic element of laughter into the picture, Atay challenges the rigidity and seriousness of the existing order, and by toppling down that which is "official," he creates a second life rather than sanctioning the existing pattern of things. Turgut is the medium of this displacement. As an anti-hero, as the fool, he uncrowns, covers with ridicule, kills the old world (the old authority and truth) and at the same time gives birth to the new in the form of fearless laughter.

His speech left the room in turmoil. Metin approached Turgut: 'You talked well, though I'm not quite sure who you were talking about'. The sobbing girl wanted to know: 'Is this pasha going to help us?' Turgut smiled. 'Let's leave those bozos out,' she continued, 'the ones who collect the protection racket. They should not join the feast that day. We all work to put food on the table. They do nothing but get fat on our money'. The lady of the house was worried, 'I hope he does not harm us,' she said, 'I am a decent woman. I have always been good to the girls, and they all like me. They can bear witness to my sins.' She collapsed in a lounge chair. The sobbing girl was determined to hear the end of the story: 'You did not tell us what happens next. If the commander takes the trouble of coming here, then there must be some reason behind all this. Someone like him visiting a place like this? Such a thing is never heard before. Why does he keep silent all the time, while we are all running in

> the streets with flags in our hands?' Her friend interrupted, 'If he does not talk at all, then he is a conceited prick.' The sobbing girl sighed, "Maybe they don't let the prince talk. Maybe there is a lot of noise, and he cannot make himself heard. I remember seeing a movie like this. Oh, how I cried my eyes out.' 'Come on, you floozy! You don't even remember what you ate yesterday'. The sobbing girl got offended and halted in mid-sentence. (240-41) [71]

The act of crowning and uncrowning works in both ways in this scene. It is not only the national day parade, as the heavy and monolithically serious symbol of progress that is being debased by Turgut's carnivalistic gesture. It is also Turgut himself who is subjected to the grotesque swing. Once he declares himself the leader of the progressive movement, he is bound to go down - the downward movement always being reflected in curse and abuse. When the prostitutes finally turn against him at the end of the brothel scene, Turgut becomes the Fool-king of the carnival, whose attributes are ambivalent from the very start since "decrowning always glimmers through the crowning". The king's attributes are turned upside down in the clown; now he is "the king of a world turned inside out" (Bakhtin, *Rabelais*, 370).

> My friends! Here I stand among friends. I am the king of this place. Let me ask you this: What king has ever conquered a country at such a low cost? I have just bribed the queen, and conquered the entire whore-land. Yet, I would like to underline this very important issue, this victory was not a piece of cake. As it is always the case with governmental takeovers, I have chosen a late and godforsaken hour of the night. I handed out booze to the guardians. I fondled the girls' legs. And I mesmerized the rest with music. Now I can put my sinister plans into practice. (*Tutunamayanlar*, 248)

In this passage, Turgut is apparently referring to a recent military coup that the country has been through. The Hamlet metaphor is still at work here in the description of the workings of a takeover: seducing the Queen and conquering the entire whore-land, is something that Hamlet would blame Claudius for.

Ankara: the masculine capital of the "fatherland" is one of the characters of the novel. In the brothel scene, Turgut while toppling down official authority also transforms the masculine attitude of the bureaucratic city into coquettish airs of a harlot, which is a form of gender transformation typical to the carnivalesque. The city becomes a woman changing hands losing its manly distance that it exhibited during the day. As Turgut spends most of his time during the

---

71 The prince here is not only a double of Hamlet in his lack of action, but also bears similarities to the portrayal of Myshkin of *The Idiot* and Christ in the "Grand Inquisitor" episode of *The Brothers Karamasov*. For a detailed discussion, see *Chapter 5*.

day trying to communicate with the civil servants in the public offices, we observe that the rows of bureaucracy are completely impenetrable:

> Turgut was good at pursuing documents and following procedures. He had a notion of what is what and knew how to guard himself. Every time he entered this country of indefinite rules, he would make sure to respect the whims of these creatures that could easily be intimidated. So, he pretended to be patient no matter what happens. With the same respectful gaze, he watched every clerk passing before him. You could never know, anyone could come in handy. You wouldn't want to be left out of the game because you failed to pay homage to a seemingly unimportant person. You would not want to get the "you-pooh-poohed-me-but-you're-in-my-hands-now" look. [...] This is a place where even janitors can sweep you away with their brooms. Do not reach out for any paper. This is the first of the Ten Commandments. Never speak unless you are spoken to. Never come up with ideas. Look ignorant. Do not overdress. Do not lean on the desk. Make them pity you, but do not carry things too far, or they will find a way of getting rid of you. Smile, wait... And never indulge in hope. (261)

The capital city, repeatedly depicted as a huge governmental building that can never be entered, assumes a claustrophobic quality to the extent that it bears the trace of a Kafkaesque bureaucracy. Anywhere else in the novel, we see the repeated image of official buildings, equally inaccessible:

> The governor's office is an old building, Olric. You can tell it because the door is in the middle. If it were a relatively newer building, the door would be somewhere on the side. In the newest of all buildings, Olric, you could never guess where exactly the door would be. We don't have such novelties in small towns like this one. They can only think of moving the door to the side to get rid of the symmetry that bores us to death. For now, the subsidy is barely enough for that much of a change. You shouldn't even trust those side doors. Even *they* would be closed to the citizens. Which door are the citizens going to take, you ask. Well, hard to tell at first sight. Without any citizens present, it is very difficult to find that door. (538)

The door of the brothel, however, is open to everybody. Being the material bodily principle, it has the power to embrace everybody. As Bakhtin emphasizes in *Rabelais and his World*, material bodily principle is the concept of grotesque realism. In grotesque realism the bodily element is truly positive, because, unlike the spiritual or the mental element, it is not devoid of content. The spiritual, the ideal, the supposedly 'Absolute', on the other hand, is just an abstraction. Being presented in a private and egoistic form, being cut off from 'the other', and at the same time claiming to be the universal, it is doomed to fall short to represent all the people. The bodily principle, however, does not refer to a single body, but has a cosmic character, and possesses the power to represent all that there is; the total of human existence. It does not refer to the bourgeois ego, "not to the private, egotistic 'economic man,' but to the collective ancestral body of all the people" (Bakhtin, *Rabelais*, 19). As Turgut challenges the limits rationality, we observe the ultimate carnivalesque moment in *The Disconnected* where such cosmic union is described:

> Although scientists can't yet determine the exact date of it's beginning, the Brass Period will be the golden period of our people. According to some theologians, this period will coincide with the second coming of Christ. During the Brass Period the distinctions between people as first-class versus second-class will cease to exist. [...] Drivers will not torture people; they will always carry enough change. Peasants will no longer squat in front of public offices under the sun with their thick wool coats. The reign of the concierges in the buildings will end. The dark-skinned man selling toys in the streets, the man selling belts who looks twenty years older than he actually is, and the man who keeps falling on the sidewalk because of his epilepsy, selling I don't know what in small bottles, and the young man with glasses selling nuts in bars, and Koco, who dances for the customers in taverns, and the senile waiter Tanas, who brings wine when you order Ouzo [...] they will all be saved from their miserable condition. Everybody will become what they want to be. [...] No one will make fun of the mentally ill: kids will be forbidden from running after the mad. [...] The condition of street dogs will improve. [...] Cunning will be abolished. Strictest measures will be taken in this regard. This heavy burden in our hearts, this pressure in our heads will be lifted. Only then will the reign of the disconnected begin, and it will last a thousand years. It will last a thousand more years, and a thousand more. (212)

The power that carnival laughter possesses lies in its dynamic quality of going beyond the rigidity of binary oppositions. As opposed to the seriousness of authority that bases its essence on the definition of a subject/object dichotomy, laughter overcomes any such definition by its constant gesture of reversal. By turning things upside down, by reversing the upper strata with the lower, it objectifies any idea that claims to be the Absolute. It fills the vacuum, and gives it content. As Bakhtin repeatedly underlines, it is only through carnival laughter that "the world is seen anew, no less (and perhaps more) profoundly than when seen from the serious standpoint" (*Rabelais*, 66). The material bodily principle embedded in laughter is, therefore, liberating. It brings anything that is idealized, romanticized, stabilized into the realm of the tangible and material. It brings the heavenly down to earth and makes it real. By familiarizing the unfamiliar it annihilates the fear involved in it. It is the antidote for dogmatism, for anything that induces fear and pity. It purifies and liberates us "from fanaticism and pedantry, from fear and intimidation, from didacticism, naiveté and illusion, from the single meaning, the single level, from sentimentality" (123).

Not only in the brothel scene, but elsewhere in *The Disconnected*, in the very person of Turgut we see the toppling down of the modernist ideal of progress, which has established itself as the Absolute. He presents us with the carnivalistic crowning and uncrowning of 'sacred texts' of modernity. Any political movement or cultural institution that takes itself too seriously falls prey to laughter; anything that claims to be the absolute is brought down to earth by the carnivalistic gesture of profanation: modern psychology, college education, law enforcement, modern commerce, and leftist social reform efforts. Turgut reminds us that the essential problem with modernity is not inequality or lack of justice, but a failure to understand the fact that the modernist project offers nothing but a tedious uniformity since it can not stand the presence of 'the Other' fearing that it might challenge the validity of its own ground. And uniformity does not pass as true equality, as a tamed and polished humanist understanding of liberty does not pass as real freedom. In this sense, Atay's novel as a whole seems to be echoing Bakhtin, who says that "fear is the extreme expression of narrow-minded and stupid seriousness, which is defeated by laughter [...] complete liberty is possible only in the completely fearless world" (41).

# A NOVEL BEYOND THE SCOPE OF BILDUNGSROMAN

In the surviving part of his work on the *Bildungsroman*, Mikhail Bakhtin places special emphasis on the outcome of the Enlightenment philosophy, which "impoverished" the world and "created a narrowed conception of the real" in the eighteenth century realism. He admits, however, that this "impoverishment" opened up new prospects for narrative and led to the development of the *Bildungsroman* by the end of the century (*Speech Genres*, 44-45).

In this manuscript, Bakhtin draws a distinction between *Bildungsroman* and the various types of traditional novel that precedes it. He emphasizes the fact that the temporal characteristics of both types of novels can be used to shed new light on the different shapes of novelistic protagonists. In the first group of novelistic schemata – that of the traditional novel (the travel narrative in the vein of Apuleius and Petronius and the adventure novel and its variations: The chivalric romance, the Baroque adventure novel, the Gothic novel) -- the hero neither has to nor is able to develop because he is caught in a static world model, where space and time adhere to the laws of suspense. In the eighteenth century *Bildungsroman*, however, which is fundamental to all subsequent forms of the realist novel, Bakhtin sees a clear connection between the novel's new world model and the nature of the plot: The hero becomes a dynamic character because he moves in a social world charged with historical dynamics. Being concerned with "the assimilation of real historical time and the assimilation of the historical man that takes place in that time," *Bildungsroman* focuses on the image of man in the process of becoming. Therefore, becoming, in the sense that the hero is not ready-made or unchanging (as he was in the travel novel, or the novel of ordeal), emerges as a distinguishing feature of the novel of education (20-21).

Focusing on the notions of "becoming" and "finalizability of meaning," Franco Moretti very aptly observes that *Bildungsroman* is the narrative equivalent of Hegelian thought (*The World*, 7). The problem posed by Hegel's *Phenomenology* is the education of the specific individual who attains knowledge of reality by becoming aware of its substance. Hegel, in the Preface to *Phenomenology* clearly states that this process of education bridges the gap between the individual and its substance, which, at the beginning of the process are detached from each other, as separate modes of existence. From the point of view of the universal consciousness, however, they are one and the same being united in one entity: a universal self-consciousness that knows its substance as itself.

> The particular individual, so far as content is concerned, has also to go through the stages through which the general mind has passed, but as shapes once assumed by

> mind and now laid aside, as stages of a road which has been worked over and leveled out. Hence, it is that in the case of various kinds of knowledge, we find that what in former days occupied the energies of men of mature mental ability sinks to the level of information, exercises, and even pastimes for children; and in this educational progress we can see the history of the world's culture delineated in faint outline. This bygone existence has already become an acquired possession of the general mind, which constitutes the substance of the individual, and by thus appearing externally to him, furnishes his inorganic nature. In this respect, culture or development of mind (*Bildung*), regarded from the side of the individual, consists in his acquiring what lies at his hand ready for him, in making its inorganic nature organic to himself, and taking possession of it for himself. Looked at, however from the side of universal mind, qua general spiritual substance, culture means nothing else than that this substance gives itself its own self-consciousness, brings about its own inherent process and its own reflection into self. (89-90)

The structure of *Bildungsroman* resembles the formation of consciousness in Hegel's *Phenomenology* in that it is *biographical*, assuming the existence of a coherent individual identity which constitutes the focal point of the narrative; *dialectical*, defining identity as the result of an interplay between conflicting forces, usually the individual and the society; *historical*, depicting identity formation as a temporal process which is represented by means of a linear and chronological narrative; and *teleological*, unfolding towards the projected goal of the protagonist's access to self-knowledge, which emerges as a consensus between the individual and the society.

Hegel's work is specifically pedagogical and biographical, setting itself similar tasks to those of *Bildungsroman:* individual consciousness is involved in a process of *Bildung* (formation/education) with the goal of attaining knowledge of itself, i.e. its substance which, at first, appears to it as external. Similarly, the discovery of the inner self in *Bildungsroman* is only possible through an exploration of the outer world. The individual, when he recognizes the contingency and uncertainty of experience, moves to another level of consciousness in the form of a more complete and determinate self. Therefore, the protagonist's move into society is essential, and should be interpreted as a move from an abstract, static, shadow-like existence to an actual and dynamic one, which is defined by contingency and change.

Hyppolyte, in his well-known analysis of Hegel's *Phenomenology,* points to the fact that Goethe's *Wilhelm Meister*, probably the earliest example of the genre, was considered to be one of the essential events by the Romantic circles in Jena, and Hegel himself was familiar with the novel. He goes even further and claims that it is possible to read Hegel's *Phenomenology* as a novel in the fashion of *Bildungsromane* of the time, because the book "for its part, is the novel of philosophic formation: it follows the development of consciousness, which renouncing its first beliefs, reaches through its experiences the properly philosophic point of view, that of absolute knowledge" (12). Obviously, when Hegel talks about absolute knowledge, he means the knowledge that gets accumulated and completed as consciousness moves further in the process. So, everything within the process derives its meaning from the final purpose that is to be attained at the end. Similarly, in the plot of classical *Bildungsroman*, all the aspects of the text gain their value in relation to the development of protagonist towards his goal; i.e., self-knowledge. In short, the meaning of events lies in their finality.

In Goethe's novel, the young Wilhelm gradually matures through his relations with people of every social class who represent a wide spectrum of moral and intellectual values. His expectations and enthusiasm is great, but as he progresses, he comes to learn his limitations and responsibilities. In the flow of his journey towards self-knowledge, he completely gives himself up to his conviction, and through a series of events, based on his relations to others, he comes to abandon his first conviction, and discovers what he took to be the truth was an illusion. The path that Wilhelm follows is his own history; and in the course of the development of his history, he discovers himself to be identical with the process he goes through, a path marked by the error of the Ego grounding itself in itself. The steps that Wilhelm goes through in the novel, therefore, resemble the triadic pattern in *Phenomenology*. He starts with a naive consciousness – in the sense that it is based on theory lacking the content of real experience – negates himself and becomes self-alienated consciousness, and then regains itself possessing the knowledge of itself as itself, i.e., as a universal Ego that is a 'we' rather than an 'I'.

Therefore, Goethe's portrayal of Wilhelm Meister is not that of the obedient vassal who follows the code of the society out of a sense of fear, but of a free individual who internalizes these code and comes to perceive the social order as his own. What renders Goethe similar to Hegel is this attempt to bring together these two conflicting themes of modernity: individuality and socialization. Lukacs, in his *Theory of the Novel*, draws attention to this very fact and states what distinguishes *Wilhelm Meister* from other types of novel of eighteenth century is its theme based on the reconciliation of the problematic individual with the concrete social reality. The structure of the plot, he says, is "determined by the necessary condition that a reconciliation between interiority and reality, although problematic is nevertheless possible" (57).

In this sense, what determines *Bildungsroman* is how novelistic youth gets tamed and moderated so as to fit into the norms of the bourgeois society (Moretti, *The World*, 7). The plotline revolves around the idea of how youth comes to an end and is transcended into a higher reality being subordinated to the idea of maturity, which usually translates as normality. Jarno, the Enlightenment man, reminds Wilhelm of the illusory nature of his empty idealism and calls him to embrace maturity while acknowledging that "youth may live for a time free from care: in the conduct of poor mortals, equilibrium cannot be restored except by contraries" (*Wilhelm Meister*, Book VIII, Chapter VII). This is exactly what happens in *Wilhelm Meister*: Goethe, while portraying the socialization of his protagonist, suggests a synthesis by reconciling major oppositions within the narrative and leading Wilhelm toward normality.

The novel explores the ways in which both the high-minded young protagonist and modern bourgeois society must be modified in order to bring about an accommodation between them. Unable to work in ways required by a society of merchants, Wilhelm goes out into the world to actualize his great expectations of becoming an actor. He wants "to be" rather than defining himself in terms of possessions as his father does. He wants to exercise his freedom, and discover who he really is. He is well aware of his middle class roots, which confine him within the limits of a life of possessions, and regretfully writes to his friend Werner: "The burgher may not ask himself: 'What are thou?' He can only ask: 'What has thou? What discernment, knowledge, talent, wealth?'" (Book V, Chapter III). If he were a nobleman, he knows, he would not have been forced to ask these questions, "but being a simple burgher, I [he] must take a path of my [his] own" (Book V, Chapter III).

Basically, what Wilhelm wants is a better society, where there is place for an individual who is asking for more than possessions. This is what leads him to his journey. As the story unfolds, he goes through a series of experiences, and comes to realize that acting, even in his own theater company, fails to fulfill his dreams of reforming German culture. He encounters an alternative both to commerce and theater in an extended family of landed gentry, which pursues practical reforms in both education and in land ownership. In the final books of the novel, therefore, he renounces the theater, discovers he is a father, and is betrothed to Natalie, who is a member of landed gentry. In short, while seeking the reformation of society, he ends up as a reformed idealist.

The classical *Bildungsroman* conceives both the individual and the society as dynamic principles. When the idealistic hero comes into contact with social reality, the individual realizes himself in a process of attaining maturity, and at the same time, the society unfolds itself, and comes to be. Self-recognition or self-understanding is always attained through a self-realization in a society. Only by moving out into the world can the protagonist become critically aware of himself as he really is. The process, therefore, is obviously a learning process, and the experiences that the protagonist goes through, though difficult and painful, are presented as the necessary steps to maturation. The synthesis attained at the end is a reconciliation of the individual with the society. The individual abandons his illusions and being confronted with social reality, he becomes a member of "this society", and the society actualizes itself through its members who, at the end of the process, appear as responsible citizens. Hence, the project at hand is not only the emergence of the new man. It is also the emergence of a new society. The novel envisions an alteration of the society, which would be possible only through the formation of its individuals. Therefore, although he is not fully aware of it, Wilhelm by choosing his own path, also shapes the future of the society as a whole: "Whether it [society] will ever alter, and how, is to me of small importance: my present business is to meet my own case, as matters actually stand; to consider by what means I may save myself, and reach the object which I cannot live in peace without" (Book V, Chapter III).

It is only at the end of the process that the society, like the individual, comes to see itself under a different light: Natalie's family and the Society of the Tower envisage a form of social organization that accepts commercialization when combined with a sense of idealism, as voiced by Jarno toward the end of the book: "From our old tower there is a society to issue, which must spread itself through every quarter of the world, and to which members from every quarter of the world shall be admissible" (Book VIII, Chapter VII). Jarno, as the spokesman of the Society of the Tower, envisions a future where the bourgeois gets reformed and globalized. Hence, the project of mediating between a high-minded young man and a form of society that falls short of his aspirations leads to the formation of a new and harmonious bourgeois community. The Society of the Tower presents a refined form of middle class as Wilhelm emerges as the reformed version of his idealist self. The Society is neither like Wilhelm's narrow-minded and materialistic father confined in a mundane life, nor like the theatrical company determined by trivial irrelevance. Wilhelm's engagement to Natalie removes him from the society of merchants and raises him into the ranks of the upper middle class. Moreover, the Society offers Wilhelm direction by accepting him into an organization with greater influence than his theater and linking his continued development to its projects: "If you like to join us, you shall have the choice of continuing in Germany to help Lothario, or of accompanying me. I conjecture you will choose the latter: to take a distant journey is extremely serviceable to a young man" (Book VIII, Chapter VII).

Yet another question arises concerning the necessity involved in the development of the individual, since the development from within appears only as a series of particular contingencies. However, at the end of the journey, from the viewpoint of the society, these contingencies are revealed to be necessary moves. Goethe, obviously, wants to present the past, the present and the future in a chain of necessity securing his protagonist's movement towards a *Bildung*.

This necessity, according to Bakhtin, is crucial in understanding Goethe's sense of time:

> This Goethean necessity was very far both from the necessity of fate and from mechanical natural necessity (in naturalistic thought). It was visible, concrete, and material, but it was a materially creative, historical necessity. (*Speech Genres*, 39)

The historical necessity that Bakhtin sees as an inseparable part of Goethe's novel, is also essential to Hegel's understanding of the Spirit opening itself up in the form of the totality of human experience. Only after the process completely unfolds itself, and manifests itself as awareness, can the individual think universality through particularity, and particularity through universality, and grasp the unity of these two moments as the synthesis. Up to this moment, time will be regarded as a chain of contingencies.

It is not really a surprise that we discover the plot of the protagonist overlaps with the larger plot of the society at the end of *Wilhelm Meister.* When Wilhelm is initiated into the Society of the Tower, he and the reader find out that the Society has followed his actions from the very beginning. The seven strangers whom Wilhelm has encountered in the narrative now all turn out to have been played by the head of the Society, the Abbé, as he sought to guide the young man's steps. In addition, Wilhelm receives a scroll containing a record of his apprenticeship; a version of the narrative that we have been reading has already been written by the Society of the Tower. The events of Wilhelm's life have been "observed, nay guided", recorded, and at least partially arranged by the Society (Book VIII, Chapter X). In *Wilhelm Meister*, the protagonist remains unaware of the Society's role in directing his life until his initiation. In the last two books, Wilhelm objects repeatedly that he finds himself in the middle of secret plots whose extent and purposes he cannot ascertain; the Society appears to exercise its invisible power on everything from his choice of marriage partner to plans for him to travel extensively after his engagement to Natalie.

The Society of the Tower, therefore, with which the novel comes to an end, becomes the perfect metaphor of the compromise of the individual with society, where self-development and integration become synonymous.

## Atay's dialogue with Goethe

While several critics classify *The Disconnected* as a *Bildungsroman* —probably a little too hastily— because of the pattern of formation observed in the main character, we will approach Turgut's development from a different perspective.[72] Novels of this genre, as I have argued above, traditionally end in a resolution between the society and the individual. Hence, the case of Wilhelm, who, being a quintessential *Bildungsroman* hero that he is, abandons his youthful fantasies and gets tamed – his entrance to the Society of the Tower and his marriage to Natalia being the culmination of his formation. *The Disconnected*, on the other hand, ends with the protagonist's slowly drifting away from the society that he initially identified himself with.

This is a very significant difference that cannot be overlooked, and it provides us with the necessary clues of how Atay draws upon the classical *Bildungsromane* and transforms them by making them his own. Obviously, Turgut's development is towards a "disconnection" from the society rather than an integration into it. As opposed to Wilhelm's "outward" movement characterized by his desire to go out into the world, Turgut's movement is an "inward" one initiated by a loss and alienating him from his surroundings.

Therefore, one might suggest that, as opposed to the finalized meaning offered by the classical *Bildungsroman*, Atay presents the reader with an unfinished manuscript, generically difficult to classify, though it could be said to parody a *Bildungsroman* in its narrative movement. The personal development and education reserved for Turgut does not lead him into the totality of experience in the form of a unity with the society, but to a descent into madness and isolation.

## Irony and the parody of *Bildung*

One of the points that Goethe and Atay have in common is their extensive use of autobiographical material. Goethe, in his depiction of Wilhelm, derives from his youthful experiences, especially his fascination with theatre. Similarly, Atay bases the background stories of both of his protagonists on his own memories of childhood and youth, as Ecevit demonstrates in *Ben Buradayım*, her comprehensive biography of Atay.

While Wilhelm's attitude toward art and literature are similar to those of young Goethe, in the novel they are already transformed into poetic material, through which the author is capable on reflecting on his youthful fantasies in an

72 Both Berna Moran and Yıldız Ecevit suggest that *The Disconnected* should be read as a *Bildungsroman*, or at least as a "novel of education," although they acknowledge the fact that Turgut's *Bildung* suggests a disintegration of the individual from the society. While Moran sees Turgut's trasformation as a "conversion" (288), Ecevit regards his formation as "a journey into his inner world" (340). See Moran, *Türk Romanı* and Ecevit, *Ben Buradayım*.

ironic manner. In a sense, the older Goethe is critically observing the romantic idealism of his own youth, and showing him the way that leads to maturity.

Irony in *Wilhelm Meister* is the outcome of this diversity in the perspectives of the narrator and the protagonist. "Dialectic is the universal irony of the world," announces Hegel (*Lectures on Philosophy*). The source of irony is that the individual, in the course of his formation, wants to attach himself to some objective cause, but cannot do so. He takes the form of pure subjectivity while still claiming to be the identity of his subjective knowing and willing, on one hand, and the objective cause, on the other. Similarly, Wilhelm until he joins the Society of the Tower, constantly asserts, negates, and reasserts himself. He is only aware of the fact that experience calls him, and spends most of his time meditating about what he is supposed to do with this freedom:

> Wilhelm saw himself in freedom, at a moment when he could not yet be at one with himself. His thoughts were noble, his motives pure, his purposes were not to be despised. All this he could with some degree of confidence acknowledge to himself: but he had of late been frequently enough compelled to notice, that experience was sadly wanting to him; and hence on the experience of others, and on the results which they deduced from it, he put a value far beyond its real one; and thus led himself still deeper into error. (Book V, Chapter 1)

From his naïve standpoint, Wilhelm does not yet perceive the fact that going out in to the world and exercising one's free will necessarily involves error. Only Goethe (represented by the Society of the Tower) sees the genesis of a new truth from the negation of an error. Thus, the synthesis in the novel turns out to be an epiphany on the side of Wilhelm, who discovers that his journey, which he regarded as the outcome of his free will, was actually a necessary step in his formation. This teleological structure of *Wilhelm Meister* puts a distance between the perspectives of the author and the protagonist. While the protagonist, as he moves towards maturity, comes to realize the contingency and uncertainty of experience, the author sees every move as a necessary step of an irreversible process directed to self-knowledge. The author wants the reader see the protagonist's ignorance, and the gap between the protagonist's naive understanding of events and his own all-knowing, all-seeing attitude. In short, there is a truth to be discovered at the end of the journey, which the author has access to while the protagonist does not.

In *The Disconnected,* on the other hand, Atay enters into a dialogue with Goethe by parodying *Bildungsroman* conventions such as the above mentioned position of the all-knowing author, who, while being preoccupied with the inherent subjectivity of his characters, also feels obliged to inform the reader about 'the truth'. One can feel this totalizing attitude all through *Wilhelm Meister*. The presence of the God-like author puts all phenomena under one explanatory concept, which kills the possibility of infinite number of readings that the text originally offers. For Bakhtin, this totality of meaning indicates a 'monologic' discourse.[73] For Barthes it should be considered a crime, because it would mean attributing "a single 'theological' meaning (the message of the Author-God)" to a text (146). Atay, on the other hand, in his playful attitude towards his material, echoes Foucault, who promotes the idea that writing unfolds like a game (*jeu*) that goes beyond its own rules canceling the author's particularity (102).

Atay seems to be in full knowledge of what Foucault means when he says the writer should take the role of the dead man, and what Barthes means when he says that the unity of the text is not in its origin but in its destination, i.e., the reader. He welcomes his own death that is marked by the moment of writing, and allows other voices to enter into his text opening the way for dialogism. Parody, as Bakhtin argues in *Problems of Dostoevsky's Poetics*, is one of the possibilities of establishing a dialogue with other voices:

> But the author may also make use of someone else's discourse for his own purposes, by inserting a new semantic intention into a discourse which already has, and which retains, an intention of its own. Such a discourse, in keeping with its task, must be perceived as belonging to someone else. In one discourse, two semantic intentions appear, two voices. Parodying discourse is of this type. (189)

In the following passage, where he talks about the birth of his main character Turgut, Atay unmistakably presents a parody of the classical *Bildungsroman* through the ironic use of various elements of the tradition. Yet, the most entertaining one is the way he ridicules the position of the all-knowing author who gets lost in the abundance of details.

> It was nearly twenty-five years ago. In the Nococksfly district of Aksaray, on Tuliprose Street, Door Nr. 54, Volume 22, Page 669, a child was born with marital status single, sex male, religion Islam. His father was Hüsnü Bey, an accountant who would retire from the Turkish Tobacco Monopoly eighteen years four months and twenty-two days later, and his mother was Mürüvvet Hanim, a housewife. Turgut was born with the help of a midwife as his father was going up and down the stairs every five minutes trying to suppress his concern. In fact, he was born, unfortunately, while his father was going down the stairs after having climbed them up for the seventh time. Some elderly women from the neighborhood were running around in the house, and Hüsnü Bey felt utterly useless among them not knowing where to put

73 Holquist in his analysis of Bakhtin's concept of dialogism draws attention to the differences between Goethe and Dostoevsky in the sense that the former is monologic striving to "perceive all existing contradictions as various stages of a unified development." See Michael Holquist, *Dialogism: Bakhtin and His World* (London: Routledge, 1990), 161.

> himself so that he would not be in their way [...] When the baby's first cry was heard from upstairs, Hüsnü Bey was thinking about the public law exam he was to enter the following day. He was an assistant accountant and a law student at the same time. And this was too much for him – way too much. Hüsnü Bey felt suffocated. Since he did not like reading, he was always confusing one philosopher with another –the only thing he knew about them was their names anyway -, and was trying to remember some phrases he read in Necmettin's lecture notes. Yet, the notes Necmettin took in class were completely illegible. One could not tell whether it was Aristophanes or Xenophon who wrote Retreat of the Ten Thousand, or one would easily confuse Dante's notion of the state with Plato's theory of the family. The greatest misfortune that befell Hüsnü Bey was his tendency to remember always the wrong names first. They say culture is not name-dropping. Culture is rather the way you use all these names properly and knowing the relations between them. Words, words... thought Hüsnü Bey although he never heard of Shakespeare. Was this what culture meant? (37-38)

What dominates this passage is the obsession with precision, an abundance of detail, and the desire to mention every single component constituting Turgut's background. The author can see into the future and provide us with details such as the date of the father's retirement, or give us the precise information one would find on Turgut's identity card like the door number, or see through Hüsnü Bey's mind and tell us that he was quoting Shakespeare though he had never heard of him. By displaying all the possible functions of an omniscient author and blowing them out of proportion, Atay goes far beyond a stylistic imitation. He rather challenges the relationship between the author and the character as presented in *Bildungsromane* by questioning the nature of truth voiced by the all-knowing and all-seeing author. He seems to be suggesting that the God-like author, even if he is a great one like Goethe, is doomed to fail not only because the amount of detail to be covered is beyond the scope of his consciousness, but also because there is no absolute truth to be represented in its fullness.

As Bakhtin would say, parody leads to polyphony in this passage of *The Disconnected*, where we can hear the voices of both authors clashing with one another. To Bakhtin, mere stylization or the type of imitation recognizable by a specialist does not make a discourse polyphonic, but in parodic imitation, polyphony does occur, because there is a clash between the original and the later discourse, in which the latter is given a new orientation (*Problems*, 189). Bakhtin goes on to explain how this is different from ordinary imitation, wherein the other's voice, while taken seriously, is not heard as an other but is merged with the author's own voice. In parody

> as in stylization, the author again speaks in someone else's discourse, but in contrast to stylization parody introduces into that discourse a semantic intention that is directly opposed to the original one. The second voice, once having made its home in

> the other's discourse, clashes hostilely with its primordial host and forces him to serve directly opposing aims. In parody therefore, there cannot be that fusion of voices possible in stylization [. . .] the voices are not only isolated from one another but also hostilely opposed. (193)

Another interesting example of how this opposition of the two voices takes place in *The Disconnected* is the way Atay ridicules the core idea of the novel of formation, i.e., experience. He borrows and manipulates the plot of the classical *Bildungsroman*, where the process of maturing is long, tough, and gradual, consisting of repeated clashes between the desires of the hero and the judgments enforced by an unbending social order. It is a learning process, through which the spirit and values of the social order become manifest in the protagonist, who is then accommodated into society by acknowledging the norms. The following passage demonstrates how this plotline works in Atay's world:

> [...] Turgut received his first formation on the street. He was in the springtime of his life, in his third year on this planet. Teeny-weeny little Turgut went out to play one morning. It was a sunny day. As it was the case with teeny-weeny little Newton who discovered the universal law of gravitation when an apple fell on his head in another sunny morning, Turgut came up with the law of the street that day, that is to say, the golden rule for the battle of life. He approached some boys playing football in the unoccupied lot next to his house — probably a little unceremoniously because he was inexperienced —, and got punched in the eye by a five-year-old bully. He rushed back to his mother running as fast as he could — as Archimedes did when he discovered the principle of hydrostatics — and started whining. To his surprise, his mother gave him the worst spanking that he ever had, which taught him the second important law of life: ' ...and thou shalt not whine!' (42)

The structure of the *Bildungsroman* is still there (a young man goes out into the world and gets reconciled with society through bitter experience), but now that it clashes with Atay's humorous voice it is not anymore what it used to be: Goethe's monolithically serious attitude towards his character has been juxtaposed to Atay's lowbrow and lighthearted approach to the adventures of little Turgut, which changes the effect considerably accomplishing a completely different aim. The whole ideology of Goethe's fiction, the conviction in the possibility of attributing meaning to experience, is reduced to the image of a three-year-old being repeatedly knocked around in his first attempt to go out into the world. Atay aims at the project of Enlightenment as a whole when he portrays Newton as a child no different from little Turgut in his discovery of the "truth".[74] Later

74 This reference is not a coincidence, Newton being the icon of the age of Enlightenment and a secular god of science, who rendered the world knowable and meaningful as in Alexander Pope's famous couplet: "Nature, and Nature's laws lay hid in night./God said: 'Let Newton be!' and all was light."

in the novel, he goes even further and comes up with another story of *Bildung* and topples down the cult of reason altogether:

> Gustav Willibald Franz Hegel was born in Stadthamburg in 1774. This small town should not be confused with Stadt-Hamburger über Reinenvernunft. (Sightseers do that very often.) The small town, where G.W.F. Hegel was born, is a little bit more to the south. Hegel was born two thousand years after the great Teuton king Gustav Willibald Illiteratus, in a very modest house on the street which was originally named Fleisher Allee, but later called Franz Hegel Strasse upon the acceptance of a decree unanimously approved by the Stadthamburg city council in 1892. His father was a mediocre butcher running a small shop in the basement of their house. Unlike his famous namesake Georg Wilhelm Friedrich Hegel, Franz Hegel did not even get a proper education; he did not even go to school regularly. When he was six, he started helping his father with the shop. [...] His immaturely terminated education consisted of reading and writing, a little math to be able to return the change and to keep a book of deferred payments, some grammar to read his Bible, and some theology to be able to tell Luther from Calvin". (152-153)

When viewed from a Bakhtinian perspective, Goethe is not only a "Newtonian" but also a Hegelian author since he envisions a clearly defined end, a *telos* that closes up his novel in absolute *stasis* (Holquist, *Dialogism*, 161). In his dialogue with the idea of *Bildung*, Atay's ironical attitude reaches its peak here when he applies the dialectical mechanism of formation to its own godfather. All the details concerning Atay's account of Hegel's alternative biography present the character of a popular festive performance: they are part of a gay and free play, but they are also full of deep meaning (Bakhtin, *Rabelais*, 207). Atay degrades the whole culture behind the idea of *Bildung* when he comes up with this passage about Hegel, portraying him as the barely literate son of a butcher, who, later in the text, becomes a very good citizen and, by pure chance, develops an interest in philosophy. Overcoming all the difficulties one by one, Hegel becomes a doctor of philosophy and starts teaching at the university until the time comes when he discovers that all his efforts were in vain and that there is no meaning to be attained at the end — simply Atay's contribution to the process of *Bildung*.

## The rhetoric of loss and madness

We have already mentioned that the dialectical concept of cognitive development is at the heart of the novel of formation. The most evident truth about the protagonist of *Bildungsroman* is that he is capable of acting – and hence erring, which would open the way for a dialectic process of learning. In *Wilhelm Meister*, the road that leads to the Society of Tower is a crooked path full of illusions, and negative consequences. In Hegelian terms this road that consciousness takes is "the path of doubt, or more properly a highway of despair" (Hegel, *Phenomenology*, 135). The use negativity is of extreme importance in the novel since it constitutes the basis of Wilhelm's *Bildung* through a dialectic movement. What makes Wilhelm move from one conviction to another is nothing but the negative character of the consequences he reaches in his experiences. His romantic idealism leads him into awkward and regrettable situations: his love affair with Mariane ends with his discovery of her unfaithfulness; his idealized vision of the theatre is impaired when he becomes part of a small company of struggling actors like Laertes and Philina, his chivalric fantasies come to an end as the troupe gets waylaid by bandits, and his dream of fatherhood collapses as he finds out that, in his ignorance, he has given rise to the death of the little Mignon, whom he dearly loves. In the end, however, all these failures get elevated and transcended into Wilhelm's fulfillment, and are viewed under the light of the final purpose of the novel attaining a new meaning. In short, they get submerged in the fabric of the protagonist's development.

Among all these stories that end in disappointment, the most tragic one is that of Mignon. In itself, Mignon's story does not play an important role in the development of the plot, but her premature death shows that she, too, is part of the fabric of illusion Wilhelm had built for himself. Wilhelm meets Mignon at an early point in his journey while attending an acrobatic show. He immediately notices the young girl, barely an adolescent, being mistreated by the leader of the wandering acrobats, who have apparently abducted her. He rescues her, and she becomes his devoted servant. It is obvious that she falls in love with him, but Wilhelm seems to be largely unaware of her affection, and is toying with the idea of becoming a father to the girl. Mignon enjoys Wilhelm's protection together with the Harper, a melancholy-wandering minstrel, who later joins them. All through the novel, she is described as a fragile and vulnerable creature suffering from alarming seizures when she gets emotionally disturbed. Eventually, when Wilhelm meets the Society of the Tower, and is reintegrated into the social world under the guidance of his ideal woman, the noble-minded Natalie, Mignon is also brought into this well-born and well-heeled company. But her seizures have become more acute, and seeing Wilhelm kiss a woman, she has a final fatal seizure. After her death, an Italian nobleman appears who identifies her in her coffin as the daughter of the Harper and his sister, i.e. as the product of an incestuous union.

In *Wilhelm Meister*, the story of Mignon, which later gets interwoven with that of the Harper, plays a significant role in the sense that it demonstrates how even madness and death get transcended in Wilhelm's *Bildung*. These two characters represent the intensity of lyric feeling, which must not, the novel appears to say, become an object in itself, and must be left behind with maturity. Moretti draws attention to the way Goethe describes Mignon's funeral turning it into a social event, and thereby rationalizing this experience, where it gets transcended into the totality of Wilhelm's education. In the funeral scene, Goethe attempts to contain within the process what actually lies beyond experience: death. According to Moretti, the transcendence of death is inescapable if one considers the teleological structure of Goethe's novel; everything should find its place in the social structure, every void must be filled, and no room should be left for the unknown or the unfamiliar that could cast a shadow to the radiant conclusion of the book.

> Thus the repugnant *mise en scene* of Mignon's burial – embalmings and choirs of angels to conceal the reality of the corpse and transform even the funeral into an 'episode' worthy of being lived. The gaze must be removed at the first opportunity from the spot that will remain empty: one must immediately move on to new tales, to new connections. [...] Mourning does not become Wilhelm Meister. (*The World*, 47)

Atay differs fundamentally from Hegel and Goethe despite the fact that he views the world also as the history of consciousness. In Atay's understanding of history, one finds multiplicity and variety rather than the totality one would find in Goethe's or Hegel's world. In Atay's world, the path that consciousness takes does not end in self-discovery, but in the self's discovery of the other. Hence, we should think of dialogism instead of dialectics.

In *The Disconnected*, unlike *Wilhelm Meister*, it is the loss of a beloved one that opens up the novel – and the world for Turgut. What ruptures Turgut's existence is Selim and his death, the recognition of radical alterity. In Goethe's world, any form of otherness, including death, is conceived in terms of negativity transcended in the process of Wilhelm's self-discovery. In Atay's world, however, the absolutely other is not defined as negativity; it presents itself as the personal other. The other is what cannot be transcended into a "higher truth". It is something whose presence disrupts Turgut's existence as a human being. It is what Levinas calls "the face of the other".[75] Being radically other, Selim escapes

75 The "face to face" relationship, as Levinas develops it in *Totality and Infinity*, is that of an ethical relationship being characterized by the presence of the other disturbing the spontaneity of my enjoyment and calling me back to the seriousness that the ethical relationship requires of me. Levinas's argument is that the other person ruptures the horizon of my intentions. The other person interrupts my enjoyment and my representation of the world because despite the "face to face" encounter, I am incapable of making him or her an object of my intentional act. See Emmanuel Levinas, *Totality and Infinity*, trans. Alphonso Lingis (Pennsylvania: Duquesne University Press, 1969) 41.

all kinds of understanding, and constantly disrupts the unity and coherence of Turgut's world. Selim's death is what calls the horizon of Turgut's existence into question.

In the course of the novel, following the footsteps of his dead friend Selim, Turgut gradually leaves the tedious comfort of his bourgeois life, and discovers himself as one of the "disconnected", who cannot hold onto life and take their place in the pecking order. The connected, people like Turgut's wife Nermin or Selim's other friends, have one thing in common: they want to move forward, get a life, possess and achieve more while Turgut doesn't. The novel traces this transformation of Turgut, and shows not only how he gradually comes to know himself, but also how he slides into madness and gets drowned in his own pathos as he approaches the end.

Yet, it would not be wrong to say that *The Disconnected* is a *Bildungsroman* viewed from the other way round, i.e., reinstating the presence of the other rather than the self. The inner monologues that Turgut delivers throughout the book are actually part of a long conversation that he carries with his dead friend Selim throughout the novel. They are dialogized in the sense that "every word in it is double-voiced, every word contains a conflict of voices" (Bakhtin, *Problems,* 237). It is true that Turgut's voice is separate from the others displaying absolute uniqueness and individuality, but whenever he talks, we also hear the voices of the others being echoed; especially that of Selim: Turgut quotes him, he mimics him, he uses his phrases (unconsciously or deliberately), and in an unending dialogue he restates the presence of Selim as the 'other'. Even from the very beginning of the novel, we hear him talking to Selim:

> He heard Burhan saying, "I don't know what to say." I don't know, either. You could have told me, Selim. Who wouldn't have listened to you in a situation like this? What did you do in the last months? Even if I didn't understand, I would have listened to you. The existence of another human being would have taken away the burden of your deadly thoughts. [...] How did we come here, Selim? [...] How can I fill this void between us? How can I learn you without you now? [...] Say something, Selim, don't be silent. Speak, tell me: That I have to read a thousand books. That I have to stay awake at nights. That I have to exercise every day and at the end I will accomplish an epsilon of progress. [...] I am ready for everything. [...] Tell me that I have to go to the British Museum, say that I have to work like Karl Marx [...] if you want I will even grow a beard. (72) [76]

Obviously, the whole passage is more about Selim and his death rather than Turgut and the way he conceives of himself. We can hear Selim's voice all through the passage: the way he once criticized Turgut for being lazy and not reading enough, the way he joked about Karl Marx and the like. This is, of

76 trans. by Ertuğrul.

course, not a matter of denying the presence (or the development) of the main character all together; it is rather an attitude on the side of the author of pushing his characters on the boundaries of their existence determined or limited by the other. Atay, unlike Goethe, does not use the authority of the author to provide any viewpoint that cannot be challenged by his characters. Similarly, the characters are given the privilege of uttering their final word about the world and about themselves. Bakhtin argues that it is only in this way that an author can employ dialogism: he can not completely erase himself, but he can force his authorial attitude to its limits by opening himself up to other forms of consciousness and displaying an equal interaction with them.

In the case of Atay, therefore, we see an author not only in dialogue with other authors, but also capable of understanding the naiveté of his characters — an approach that is in total contrast with the judgmental attitude displayed by Goethe. When Atay becomes ironic, which he often does, it is not because he denounces the naïve worldview of his characters, but because he regrets that they have lost their innocence and failed to keep contact with their immediate selves. For instance, while Goethe proudly announces Wilhelm's mature love for Natalia and makes his protagonist review his former adventures as a series of affairs being deficient one way or the other, Atay portrays Turgut as a character suffocating within the boundaries of marriage tainted with bourgeois habits. As opposed to Wilhelm's acknowledgement of all the girls he loved before ("Thus did I love Mariana, and deceive myself so dreadfully; I loved Philina, and could not help despising her. Aurelia I respected, and could not love; Theresa I reverenced, and paternal tenderness assumed the form of an affection for her" - Book VIII, Chapter VII), what we have in *The Disconnected* is Turgut's resentment of a marriage that alienates him from his true being. On another boring Sunday, we see him looking at the mirror and examining himself:

> Nermin was reading the Sunday papers in the living room. On his way to the couch, Turgut's eye fell upon the mirror. He surveyed himself for a while. I'm getting chubby, he thought. [...] Very soon my big blue eyes will become invisible in this round hollow dough-like face. What about the hair? I have to do something before it's too late. Nothing can be said about the mouth and the nose, though. He cast a sidelong glance at his wife: Was she aware of this thorough examination? [...] Mr. and Mrs. Turgut Ozben, they appear to be very young in this picture. Who? Turgut obviously. How about his wife? Well, she does not appear at all. What do you mean she does not appear? She wears so much make up that she is lost beneath it. Turgut, who are you talking to? I am talking to myself, Turgut. (68)

While commenting on the narrative discourse in Dostoevsky's novels, Bakhtin refers to Raskolnikov's constant monologic discourse which flows all through the novel and which the author presents in the form of an 'internal dialogization': "He does not think about phenomena, he speaks with them. In this way, also does he address himself (often in the second person singular as if to another person), he tries to persuade himself, he taunts, exposes, ridicules himself and so forth (*Problems*, 237). Here, Turgut finds himself in a dialogical moment similar to that of Raskolnikov as his social self gets engaged in a dialogue with his inner self. This dialogized internal monologue continues in a memorable passage a little further in the novel, where he sees himself through the eyes of Selim, and realizes that he has become another sheep of the flock.

> I am weary of this world, Nermin. I wish I had started talking to you about my weariness earlier. Little by little I could have told you all before things got out of control. Now it is too hard to talk. [...] He stood up, walked towards his wife, and sat next to her. He held her with one arm from behind, and rested his head on her shoulder. Nermin did not move but smiled and asked: "Name an animal beginning with an 's'." "Sheep," he said trying to suppress the desire to scream. [...] "It does not fit. And it ends in an 'l'," said Nermin in a melancholic voice. "Serval," said Turgut as if in a hurry. I am still capable of coming up with the right answers, he thought. This means I haven't lost my composure yet. Who would have thought of servals? Millions of people have never even heard of this animal. "Cow," said Selim in his mind. Selim who never leaves him alone. "A cow that is scared of thinking, a cow that forgets how to think because he is scared. A cow that can think of nothing but how to play the game according to the rules now that he is married. A cow that is forever on duty in the apartment of love." (69)

The choice of the animal is very typical here. Serval. Who would think of servals, asks Turgut, in an attempt to persuade himself of his own uniqueness as well as that of the animal. Yet, the eyes of the other, Selim's voice, never leaves him alone. As he sees himself through Selim's eyes, his fantasies of individuality get shattered. A cow, says Selim. A domestic animal as opposed to Turgut's idealized wildcat. A boring animal. An animal that lives in a flock of his like. This is the way Turgut sees himself through the eyes of his other. And he knows that once he cuts his ties with the world he has become part of, he will leave the familiar behind and enter the world of the unknown, where the simple reasoning of his simple life will not function. And this is exactly what happens in *The Disconnected*, as Ertuğrul argues:

> What is at stake here is the ego's panic in the face of something that disturbs the enjoyments of life, the fear of losing the sense of security one finds in the world and in the economy of meaning that sustains the daily. This would mean the loss of resistance against the unfamiliar and the uncanny that might overcome one if one leaves the realm of the home and everyday—in short, the realm of ideology. In other words, what is at stake in this resistance is nothing other than the loss of the world and ground as the referential frame in which we can more or less make sense of our lives. The danger, as Turgut senses, is absolute in hearing the call, since it leads to

> the shattering of the familiar and opens up the world no longer as the correlations of answers but as a realm of unanswered questions. (635)

As Turgut leaves the comfort of the flock of cows, hearing the call and responding to it, as Ertuğrul says, he gets more and more engaged in the conversation with Selim facing the limits of his existence and going beyond the boundaries of his Ego. This is nothing but madness, which marks the end of the novel. It would be interesting to compare *The Disconnected* with *Wilhelm Meister* also in this respect, because madness in *Wilhelm Meister*, cannot be tolerated at all. The Harper's madness is regarded as a threat to the social order in general, and Wilhelm's *Bildung* in particular, because insanity rules out any relation with the society – and hence the possibility of mediation. In fact, refusing to come to terms with the society is presented as the source of madness. As the Clergyman observes, "nothing more exposes us to madness, than distinguishing ourselves from others, and nothing more contributes to maintain our common sense, than living in the universal way with multitudes of men" (Book V, Chapter XVI). Thus, the Harper must either be expended (like Mignon), or saved and reintegrated into the society. Goethe, having already given up on Mignon, chooses the latter and keeps the Harpist, but transforms his otherness into the totality of rationality. In the last chapter of the book, by portraying the Harper as an unfortunate man miraculously cured of his insanity, Goethe presents the socialization of an isolated and lonely individual, which serves the final purpose of the story.

> [...] the Doctor in the evening entered with a stranger, whose form and aspect were expressive, earnest, striking, and whom no one knew. Both stood silent for a space; the stranger at length went up to Wilhelm, and holding out his hand said: "Do you not know your old friend, then?" It was the Harper's voice; but of his form there seemed to remain no vestige. He was in the common garb of a traveller, cleanly and genteelly equipt; his beard had vanished; his hair was dressed with some attention to the mode; and what particularly made him quite irrecognisable was, that in his countenance the look of age was no longer visible. Wilhelm embraced him with the liveliest joy; he was presented to the rest; and behaved himself with great propriety. (Book VIII, Chapter X)

This last remark, "behaving oneself with propriety," is the core of the whole ideology that lies behind Goethe's novel. The Harper, as the last manifestation of otherness in the book, is transformed into propriety, which emerges as the essence of the society. Hence, like Wilhelm, the Harper also finds a home in rationality and maturity. Turgut, on the other hand, validates his homelessness in his madness, which gradually acquires a tragic aspect of isolation.[77] Turgut's

77 Bakhtin refers to this duality concerning madness: "In folk grotesque, madness is a gay parody of official reason, the narrow seriousness of official 'truth'. It is a 'festive' mad-

problem is that he cannot hold on to the world, that is to say, he cannot behave with propriety.

The disconnected, as depicted in the person of Turgut, is presented as an individual who is locked up in his own consciousness, in his privacy, which he can hardly communicate to others. In fact, any communication with the others emerges as a problematic issue in the case of the disconnected killing the possibility of mediation. Being an intellectual, and being equipped with an awareness of his own fallibility, Turgut is capable of seeing himself from a distance. His consciousness always gets in the way, becomes an obstacle, and prevents him from acting. This is what paralyses Turgut as opposed to his more naïve counterpart Wilhelm, who is not endowed with such awareness. The disconnected, obviously, is not an acting consciousness; it is a consciousness that reflects upon itself.[78] This is the tragedy of the modern man, the intellectual, who wants to stop and think about the limits of his own existence when all the others act. The cult of success and action, the dynamo of modernity, fails to satisfy the intellectual.

## Time, space and meaning: the novel as chronotope

Bakhtin, in his analysis of *Wilhelm Meister*, draws attention to the fact that human emergence is no longer man's private affair: the character emerges along with the world, and he reflects the historical emergence of the world itself. The *Bildung* of the individual "begins to surmount its private nature (within certain limits, of course) and enters into a completely new spatial sphere of historical existence" (*Speech Genres*, 24). According to Bakhtin, everything we see in the novel "bears the stamp of time, is saturated with meaning in time." Yet, Goethe's time is localized in concrete space, which makes everything in his world dependent on both time and space.

> In Goethe's world, there are no events, plots, or temporal motifs that are not related in an essential way to the particular spatial place of their occurrence, that could occur anywhere or nowhere (eternal plots and motifs). Everything in this world is a *time-space*, a true *chronotope*. (*Speech Genres*, 42)

---

ness. In Romantic grotesque, on the other hand, madness acquires a somber tragic aspect of individual isolation." The madness of the disconnected is closer to the latter in that he is more and more detached from outside reality not being able to transform it, in that he cannot take hold of the world. The intellectual, being presented in private form, being cut off from the society, is doomed to fall short of representing all people.

78 See *Chapter 5*.

Therefore, the world does not only become historical after Goethe, but also gets localized where meaning is to be discovered in the in the unity of space and time. In *Wilhelm Meister*, Goethe achieves a visible fullness of time in the formation of his main character, because Wilhelm's individual development is situated within a historical process, which is inseparable from the natural setting, and "the entire totality of objects created by man, which are essentially connected to this natural setting" (33). In this sense, Bakhtin's notion of *chronotope* overlaps with Hegel's understanding of *Zeitgeist*, which views the "spirit of the times" as the mentality, social life and cultural products of an age. Therefore, Goethe's project in *Wilhelm Meister* is as ambitious as that of Hegel in that he suggests an all-embracing synthesis: he leads his protagonist to a journey, through which he can become aware of himself as *Zeitgeist,* and thereby rise to maturity, transcending and transforming also the society that he lives in.[79]

Atay's time consciousness is another aspect of his dialogue with Goethe, because his writing possesses a similar space-time quality. In *The Disconnected*, Atay does not only draw a universal picture of the modern individual, but also portrays the life of the Turkish bourgeois as it is localized in the big cities of the 70s. In the following passage, while describing Turgut's entrapment in the "comfort" of his everyday life, Atay draws a wonderful sketch of the uniform, tedious, and pretentious lives of the bourgeois. The surreal quality of the passage is probably never equaled – with the exception of Buñuel's *The Discreet Charm of the Bourgeoisie.*[80]

> Later, for days and days, he was carried away. He went back to the insignificant events of his daily life. Days passed one after another without thinking of Selim. Night after night, he slept next to his wife, taking refuge in her warmth. He washed... He shaved... He got dirty again. He bought a new pack of razor blades. There has been a set of "overall cleanups" in the house. He spent nights with his friends. Friends Selim did not know. Friends from the office, friends from the family circle. Days that resemble each other, days that do not make much sense, days you

79 When Hegel speaks of *Zeitgeist* or the *Geist der Zeit,* he has in mind not only a given age, but also a given people (*Volk*) that share a common spirit. The spirit of the age, thus, is a phase of the World-spirit (*Weltgeist*).

80 "The Discreet Charm of the Bourgeoisie" (1972) is about a group of people who constantly arrive for dinner and sometimes even sit down for it, but are never able to eat. They arrive on the wrong night, or are alarmed to find the corpse of the restaurant owner in the next room, or are interrupted by military maneuvers. Atay, like Buñuel, is aware of the fact that dinner is the central social ritual of the middle classes, a way of displaying wealth and good manners. It also offers the convenience of something to do (eat) and something to talk about (the food), and that is a great relief, since so many of the bourgeoisie have nothing much to talk about, and there are a great many things they hope will not be mentioned.

> cannot label with a date. Days followed other days. It became Monday, then Sunday, and then Monday again. Then there came another Sunday. It was impossible to keep track. Then there came another Sunday. You get up late. Have a late breakfast, or brunch if you like. Read Sunday papers, do crossword puzzle. The same goddamn puzzle. Invite friends for dinner. Or visit friends for dinner. Go to other people's places and eat there. Homes that look different from yours at the first glance, but in truth, are just the same. Did we have dinner at our place, honey, or did we go to Kaya's? Or was it Mehmet's? What difference does it make? We're always eating in the same place anyway: it is the same hectic, I always wear the same tie, and all my white shirts are identical. My trousers get wrinkled always at the same spot. Did I spill my food over Kaya, or did Kaya spill his over me, or did he spill it over himself? No, I spilled it all over myself. What difference does it make? Somebody spilled food over somebody else. I am Kaya, and Kaya is Mehmet. Once Turgut, Kaya, and Mehmet are together… It is like the reflection of the same image in three different mirrors. Mehmet's wife got confused and called me Kaya when she actually meant Turgut. She just said it. Names are to tell the difference between separate creatures. Names are not for us. We are the same species. We belong to the family of Kayamehmetturgutaens. You see! We eat with our front paws, we have a pair of antennae on our heads, and we walk on our back paws. We belong to the subspecies that has two holes, and are a class called theonesthatspendalltheirnightstogether. Our females make homes, our males make a living, and storks bring our babies. And when the season changes, we move to our summerhouses as migrant birds do. (297)

This passage is also interesting in the sense that it presents a temporality that involves no idea of progress. While Hegel and Goethe regard the history as a rational whole formed by the accumulation of experience that consciousness goes through, for Atay history is defined in terms of the lack of such a totality. In this passage, he destroys the chronology of the past, present and future and leaves us with a constant repetition of evading the moment of the recognition of our individuality. This is what Atay knows, and Turgut comes to acknowledge in the course of the novel. He finds himself in a nightmare in which he keeps repeating the same moment: the moment of evading his authenticity. He also discovers that he is replaceable by others. It does not really matter whether he is Turgut or Kaya or Mehmet. Like all the others, he possesses things and acts in accordance with the rules presented to him by outside reality —by the public world, by the 'they', as Heidegger would say. [81]

The mechanical quality of repetition in this passage is also an indication of a new understanding of time. As opposed to the comparatively natural time con-

---

81 According to Heidegger, in the general strategy of inauthentic Dasein, our sense of vulnerability and powerlessness becomes 'manageable' by being projected onto the world. The treats to our existence are now viewed as threatening to us from within the world. Our entire future is – mistakenly – seen as a pursuit of a secure acceptance by the world of the 'they' (*das Man*).

sciousness of Wilhelm, Turgut is trapped in a post-industrial understanding of time where everything possesses a factory-quality in its mechanical repetition and uniformity. Turgut, in this scene, reminds us inescapably of Charlie Chaplin of the *Modern Times*.[82] Like Chaplin at the assembly line, Turgut is caught in the grip of a kind of mechanical seizure, which is against his very nature and turns him into an automaton. He suffers from anonymity, lack of improvisation, and a terrible feeling of predictability. The repetitive quality of the assigned tasks keeps him under their spell, and he obsessively measures time through a set of routine activities. In fact, like the giant clock-face that fills the screen at the beginning of *Modern Times*, which signals from the start that this film will register not just "the times" but also modern time itself, Atay makes sure we can hear the ticking of the clock all through novel indicating the temporal pressure of an accelerated world:

> Six hardwood-floor-waxing have passed since then. No, it wasn't that many. It must be only two car-wash-and-oil-change. No. Definitely more than that. There have been at least four aimlessly-moving-the-furniture-around. Let me see: I'd better do some calculations. One buying-a-flat equals six moving-the-house. And then we have two swapping-the-bedroom-with-the-study. Yes, it adds up to exactly three washing-the-curtains. I remember it perfectly well: when it all started, I had newly bought the curtains. It is an interval you cannot measure with traditional units of time. I had placed the armchairs in front of the window. Hard to keep in mind: furniture flies like the wind. Back then the clutch was still fine. Those were the days! There was not even one single scratch on the hardwood floor. We're getting old: the furniture is wearing out. So, you're saying that it has really been four run-away-maids! I don't understand. I really don't't! (300)

Obviously, the bourgeois obsession with time overlaps with a passion for objects that have to be taken care of and renewed. In addition to the feeling of belatedness that gets integrated into the bourgeois life, possessions that occupy a central position in that life become a tool of measuring time.

The chronotope, therefore, not only functions as the primary means for materializing time in space, but also emerges as a center for concretizing representation, as a force giving body to the entire novel. All the novel's abstract elements —philosophical and social generalizations, ideas, analyses of cause and effect— gravitate toward the chronotope and through it take on flesh and blood, permitting the imaging power of art to do its work (Bakhtin, *Dialogic*, 250). This representational significance of chronotope becomes obvious if we consider the work Atay accomplished using specific objects in his depiction of the bourgeois obsession with property and propriety, the symptoms of which are spread all around the novel. This obsession finds one of its best expressions in the follow-

---

82 Charles Chaplin, *Modern Times* (1936)

ing passage where several voices, seamlessly attached to each other, are talking about the conventions of the middle class life in the 70s:

> Your face looks familiar. Have we met before? Were we together up on the mountain last winter? The mountain? I haven't been to the mountain for the last two years. It cannot be. Then, we must have met in the spa at Termos. I go there every year. I don't think so: I was visiting the Nefes ruins last year. My wife collected some beautiful stones when nobody was looking. Look, I have a special showcase made for the display of these stones. And we put the amphora next to the showcase. The villagers sell those stones, did you know? Pretty cheap, too. Not that I'm interested. My wife has a soft spot for them. The whole house is full of stones. Most of them are stuck in a chest in the study. The living room is small, you know. Not enough space to put all these stones. So, the chest is doomed to remain locked. I wonder... Have we met in Herdek? Not that it is highly probable. We don't go there anymore. For one thing, it gets really crowded in summer. You have to book months in advance. Then... it is also quite dirty. Last time, we could not sleep because of mosquitoes. [...] Anyways, there are campers everywhere: civil servants, teachers. A swarm of teachers. Primary school teachers, a lot of women. At every single corner. You go to a restaurant, and there they are eating your food and letting you starve. They are like ants invading the whole place. What savage manners, what vulgar words! All those horrible blouses and garish shorts knock you down with laughter. They lie under the sun for hours and walk around with their scalded bodies. In the streets, on the beach, piles of terribly burnt flesh: It makes you sick. They fill the coasts with tents: hundreds of tents, thousands of tents, millions of tents. They have this secret plan of mapping Turkey's coastal line with tents. And they get the best places. Sometimes you drive for miles, and you cannot find a patch of sand on the seaside to put your picnic basket. I believe you are still thinking about where we must have met before. Yes, you're right. That's what I am thinking of. It's bugging me, I have to figure it out. [...] What brand is your camera? It is not something well known. I ordered mine from Japan. These Japanese guys are amazing. They made this machine: You know, it is unbelievable. You cannot take the pictures you take with that machine with Contraflex. Well, I agree that Contraflex is a good camera and has its virtues. But you should see the photos I took with this Japanese miracle. I wouldn't trade it with anything. I am really interested in photography. I wrote to every single company in Europe, America, Asia, Africa, Antarctica: they sent me catalogues. They were very much concerned about my requirements. That's also how I bought my tape recorder. It is an ST 527. Twelve speakers. Distinguishes every single sound. Let's say, you're going to listen to a symphony. The violins are playing somewhere on the table, the wind instruments above the bookshelf, and the bases are coming from within the cupboard. And my radio is tip-top: tape recorder-turntable-radio-sewing machine-electric iron. All in one. (300-305)

Details about everyday life are spread all through the novel both in *Wilhelm Meister* and *The Disconnected.* Yet, while offering a sense of familiarity and almost a domesticated aesthetic pleasure to Wilhelm, they definitely oppress

Turgut. Goethe's work has the space-time quality and represents the 'spirit of the times' with which Wilhelm can identify himself. We see him yearning for the unity of his childhood when he sees his grandfather's paintings in Natalia's house.

> The presence of the pictures and statues, which he knew so well of old, alternately attracted and repelled him. Nothing that surrounded him could he lay hold of or let go; all things reminded him of all; the whole ring of his existence lay before him; but it was broken into fragments, and seemed as if it would never unite again. These works of art, which his father had sold, appeared to him an omen that he himself was destined never to obtain a lasting calm possession of anything desirable in life, or always to be robbed of it so soon as gained, by his own or other people's blame. (Book VIII, Chapter VII)

Possessions and objects are of utmost importance also in *The Disconnected.* However, as opposed to Goethe who transcends the nostalgic moment above and provides that Wilhelm gets reunited with possessions from the past, Atay uses everyday objects to represent the suffocating atmosphere of Turgut's marriage. This he does deliberately through a detailed depiction of the furniture in his apartment. At the very beginning of the novel, he reserves pages and pages to comment on details like a couch bed, a cigarette case, a lighter in the shape of Aladdin's lamp, and silver ashtrays shaped like wine leaves (12-13). A full paragraph goes to the description of a hassock in the bedroom. A hassock, the function of which remains unclear for Turgut until he climbs onto it to reach the far end of a bookshelf. All these objects are poor imitations, uniform copies. They are practical, ugly, and anonymous —like the people who use them. When Turgut says all the apartments look the same, he means that they all have the same Aladdin lighters, couch beds and wine leaf ashtrays.

In Atay's world, like in Goethe's, every single object, every construct is situated in time, but the problem is whether Turgut can identify with the *Zeitgeist*, as Wilhelm does. Hardly possible. How can he identify himself with cigarette cases brought from Germany that play Beethoven's 9th Symphony when you open the lid, or with toilet cabins that play Bizet's Carmen in the background when you are emptying your bowels? (305) The artificiality, the ugliness, and the banality of these objects are constantly put forward in *The Disconnected.* In fact, the whole ideology of pleasure embedded in the comfort of daily life disgusts Turgut. The possessions are usually referred to as obstacles between him and Selim. Turgut remembers him saying "I wanted you show me tolerance, you showed me your buffet instead" (16).

One cannot help but notice the striking effect of *kitsch* that dominates the whole novel, which helps Atay convey Turgut's feeling of alienation as opposed to the sense of comfort that is granted to Wilhelm. In *The Disconnected*, the 'spirit of the times' is characterized by *kitsch*, the aesthetics of the middle class, which Turgut finds hardly palatable, because it "raids all sorts of aesthetic material to construct what will be the typical household of modern times" (Moretti, *The World*, 36-37). Even when portrayed as an adolescent, he is aware of the banality of the middle class objects that surround him, and he resists these cheap taste as he resists evil:

> Evil breeds evil. Banality eats up one's soul. Undoubtedly, the overdeveloped countries know how to make something even out of evil, and find a way to export it to underdeveloped countries. By rationalizing it, or freezing it in the works of art, they place it in life, and find a vitality in evil. Here, the only protection against evil is letting it slide over you. Being an underdeveloped primary school student, this was the only thing I could achieve. I let it slide. I was indifferent to evil, I did not let it enter my soul. I had to eat the black bread, but I could live without reading bad poetry. (60)

Later in the novel, Turgut admits to Selim that he was doomed to remain an observer, because he could never actively take part in a world of banality. He had to "let the world slide" over him "Yes! Like an evil spirited virgin, I saw everything but I did not let it stick on me" (63). Throughout the novel, it becomes more and more obvious that Turgut feels as if he is going to be devoured by the dullness and cheapness of the bourgeois life. His escape from the "connected", therefore, should be regarded as breakout from the world of unending banality, which "eats up one's soul." One notices the amount of relief he feels the day he left his middle class life behind:

> We are awake, Olric. He stood up, shaved, got dressed. Turned the radio on. A bank wished them good day. Good day to you too, dear bank. We have left the nightmares behind, Olric. We will leave with the rising sun. He did not ask for breakfast. His suitcase was packed. The children were asleep. He watched them for a while. He felt a slight dizziness. Like the confusion one feels in the morning after spending the night in somebody else's place. He looked at the furniture, at the walls with the eyes of a stranger. One easily finishes the chores. Take care of yourself. Drive safely. I will. I want to reach the city as early as possible. I'd better be going. He kissed his wife. So long. Good-bye. Easy does it if you keep the conversation short. He walked down the stairs. The janitor gave him a respectful nod. He bowed and opened the gate. He reached for the suitcase. Turgut did not let him carry it: it is absolutely unnecessary to complicate things even further. You only need to open the door. If you help me further, then we will have to carry a useless conversation. He opened the trunk, placed the suitcase next to the box —like the cold-blooded bank robbers in the movies. The audience does not know what it is in the box. The players do not know it, either. He closed the trunk. Nobody can stop this box from being taken away anymore. After a little while, he will be driving away from the house, he will turn the corner and disappear. The scene will change. A mild autumn breeze ca-

ressed his face, he felt the coolness of his aftershave. He waved to his wife at the window; he opened the door of the car slowly moving the key in the latch. People who do that sort thing are not as cold-blooded as they look, Olric. All robbers eventually die of heart attack. It requires some skills even to look cold-blooded, Milord. Thank you, Olric. He started the car. He opened the window and waved to his wife again. I am a great admirer of your cold-bloodedness, Milord. We have only one minute thirty-five seconds left, Olric. In one minute, we should be at the corner. He released the hand brake. He shifted into gear pressing the clutch. We don't need to look back now, Olric. I am getting nervous, Milord. We're moving, Olric. I am gently removing my foot from the clutch and pushing on the gas pedal. They passed through the street slowly, and turned the corner. Maybe they are spilling some water behind our back at the moment. He drove faster. Bon voyage, Olric. Bon voyage, Milord. God bless our Lord! (518-519)

## Bildung or Un-Bildung

It is true that Wilhelm attains fulfillment at the end of the novel, now that he finds a way to reconcile his abstract idealism with the concrete demands of the society, but what he sacrifices for this happiness is his most immediate self which can come into contact with people like Mignon and the Harper. Though the attainment of happiness is the primary goal of the classical *Bildungsroman*, says Moretti, it does not come for free. On the contrary, the cost of living in harmony with the society is rather high. The protagonist pays it with his freedom (*The World*, 9). As all the negativity, all his suffering, gets annulled and transcended into happiness, Wilhelm's free will is swallowed up and assimilated by the society. This is the end of his story, and the end of his life as a free individual. Once he becomes a loyal citizen and a devoted husband, he enters the realm of normality and loses his uniqueness.[83]

Negativity for Goethe is the dynamo of the process, a force that moves the mechanism of development further, whereas it is the essence of being for Atay. It is not a means, it is the end itself. In this sense, there is no development in *The Disconnected* because there is no such thing as accumulating experience that would lead towards an Absolute, a rational whole. The only experience is the anxiety that spreads from the truth that our lives are determined by a negativity over which we have no control. At the very end of his journey, the truth Turgut comes face to face with is that every single moment of his life is the same in that

83 Ironically, this was not how Goethe himself ended up. He lived up to the demands of being a poet, while urging the others to dream of nothing else other than being a good citizen. In this sense, maybe we should withhold from Goethe the authenticity that we grant to Atay.

it is a postponement of the possibility of death one way or the other. This is why, as Goethe views failure as a moment that can be transcended into a higher truth, Atay regards it as the core of our being.

One can successfully argue that *The Disconnected* starts at the very point where *Bildungsroman* ends. It is true that Turgut goes on an existential journey following the death of his best friend, but this journey is hardly one comparable to that of Wilhelm. Even if there is a formation on the side of Atay's main character, it can be called a process of "unlearning" rather than a process of learning. The novel starts at the point when the protagonist is devoured by the totality and assimilated by the bourgeois community, and we observe Turgut striving to go back to his immediate self-uncovering the things that have obscured the core of his very being. As opposed to the consensus reached at the end of *Wilhelm Meister*, we are presented with an open-ended finale in the case of *The Disconnected*, where Turgut simply takes off in search of his true being.

# "HUNDRED VISIONS AND REVISIONS": SELF-CONSCIOUSNESS AS THE ARTISTIC EXPRESSION OF MODERNITY

Modernity has its roots in the Enlightenment thought, the seeds of which have been planted by Descartes, who introduced the notion of the subject that involves a duality in itself, known as Cartesian dualism. The *cogito* in the Cartesian system was defined as a knowing subject, the object of whose knowledge turns out to be itself. The question whether it is possible for the subject to know itself marks the beginning of what might be called "philosophy of self-consciousness" – and also of the advent of modernity.

The legacy of Cartesian dualism is subjectivism that time and again emerged in the course of modern European philosophy. In one sense, the modern subjectivism that began with Descartes marks the beginning of a new era in history. With the Cartesian gesture, Western philosophy and cultural life all together, took a new turn, where subjectivity or consciousness became the foundation of all that there is. Taking form as the self or ego, subjectivity became the basis of a new humanism, accenting the scope for human beings to make their own world on earth – thus, shaping the Enlightenment project and eventually, the idea of progress and the emergence of a modern understanding of time. Hence, the main features of modernity, as Calinescu names them:

> Modernity in the broadest sense, as it has asserted itself historically, is reflected in the irreconcilable opposition between the sets of values corresponding to (1) the **objectified**, socially measurable time of capitalist civilization (time as a more or less precious commodity, bought and sold on the market), and (2) the personal, subjective, imaginative *durée*, the private time created by the unfolding of the "self." The latter identity of time and self constitutes the foundation of modernist culture. (*Five Faces*, 5)

The traditional view of Descartes as the origin of modernity and the *cogito* as the initial gesture to mark the beginning of a new era was perhaps best summarized by Hegel, who claimed in his *History of Philosophy* that when we come to Descartes we come home to ourselves, out of otherness, home to subjectivity.[84] As we have discussed in the previous chapter, Hegel's main task in the *Phenomenology* was to represent the journey that leads consciousness to self-

84 From Hegel's *Lectures on The History of Philosophy*, translated by E S Haldane from Michelet's compilation of Hegel's Lectures, first given in Jena in 1805, but closer to the Heidelberg text of 1816-7, first published 1892, and reprinted by Routledge & Kegan Paul, 1955.

consciousness that is aware of itself as being all reality, and that recognizes and exercises itself as that reality. We have already mentioned that the protagonist of *Bildungsroman* ends his journey with the attainment of such self-consciousness —a subjectivity that can be regarded as the culmination of modernity. From a Hegelian perspective, when the individual attains self-consciousness, this means the attainment of social consciousness indicating a reconciliation of the individual with the society and a corresponding increase in happiness for both. However, rather than being a basis for happiness, as Nietzsche sees it, the increase in the level of consciousness turns out to be a danger: "anyone who lives among the most conscious Europeans even knows that it is a disease" (*Gay Science*, 354).

As opposed to the Enlightenment philosophers, such as Locke and Kant, Nietzsche does not conceive of self-consciousness as a blank page upon which one's experiences are eternally recorded, or as a transcendental principle of self-possession. Neither does he agree with Hegel that self-consciousness is a step in the process of *Bildung* attained through negativity, i.e. suffering. In his view, suffering is not something that can be elevated and contained in a higher truth, on the contrary, it is all that there is for consciousness to experience. All consciousness is a social phenomenon that reflects historical conditions; in the modern age, it takes a particularly painful turn. With the advent of modernity, we see the development of an externalized self, which is associated with a scrutinizing subjectivity. The undertaking of the modern novelist is what Stephen Spender, in *The Struggle of the Modern*, formulates as the representation of this "critical awareness" rather than action:

> The Voltairean "I" of Shaw, Wells, and the others acts upon events. The modern "I" of Rimbaud, Joyce, Proust, Eliot's *Prufrock* is acted upon by them. The Voltairean "I" has the characteristics —rationalism, progressive politics, etc.— of the world the writer attempts to influence, whereas the modern "I" through receptiveness, suffering, passivity, transforms the world to which it is exposed... The Voltairean egoists are contemporaries without being, from an aesthetic or literary point of view, moderns. What they write is rationalist, sociological, political and responsible. The writing of the moderns is the art of observers conscious of the action of the conditions observed upon their sensibility. Their critical awareness includes ironic self-criticism. (71-72)

As he compares "the conscious I" of the enlightenment with modern self-consciousness, Spender mentions Prufrock among the modern characters equipped with such awareness. One has to remember that Prufrock's self-conscious indecision is a carnivalized version of Hamlet's dilemma, which sends us back to one of the earliest figures of modernity. Prufrock, like many of the Dostoevsky characters, represents a divided interiority that results in a constant dialogue within the self. Prufrock is capable of seeing himself from outside, from the eyes of the others, and this is exactly what paralyzes him. It is nothing but this awareness of his own fallibility that is the source of Prufrock's pathos and his "hundred visions and revisions." What characterizes the modern man is not only that he lacks the grandeur of the tragic hero, but also that he is aware of his impotence.

This state of consciousness is precisely what Dostoevsky's Underground Man finds himself in. His self-consciousness is an incurable disease. He is one of the most learned and cultivated characters of literature, but his knowledge serves only to make him aware of questions he is incapable of answering. His virtue is coupled with disgust of his own banality. He is sincere, but he uses his sincerity to reveal his canniness, and his obstinacy to demonstrate his unpredictability.

> And yet he really is knowledgeable, candid, and persistent —even virtuous in his peculiar way. If he cannot achieve the freedom of love or of self-denial or of self-mastery, at least he can proclaim that he is far more alive than his audience. In all his individual ambiguity and torment, he exists, as they do not in their complacent social identities. Even though he can express his freedom only by perversity, he clings to it with some joy and pride; for in that minimal form he still touches upon the value of selfhood that others have asserted more confidently and perhaps with less right to make the claim. (Ellmann, *Modern Tradition*, 689)

The Underground Man is the toppling of the Enlightenment ideals; rationality, science, social development, and the search for fundamentals. He challenges the whole body of western thought confident in a type of solemn knowledge that normalizes, familiarizes and tames anything that tends to remain alien bringing it to the realm of rationality. In fact, he marks the moment in history when the Hegelian project of *Bildung* completely collapses. In his unclassifiable ambiguity, the Underground Man takes a position which defies dialectics altogether. His self-consciousness is definitely not comparable to that of Wilhelm who, as the perfect bourgeois, identifies himself with history, which he sees as a succession of progressive moments. In the case of the Underground Man, Wilhelm's faith in progress is nowhere to be seen. Holquist underlines the Underground Man's awareness of history as rather that of a "late-comer" that has seen the end of time.

> [...] the underground man is conscious of the theoretical conclusion that modern man must be the pinnacle of history as it has come to be understood in the nineteenth century (its meaning will be revealed in its own process); but he is also aware that he does not *feel* like the heir of the ages. He not only, like the bourgeois, recognizes the incompatibility of such history with his own experience, but he goes beyond the bourgeois in seeing clearly what the implications of the conflict are. He

> does not try to keep the old, organic sense of history —history as the guarantor of identity— alive by deception, as does the bourgeois. Rather, he abandons it as an inadequate source for understanding himself. And he does so, because in his rejection of any system (science as well as history) as a means by which to understand himself, he abandons the primary assumption of older conceptions of identity based in history. (Holquist, *Dostoevsky*, 49)

This is why the Underground Man finds it impossible to identify himself with the history of the world. As opposed to Wilhelm, who sees progress and harmony when he looks around, the Underground Man sees irrationality and chaos everywhere, which definitely does not fit into the theoretical program of modernity, summarized best in Hegel's well-known formula rendering all reality as rational.[85] In short, the difference between the protagonist of the classical *Bildungsroman* and the Underground Man is that the latter is endowed with an awareness that sickens and paralyzes him rather than making him a functional part of the society. While the heroes of the Enlightenment seek the objective and the universal in their path towards knowledge, the modern protagonist drowns in his own subjectivity, which finds its best expression in pathos. The Underground Man emerges as a key figure in demonstrating this pattern in modern literature.

Therefore, we will consider the Underground Man and his acute self-consciousness not only as a template for understanding the protagonists of Dostoevsky's later novels, but also as a central theme in demonstrating the Dostoevskian problems of Atay's poetics. In this chapter, while arguing how Atay presents his own account of modern self-consciousness in a constant dialogue with Dostoevsky, we will also focus on the ways he elaborates on the amount of suffering that derives from the impossibility of grounding oneself in one's own subjectivity in *The Disconnected.*

---

85 In the *Phenomenology of Spirit*, Hegel describes Reason as self-consciousness, and self-consciousness as Reason. Self-consciousness becomes all reality, in that Reason is the conscious certainty of being all reality. The Absolute is a universal reality which is conscious of itself. Hence, according to Hegel, all reality is Reason. Whatever is real is rational, whatever is rational is real. The reality of Reason has a universal necessity. Whatever is irrational cannot have a conscious certainty of its own reality. See G.W.F. Hegel, *The Phenomenolgy of Mind*, trans. by J.B. Baillie, (New York: Harper & Row, 1967), 274-276.

# Dostoevskian problems of Atay's poetics

## "Man in Man"

Atay, like his protagonist Selim, was well read in Russian literature, and particularly Dostoevsky, whom he truly admired as the greatest of all novelists and a real virtuoso in mapping human nature, the *terra incognita*. Therefore, it is no big surprise that Selim emerges as an amalgam of several Dostoevsky characters. The portrait of Selim as a young man bears a striking similarity to Dostoevsky's passionate young characters, such as Kolya of *The Brothers Karamasov* or Ippolit of *The Idiot*. At times, he is as altruistic and saintly as Prince Myshkin or Alyosha. At times, he fights against his devils like Raskolnikov, Stavrogin, and Ivan Karamazov. However, what make him an unforgettable character are his keen self-consciousness and the resulting paralysis as in the case of the Underground Man.

Selim is obsessively concerned about the way he is being perceived by others, and in fact, he is tormented because of his acute self-consciousness, which equips him with the ability of seeing himself through the eyes of the others. What Bakhtin says about Dostoevsky applies with equal force to Atay, especially when Selim's consciousness is concerned: "What is important to Dostoevsky is not how his hero appears in the world but first and foremost how the world appears to his hero, and how the hero appears to himself" (*Problems*, 47). Following the footsteps of his mentor, Atay refrained from viewing his heroes as some solid and unchanging material that can be "fixed in a formulated phrase," and characterized as such. On the contrary, he fully understood that what he was supposed to characterize was not "the specific existence of the hero, not his fixed image, but the sum total of his consciousness and self-consciousness" (48).

The very term "self-consciousness," implies an inner division within the self.[86] When the self constitutes both the knower and the known, then these parts pursue and undermine each other and produce a "negative" state of self-alienation. Dostoevsky, very much like Kierkegaard, seems to think that the state of self-division, "ironic" or "negative," is part of the very definition of personal existence (Ellmann, *Modern Tradition,* 687). We cannot escape from it, by an easy Hegelian synthesis, because the tension of individual and universal must remain if the universal is to be apprehended at all. Truth is given only to the "subjective" thinker, who becomes more and more capable of genuine knowledge as he comes to understand his finite and changeable human nature.

86 Hegel interprets the intrinsic duality of self-consciousness as a conflict between a "changing" or individual aspect of the self and a "changeless" or universal aspect.

Almost all Dostoevsky characters seem to be equipped with the capacity of immense suffering that arises from the very fact of their being human. Raskolnikov, for instance, suffers because he knows that the particular content of his action is not adequate to the universality that he demands to be recognized in his deed. His problem is not that he committed a murder, but that he wants this particular action to be recognized as universal truth, that he wants to overcome his finitude. He grounds himself in himself, but at the same time he demands his own truth to overlap with the universal truth, the good. The contradiction here is between the universality he states in his words and the particular content of his action. *Crime and Punishment* opens with this very conflict between the finite and the infinite, between the particular and the universal.

The immense effort on the side of the protagonist to distinguish himself from the others, Raskolnikov's self-assertion, makes it easier to understand why Bakhtin claims that Dostoevsky's hero is a "pure voice; we do not see him, we hear him" (*Problems*, 71). One feels obliged to agree with Bakhtin that Dostoevsky is less concerned with the physical world and nature compared to many other novelists. "Dostoevsky's hero is a man of an idea; not a character or temperament, not a social or psychological type" (133). Or as Berdyaev puts it, "the hero of the Letters from the Underworld is an idea, Raskolnikov is an idea, Stavrogin is an idea, Kirilov, Shatov, Verhovensky, Ivan Karamazov—ideas" (*Dostoevsky*, 35). A distinguishing feature of polyphonic form is that the "I" and the idea are of a piece; what is said of the I may be said of the idea. Indeed, as Bakhtin puts it:

> At that point of contact between voice-consciousnesses the idea is born and lives. The idea—as it was seen by Dostoevsky the artist—is not a subjective individual-psychological formation with 'permanent resident rights' in a person's head; no, the idea is inter-individual and inter-subjective—the realm of its existence is not individual consciousness but dialogic communion between consciousnesses. The idea is a live event, played out at the point of dialogic meeting between two or several consciousnesses. (*Problems*, 88)

As at one point in the book, Bakhtin also admits, not all persons are equally favorable material for the representation of self-consciousness, but Atay intentionally sought (and found in the portrayal of Selim) a hero, whose primary task would be becoming conscious, "the sort of hero whose life would be concentrated on the pure function of gaining consciousness of himself and the world" (50).

In fact, the whole idea of not being able to "hold on to the world" is the outcome of this very same self-consciousness, and therefore a Dostoevskian theme —elaborated, probably for the first time, in *Notes From the Underground*. The Underground Man is the archetypal example of all "the disconnected." In fact, nothing explains better what it means to be "disconnected" than the following episode: The Underground Man is one day in a tavern, when a powerful officer picks him up and moves him out of the way. The narrator is humiliated to have been treated so lightly, and cannot sleep for fantasies about how he will revenge himself. The officer walks every day down Nevsky Prospect, as the narrator follows him from a distance. He decides that he will walk in the opposite direction and that when the two men meet, he will block the officer's way not giving an inch. But day after day when the moment of physical encounter arrives, he weakens, and moves out of the way just as the officer strides past. At night he wakes up obsessed with the question: "Why is it invariably I who swerve first? Why precisely me and not him?" Or as he says later while talking about his fellow clerks, "I alternated between despising them and thinking them superior to myself [...] but whether I despised them or thought them superior I dropped my eyes almost every time I met anyone" (*Underground*, 30-36).

Atay's protagonist Selim faces the whole world as the Underground Man watches the officer go by every day. In fact, Selim enters every social environment as the Underground Man walks toward the officer or his fellow clerks; that is to say, he does it for another reason: because he needs other people in order to confirm himself. On one hand, he desperately wants to be taken seriously, on the other hand, he looks down upon people who value him. The ambivalence in his attitude towards the others, a motive that dominates the whole body of the novel, stems from this conflict. Selim both wishes to remain as an isolated individual, stick to his own morality, be his own ground, and at the same time desires to be recognized by the others in order to universalize his position. The desire for recognition dominates his relation to almost all the characters in the novel, Süleyman, Metin, and especially Esat, who seems to be familiar with his inner contradictions:

> He felt he was either taken too seriously or completely ignored. And then he would at once forget what other people did to him. He would also forget what he did to other people. He could never stand the pain of having been rude to others. 'I am so sincere in my anger that people should not get offended when I'm mad at them. They should rather admire my sincerity', he would say and laugh in a disarming way. "Either spoil me, or kick me out!' he would yell 'I am tired of people only halfway sincere. Nobody will stay but one. Fine with me: One is plenty.' Then he would shout again, 'I am a sinner, hit me!' He was reading Dostoevsky back then. (347)

Selim's desire for recognition, inescapably, reminds us of the Underground Man, who calls himself "a retort man," a man who comes "not from the bosom of nature but from a retort" (*Underground*, 13). Men of limited consciousness (like the officer in the *Notes*, or Selim's friend Metin in the *Disconnected*) are able to convince themselves of their own ground as the source of a rational universe, that there is reason beyond their being there. In fact, they take their actions as the ground for all that there is. This is what nature intended, because if men were to realize the futility of their action, they would be paralyzed. They would no longer act and thereby destroy themselves by their own omnipotence. Such is the nature of the higher level of consciousness, the 'illness', which consumes the Underground Man and Selim. Having a higher level of consciousness, they see that the ultimate causes of all reasons are external. The inside (the ego) cannot possess its own ground, it will always be determined by the outside (the others).

The orientation of one person to another person's discourse and consciousness is, in essence, the basic theme of all Dostoevsky's works, as Bakhtin, who posited it as the fundamental principle of Dostoevsky's work; i.e., dialogism. In the *Notes from the Underground*, on the other hand, we have a perfect demonstration of "dialogized self-consciousness," where we are faced with a complicated relationship of the Underground Man with other consciousnesses since it is crosscut "by an equally intense relationship to his own self." In *Problems of Dostoevsky's Poetics*, Bakhtin observes that from the very beginning the Underground Man's confessions are dialogized in the sense that they are laden with the anticipation of the opinions of others. What the underground man thinks about most of the time is what others think or might think about him, and the way he tries to keep one step ahead of every other consciousness, every other thought about him forces him into a vicious circle:

> What he fears most of all is that people might think he is repenting before someone, that he is asking someone's forgiveness, that he is reconciling himself to someone else's judgment or evaluation, that his self-affirmation is somehow in need of affirmation and recognition by another. And it is in this direction that he anticipates the other's response. But precisely in this act of anticipating the other's response and responding to it, he again demonstrates to the other (and to himself) his own dependence on this other. (229)

We observe the same self-castrating attitude in the portrait of the adolescent Selim, as voiced by Esat. Selim's attitude toward himself is inseparably bound up with the attitude of the others toward him, "his consciousness of self is constantly perceived against the background of the other's consciousness of him" (*Problems*, 207). Selim depends on the consciousnesses of others; he fears the opinions of others, no matter how much he despises them.

> 'Or you could force me to face the truth that I could make nothing out of these books that would help me to get on with my life and build my personality. What can I do? No matter what books I read, the greengrocer still pulls a fast one on me and stacks all the rotten apples in my bag. I can't stop him from cheating. The old shark deceives me although I do not have faith in him. Then how am I going to stop the

> betrayal of old friends I have always believed in: this is totally hopeless. My friends are mocking me. [...] Perhaps even the books don't want me to cling onto them so tightly. Maybe they are also mocking me for my overplayed sobriety. I know, I know... Even books don't take me seriously. They despise me as whores would look down upon merchants too generous with their money.' (334-335)

Selim, like Raskolnikov, owes a lot to the Underground Man in his desire to stand out among others voicing his claim to universality. Like the Underground Man, who claims his place in the sun, or like the proud Stavrogin, who cries in fury that he did not 'represent himself' this way or the other, and that he was very much himself when he wrote the scandalous confession, or like Ivan Karamasov, the most introspective of all the brothers and probably the most cultivated Dostoevsky character, who discovers at the end of the novel that he can not live up to his ideas, Selim suffers because he is aware that he can not be compatible with himself no matter how hard he tries: "I can not be all those characters at the same time. They just get muddled up in my mind. I become a laughingstock. Moaning and groaning he would pace the room. 'I am a contemptible creature, I know,' he would say" (347). Like the Underground Man, who suggests the questioning of the world in which we are imprisoned by the rigid laws of 2 + 2 = 4, Bakhtin asks us to review our basic notion of self-identity:

> A man never coincides with himself. One cannot apply to him the formula of identity A = A. In Dostoevsky's artistic thinking, the genuine life of the personality takes place at the point of non-coincidence between a man and himself, at his point of departure beyond the limits of all that he is as a material being, a being that can be spied on, defined, predicted apart from his own will, 'at second hand.' The genuine life of the personality is made available only through a dialogic penetration of that personality. (*Problems*, 59)

Not all the characters possess the divided interiority we observe in Selim.[87] Metin's discourse is truly monological, and Turgut's wife Nermin is as flat as a pancake —if one wishes to pay homage to Forster for his famous distinction.[88]

---

87 For Bakhtin, the self "never coincides with itself" because it is always in the process of becoming, because the final word has not yet been spoken, nor will it be spoken by man. However, an author may alsa choose to represent some of his characters limited within the one-sided seriousness of a monological discourse.

88 Forster's distinction is meant to categorize the different qualities of characters in literature and examine the purposes to which they are put. A "flat" character, according to Forster, can be summed up in a single sentence and acts as a function of only a few fixed character traits. "Round" characters are capable of surprise, contradiction, and change; they are representations of human beings in all of their complexity. Forster's aim, however, is not to elevate the round at the expense of the flat, although he admits that the round is on the whole always a more interesting creation. Instead, he argues that

Nermin is Turgut's anti-thesis. We hear about her immediately after the novel opens. We feel her presence, and so does Turgut. Unlike Turgut, Nermin has no contradictions, does not possess a divided interiority, and does not come up with a self-assertion that has a claim of universality. In fact, she does not hold opinions. She does not own ideas. The relationship between the particular and the universal is turned upside down in Nermin's person. She has no claim to 'own' universality, because she lives in peace with what she holds to be the universal, the commonplace logic of the middle class, which she 'belongs' to.

Turgut, on the other hand, emerges as a double of Selim. Like Selim, he cannot be defined because he cannot be confined to the convention that rules Nermin's life. The fixed and finalized forms of a pretentious bourgeois society get destroyed as they are internalized and transformed, as they are made into features of Turgut's internal life. Thus, he is constantly at odds with anything that might settle matters, forever engaged in a dialogue between the internal and the external, between the 'I' and the 'they', between what is internal and what comes from outside.

This *they-self* against *I-self* is the most important axis of *The Disconnected* as it is the case in *Notes from the Underground.* The Underground Man, no matter how much he wants to blend "into the common rut," feels completely isolated from his fellow clerks: "Another circumstance, too, worried me in those days: that there was no one like me and I was unlike anyone else. "I am alone and they are EVERYONE," I thought--and pondered" (*Underground*, 36). Selim, who talks about the 'they', voices the isolation of the disconnected: "Who were they? He had no idea. The ones who made me like this, he would say. The ones that keep coming under different names in every single epoch of my life. The ones who are actually one and the same person. You know, it's them!" (362).

Who are the others? Evidently, those that are connected. The ones who never swerve first, drop their eyes, or hesitate. The ones who coincide with themselves. The ones who fit into the project of modernity in the sense that they can be completed and presented as part of a rational whole. Paying homage not only to Dostoevsky, but also to Gogol who created the archetypal clerk Akaky Akakievich in his well-known story *The Overcoat*, Atay provides us with an unforgettable portrait of the 'they' in the natural setting of the modern world: the office.

> Some clerks picky with their shirtsleeves were about to wear armbands; typists were refreshing their make up, licking their lips, polishing their crimson nails; the middle

---

there are compelling artistic reasons for a novelist to employ flat characters. See E. M. Forster, *Aspects of the Novel*, Abinger Edition [London: Edwin Arnold, 1974].

> aged were stretching their foreheads with their fingers to prevent it from sagging; the ones older than forty-five were complaining about the new generation whereas the younger ones were making a fuss about the counters covered with dust; there were flies everywhere hovering undisturbed above the desks. The office, that gargantuan body, was slowly stretching and waking up. Supervisors were not yet at the office, they were at the bus stop waiting for the bus to come. The managers were having breakfast at home, and the general managers were still in bed. Some clerks lucky enough to get sick leave were enjoying themselves doing some repair work at home. There were moments in the office when hands seemed to move towards a document, to a book of records, but such moments did not last, they got interrupted by a joke, a newspaper extended by a coworker sitting at the neighboring desk, or a cup of tea served by the janitor. [...] Every movement indicated tenderness, a polished worldliness. Nobody was in a hurry. Nobody thought anything unanticipated could happen. They expected all mornings to be like all the other mornings. (260)

These characters obviously have no claim to individuality. In fact, they would regard any form of eccentricity as the plague. What characterizes them is stability and dullness. As opposed to these characters that seem to be frozen in their timeless everyday reality, there is always something more to Selim that we have not seen yet. As readers, we expect him to surprise us and he does. In fact, he himself is aware of the impossibility of being one thing at a time. He knows that he will be completely renewed and regenerated: "Suddenly he jumped out of the bed and shouted: 'Selim is dead. Long live Selim!' 'Don't you pity the old Selim?' I would ask. 'There are so many of them, I don't know which one to grieve for', he would say. 'Besides I'm scared of the dead. I think they will infect me with death'" (355). Selim's fear of death can also be read as a fear of stagnation. He is scared of being frozen solid which would kill the possibility of revealing himself to himself as something new; i.e., the possibility of discourse. As Bakhtin puts it, "in a human being there is always something that only he himself can reveal, in a free act of self-consciousness and discourse" (*Problems*, 58).

His consciousness of a word yet to be uttered sustains the character's dialogical movement inward, to the discovery of the "man in man," as Bakhtin calls it (58). The "man in man" is another expression of the character's divided interiority. The character, since he is in a constant state of a dialogue with himself, always lives at the threshold of the yet-to-be, and can never synchronize with himself: "He is continually in the process of reemerging from the shadow of the not yet, for self-consciousness is consciousness of the not yet, of the future anterior of what the character shall have been, in the light of what he is becoming" (Patterson, *Bakhtin and Berdyaev*).

Ironically, however, self-assertion, as in the case of Selim, is doomed to fail, since consciousness discovers its own arbitrariness. When he acts he comes to realize that he cannot occur at the same time with himself. Hence, he is not in full possession of himself, which constitutes the ground of his self-assertion. Selim finds himself face to face with the truth that, one way or the other, he is constantly "too late" for himself. This dialogical inwardness is Bakhtin's artistic interpretation of the loss of ground, which has to do with the time consciousness of modernity, i.e. belatedness. Ertuğrul sees this accurately as an existential point about the life of the self as well as the destiny of the modern epoch:

> What we call modern is essentially an experience of the loss of origin, the loss of the transcendental structure that guarantees the meaning of the human sojourn on earth. The modern epoch is opened up simultaneously as the absence of origin and an attempt to ground it at the level of subjectivity. In this sense modernity is always belated vis-á-vis itself. (629)

Ertuğrul continues her argument claiming what is revealed in the works of Atay, as in the works of Dostoyevsky, Joyce, Beckett, and Kafka, is the impossibility of subjectivity as the ground of meaning. This is probably why, Atay, like Dostoevsky, "represents a person on the threshold of a final decision, at a moment of crisis, at an unfinalizable and unpredeterminable turning point for his soul" (*Problems*, 61). The moment of crisis is the moment when the other interferes with the hero's vision and disrupts his existence calling him to the question of ground. In the dialogical structure of Atay's novel, counterpoint, therefore, signifies turning point. When the hero comes to the threshold, it means he comes "face to face" with the other, i.e., with his own limits —man's finitude being engraved in the face of the other.[89]

## The fallen angel

Very few authors – probably none – can match Dostoevsky in demonstrating the pain of asking the question: What is the ground of our existence? Dostoevsky

89 The "face to face" relationship as Levinas develops it in *Totality and Infinity*, is an ethical relationship being characterized by the presence of the other disturbing the spontaneity of my enjoyment and calling me back to the seriousness that the ethical relationship requires of me. Levinas's argument is that the other person ruptures the horizon of my intentions. The other person interrupts my enjoyment and my representation of the world because despite the "face to face" encounter, I am incapable of making him or her an object of my intentional act. Being radically other, the other person escapes all kinds of understanding, and constantly disrupts the unity and coherence of my world. Thus, Levinas argues, to account for temporality we must go beyond talking about the horizon of being and talk about that which calls into question that horizon: the other person. See Emmanuel Levinas. *Totality and Infinity*, trans. Alphonso Lingis, (Pennsylvania: Duquesne University Press, 1969).

dares to look for the phenomena behind the surface of appearances – at what lies hidden behind what we find familiar and regard as natural. He is authentic in the sense that he does not take over the ready-made interpretations that he finds in his environment. And he demonstrates the pain arising from the experience of coming to terms with our finitude. Dmitry Karamasov asks "Why are the people poor? Why's the baby poor? Why's the steppe so bare?" Ivan Karamasov, echoing his brother, says he does not want to live in a world where innocent children are dying. Yet, none of these characters are capable of suffering for others – or for the human condition, in general – as much as Prince Myshkin does.

*The Idiot* remains unique among all Dostoevsky novels in the way it elaborates the question of ground centralizing the issue around a Christ-like character, and portraying him as a complete failure. Unlike *Crime and Punishment* and *The Brothers Karamasov*, the novel offers no reconciliation at the end. Both Raskolnikov and Dmitry go through a process of moral *Bildung* and reach salvation after they give up their pride and open themselves to the presence of another, whereas Myshkin not only fails to save people from their demise, but also destroys everything that he touches. Dostoevsky's "truly good man" is unable to bring his goodness to the society without also bringing on disastrous results. He does not bring light into the lives of the people he touches, instead he brings darkness. Murray Krieger says Myshkin suffers from a 'psychosis of humility' and gives to all those around him a moral burden greater than they can carry (43).

With the portrait of Prince Myshkin returning to his madness at the end of the novel, Dostoevsky provides us with a Jesus that is reduced to a miserable failure. No one in the book is capable of loving Myshkin, 'the good man' or 'the Godman'. Neither can they accept the love that he offers. He is wandering from one person to another in the hope of touching the good part of their souls, but in his desperate search he brings out the worst in their nature. Rogozhin commits murder, and is sentenced to fifteen years of hard labor in Siberia. Nastasya is never able to give up her self-contempt and falls prey to Rogozhin's uncontrollable desire for her. Ippolit makes a fool of himself in his unsuccessful suicide attempt, and dies in agony without being able to have faith in anything. Aglaya becomes the victim of her own interest in appearances, and runs off with a Polish Count, who is later discovered to be a scoundrel. After his talk with the Prince, General Ivolgin sees what he really is – that is, a foolish old drunkard who invents stories to restore his prestige – and dies literally out of shame. Ganya discovers that he actually is what he has always been scared of becoming: a mediocre man with delusions of grandeur.

By portraying a Christ figure completely stripped off his divine qualities in the person of the Idiot, Dostoevsky challenges the myth of incarnation. Prince

Myshkin is a Christ figure with all the human side exposed, the divine side invisible or negated. As Barbara Fister points out the Christ figure Dostoevsky gives us in Myshkin is "one who is undeniably human, vulnerable to suffering and death, not a deity in human form offering us redemption. (Fister, "The Holbein Christ")

The myth of incarnation plays a very significant role in *The Disconnected.* Selim emerges yet as another Christ-figure equipped with an immense capacity for suffering, but also locked up within the impossibility of transcending that pain.[90] What makes Selim comparable to Dostoevsky's good man —or "God-man"— is that he unmistakably fails to communicate the message he bears. Like Prince Myshkin, Selim is a complete failure. His heartbreaking tenderness and acute sensitivity, his gentle nature and fragility simply make him powerless in the eyes of others. In fact, the way Turgut sees it, he is an angel —fallen into a world of egotistical barbarians for whom the message that he bears does not possess any meaning. He is a savior who cannot even save himself. Actually, the message that he bears is what renders Selim impotent; he is castrated by his own selfless existence. In the notes he wrote to his own poem, he explains why he is cut off from the life of the others:

> *Stanza 263: I have no claim on life...*
>
> Selim's instincts were underdeveloped. He had no idea about self-interest. Yet... those who doth not have a claim on life shall be forgotten. Those who choose to stand in the shade shall remain in the shade forever. Those who seek secrecy in their good deeds shall be surprised to find the only success of their lives. No one will ever bother to notice their presence. One day, when they die, they shall completely disappear leaving not a single trace behind: not a memory, nor a work, not even a tearful eye. Even their obituary will be left in a remote corner on the seventh page attracting nobody's attention. Those who have no claim on life shall have no claim on death. (175)

As Selim tries to communicate a reality other than theirs, his friends do not want to hear what he says, and he becomes their toy if not their enemy. Before he kills himself, we see him abandoned not only by his 'devoted' followers, but also by the message itself. The myth of incarnation proves to be a bad joke, and Selim as the Christ-figure turns into a dark emissary who, in his search for the light, destroys not only himself but also the possibility of meaning.

---

90 In fact, Selim is not the only Christ-figure in Atay's works. What might be called the "Idiot-theme" also emerges in one of his short stories: *Beyaz Mantolu Adam* (The Man with the White Coat). With its depiction of a beautiful soul canonized in its immense capacity for suffering, the story is actually a homage to Dostoevsky's *Idiot.* See Oğuz Atay, *Korkuyu Beklerken* (Waiting for Fear), Istanbul: İletişim Yayınları, 1988.

Gürbilek, in her essay "*Kemalizmin Delisi Atay*" (Atay, the Fool of Kemalism), points to the fact that Selim's failure in life is caused by an acute self-consciousness and adds that this is one of the peculiarities of Atay's characters. According to Gürbilek, this is what dominates Atay's writing in general:

> What attracts us to Atay's characters today is that they are rather clumsy in the sense that they are not well versed in life, that they are "unworldly". Selim Işık of *The Disconnected* and Hikmet Benol of *Dangerous Games* are such characters, who spent their time thinking rather than acting, who suffer from a lack of what maybe called "*science du monde,*" and who, therefore, have to remain forever in their childhood being locked in their homes and within the limits of their minds. It seems as if everything has been determined beforehand: Selim 'the bookworm, the day-dreamer, the pale shadow of life' has never been able to join the football team, become a prefect, or overcome his high anxiety and climb the mulberry tree to follow his high school sweetheart. Neither can he become a part of life conquering the fear of being mediocre. (*Yer Değiştiren Gölge*, 30-31)

Parla also draws attention to Selim's portrayal as a timid, naïve, and fragile young man, and she says that we should regard this as a clue to understand the allusions to *The Idiot.* A constant feeling of defeat is what characterizes his adolescent years. "I may be inferior, but I have no inferiority complex," he says proudly, but we can imagine what kind of a life this oversensitive man might have led in the world of, what seems to him as, brutes.

> Selim Işık has nothing to do with the "masculine" identity delineated by Turkish culture. He is more of an *idiot*; an 'idiot' with a vague sexual identity and a feeling of insignificance. In the last stages of his depression, when he identifies himself with Christ, his asexuality and idiocy get finally confirmed. (*Don Kişot*, 221)

Like the beautiful Myshkin, Selim gets attracted to sufferers, especially to those at the bottom of the social scale. He can easily communicate with simple people and feel for them without toying with the idea of superiority – unlike Turgut, who, apparently, is not as innocent as Selim as he later realizes. "Can we stay clean?" he asks at some point in the novel, which turns out to be one of the most important issues in *The Disconnected.* Selim is the one who managed to remain "clean" —or who could not be anything but "clean"—, but this is what cost him his life in the end. The following episode about the conductor's daughter is of great importance in the sense that it shows Selim's purity —as opposed to others, whose souls got tainted with self-interest, greed, or overrated self-importance. The story is remembered and told by Turgut who regrets having failed to understand Selim. He recalls visiting a slum area years ago when they were both engineering students working on the field. Here is the episode about the conductor's daughter:

It was a hot day. We were working on top of a hill. We were mapping the area. It was a poor neighborhood with nothing but ramshackle houses and a few trees. Some of our friends had scared the hell out of the onlookers telling them stories of a new road to be constructed which would require the pulling down of their houses. One could sense that those poor people were intimidated by our presence. Then, a dark-skinned man emerged from one of the houses. Later we found out that he was a conductor working for the city buses. Taking him for the leader of our group, he approached Selim, and spoke to him in a respectful manner. They had some small talk. The conductor had a beautiful daughter: as dark as his father. A young girl with a disarming timid smile. She made coffee for both of us and served it with some water. Even today when I close my eyes, I can see water drops gliding on the surface of the flower decorated glasses. And I know, if Selim were here now, he would have told me in the same manner about the refreshing coolness of the water we drank that day. The boys later picked on Selim saying that the conductor was ready to give him his daughter. "He set his eyes on you," they said and roared with laughter. What a shame! I left a totally wrong impression on Selim that day. I laughed with the boys. He sat together with the conductor in the shadow of the house. They turned their backs to us and talked for a long time. Who knows what they talked about! I only remember about the water and coffee. Selim would be surprised to hear me say these. But as we were laughing at him, as he was talking to that conductor in the shadow, I think he gave serious thought to marrying that girl even if it occurred to him only for a moment! And I'm sure he never forgot thinking about it. I believe he thought about it in a beautiful way, in a way that would hurt nobody's feelings. In those days, I had no idea how seriously Selim took anybody who approached him with sincerity. [...] If it were possible, he would have married the conductor's daughter. He would have married every single girl on the street. He would have made friends with the conductor and everybody else. Not for the sake of doing it, but he would do it truly and sincerely. When he found out that he could not do it, when he discovered the impossibility of living as Selim, when he understood that he was not able to live those little moments to their end in the flux of life, he fell in such a great despair and fear [...] (578-79)

This episode is interesting in the sense that it bears echoes from Prince Myshkin's stories told to Madame Yepanchin and her three daughters when he first met them. One of the stories he tells them is about a young Marie, an outcast of the village where Myshkin lived in Switzerland. The story of Marie is about his compassionate Christian love. The story goes as thus: Marie was ostracized from the village community (including her mother) for having once fallen to sensuality (she was seduced and wronged by a traveling salesman). Myshkin alone took pity on the unfortunate girl and made efforts to restore the village children's love and respect for her. At the time the girl died, she was surrounded by the boundless love of the children. The story of Marie, which resembles the biblical story of Mary Magdalene, gives the reader the first clues that Myshkin was intended to be a Christ-figure. It also plays a role as a measure of comparison in the novel: Myshkin's compassion to save Nastasya, another victim and sufferer of seduction, from her destructive pride and apathy.

Like Myshkin, who tells probably the most improper story to a group of middle class women, Selim remains an outcast in a group of friends who are not capable of understanding his sincere desire to be close to the ones who suffer. The feeling that emanates from Selim is worlds apart from the atmosphere that reigns in Turgut's circle of friends —who later emerge as families of newly emerging Turkish middle class, equipped with the desire of being recognized by their likes, hence with all the hypocrisy of bourgeoisie, like the Yepanchins of *The Idiot.* Selim approaches everybody with the same frankness, and does not seem to be aware of any class difference, or social obligations. He talks to them in the same way he has been talking to Turgut, with great sincerity, which is obviously not acceptable by the class-conscious bourgeois of the novel. Atay makes it clear to the reader through Selim's attitude that he is an alien among others because of his inability of pretense —the prognostic sign of middle class. Therefore, for the most part of the novel, as it is the case in this episode, whenever Selim appears on the scene, we feel like we are watching a creature from outer space. Being Selim means to be immune to all kinds of pretense, to be able to keep that innocence, and to "stay clean," as Turgut later realizes, and finds it hard to convey to others:

> I wish you had left your eyes to me when you died. Now Being-Selim is left to the hard words spoken between two people. Even if we get a big funding how can we gather together all the Being-Selim? How can we gather your sweating over the lecture notes for economics in the heat of the summer to help your friend when everybody was at the seaside? Where can we collect your worries, your pain while you were working on them? How can the guide at the Museum of Selim express all these? How is he going to remember everything? And also, would his voice be as we want it? What if he skipped the most important moment? What if one of the visitors wanted to look at the fly that flew through the window right at the most important moment? We can't afford such a danger. What would Being-Selim be in the hands of the ignorant museum guide when even we couldn't find the words to express it? Even if the highest-ranking staff, how can I say, the presidency, were assigned to this task, we couldn't find a fitting person for this job of keeping. I wish you had trained me before you went. I wish you had found for me a way to say the difference between your death and others. Now there is nothing but the pain of carrying you inside me. The pain is growing as time goes. What will I say if someone stops me in the street and asks? Everybody will be relieved: they will say, after all there was nothing, since you can't tell, explain, express! They will return to their daily tasks with peace! I wish they all went blind by the excess of peace! Let the museum be

> closed also! Let no more Selims come to this world; let them live their scientific lives! Let a god-dammed peace of mind fill the whole world! (329)[91]

The "peace of mind" that Turgut is talking about here is the relaxed carelessness of the middle class. It is what Tolstoy calls the happiness of a well-fed cow in *The Kreutzer Sonata*. This is what Dostoevsky calls the cheerless contentment of "ant heaps" in the famous episode of the *Grand Inquisitor*. This is how Turgut and his friends live. However, what defines Selim is his isolation from community in general, and from his friends in particular. In this sense, he is an '*Idiot' per se*:

> We are now able to speculate further as to why Dostoevsky chose (even before he had written it) as a title for this novel *The Idiot*: He does so to emphasize the subjectivity of his Christ figure. 'Idiot' goes back to Latin *idiota* to the Greek word meaning private person (that aspect of a man separate from any collective identity) [...] Myshkin, then, as idiot, stands for the isolated individual. (Holquist, *Dostoevsky*, 111)

The passage about the conductor's daughter is also important in the sense that it demonstrates Turgut's betrayal of his best friend and the feeling of guilt that follows: The way he joins the others in their cruel joke on Selim is unforgivable and Turgut is aware of his crime. "I laughed with them," he says not being able to come up with an excuse for his baseness. His friends – especially Turgut's – attitude towards Selim is marked by betrayal. In fact, they all are fond of him; Turgut obviously adores him. But when others make fun of Selim, he puts a distance, especially because often Selim takes insults quietly like a meek child. Like Aglaya who yells at Myshkin saying, "Why are you abasing yourself, setting yourself lower than them? Why have you got everything twisted up inside, why is there no pride in you?," the young Turgut of this episode wants to shake Selim up and remind him of his status as a young promising engineer, who is no match for a conductor's daughter. Turgut's deceitfulness stemming from his wish to belong to the group is no different from Aglaya's hypocrisy emanating from her desire for social acceptance, which results in the abandonment of the loved and cherished idol.

Hence, Atay's dialogue not only with Dostoevsky, but also with the central myth of Christianity: Peter was scared of being killed, Turgut is scared of being ostracized.[92] Deep inside, he knows that, like many other characters in the book,

91 Trans. Suna Ertuğrul.

92 According to the Bible, Christ is not only betrayed, but also denied by his disciples. The night before he is crucified, Peter says that he is ready to go with him both into prison and to death, to which Jesus replies "I tell thee, Peter, the cock shall not crow this day, before that thou shalt thrice deny that thou knowest me". (John, 22:34) And this is what

he has been ready to give up on Selim at the first moment of crisis. In this sense, he is like Christ being betrayed, denied and completely abandoned by his disciples. His loneliness makes one think of the prophetic remark of the Grand Inquisitor telling Christ that he will burn Him the following day, and that "the same people who today kissed your (his) feet, will at the first sign from me rush to rake up the coals at your (his) stake tomorrow."[93]

In this scene with the conductor's daughter, we are also faced with Selim's loneliness and his incapability of communicating the faith he has in the possibility of transcendence: going beyond the boundaries of the ego and loving someone only out of compassion for another being. Like Dostoevsky, who says it again and again at various instances in *The Idiot*, Atay also believes that faith is silent. In this sense, Selim, like Myshkin, is completely isolated in his faith. The possibility of loving a conductor's daughter is not something that he can communicate to a young Turgut, or other people who are equally riveted in their own egotistical selves. Therefore, what Kierkegaard says about Abraham applies to Selim:

> Abraham keeps silent – but he cannot speak. Therein lies the distress and anguish. For if I when I speak am unable to make myself intelligible, then I am not speaking – even though I were to talk uninterruptedly day and night. Such is the case with Abraham. He is able to utter everything, but one thing he cannot say, i.e. say it in such a way that another understands it, and so he is not speaking. (112)

This silence bears a horrible loneliness in itself. Selim's search for a home ends up in a dreary picture where he discovers himself completely isolated, deserted

---

he does when they ask him whether he was together with Jesus of Nazareth: "Then began he to curse and to swear, saying, I know not the man. And immediately the cock crew". (Mathew, 26:74)

93 In some ways, Myshkin and the Christ of the "Legend of the Grand Inquisitor" are similar. Both are abandoned by their disciples, both suffer criticism and insults meekly, and they both are silent on the essential questions incapable of offering answers or creating miracles. The Inquisitor bases his charges on the fact that Christ has unkindly burdened mankind with questions that it dares not answer, and Aglaya Yepanchin accuses Myshkin of similar cruelty: 'You have no tenderness: only truth and that's why you're unfair'. Mankind does not want to hear the truth that Christ has to offer. Freedom of choice, in the eyes of the Inquisitor, is a burden that man can never bear "... a tranquil mind and even death is dearer to man than the free choice in the knowledge of good and evil. There is nothing more alluring to man than this freedom of conscience, but there is nothing more tormenting either." What man seeks on earth, however, is only someone to worship, someone to keep his conscience, an authority that he can obey. Both Myshkin and the Christ of Grand Inquisitor lack this authority. Their only power is in their powerlessness, as Kierkegaard would say, which is not recognized by their followers.

and incurably human in his vulnerability, which is stated over and over in *The Disconnected*:

> "In the beginning was the Word" says the Gospel according to Saint John. But in the beginning there was loneliness. It was before the Word. And loneliness continued to exist even after the Word. Loneliness. It began when the Word came to an end. It began before the Word was said. [...] Selim Işık's loneliness was feeding on words. (129-130)

Man's loneliness and abandonment on earth, and the question of faith is one of the central issues in *The Idiot*. Dostoevsky makes a perfect use of the reproduction of a Holbein painting Myshkin sees at the Rogozhins to portray the abandonment of man on earth.[94] Myshkin says 'One could lose his faith looking at this painting', whereas Rogozhin says that he likes gazing at it. The painting depicts Christ immediately after he is taken from the cross and laid into his tomb. As opposed to the general tendency of portraying Christ with his face still beautiful and shining under divine light, this one is 'a faithful representation of the dead body of a man who has undergone unbearable torments before the crucifixion, been wounded, tortured, beaten by the guards, beaten by the people, when he carried the cross and fell under its weight, and, at last, has suffered the agony of crucifixion'. This is the portrait of Christ as a human being who suffered the cruelty of his fellow brothers, and abandoned by his Father. Ippolit, the young nihilist, talks about the painting in the long farewell letter that he reads aloud echoing Smerdyakov of *Crime and Punishment*, who asks what if what we call beyond is nothing but a dark room full of insects:

> This blind, dumb, implacable, eternal, unreasoning force is well shown in the picture, and the absolute subordination of all men and things to it is so well expressed that the idea unconsciously arises in the mind of anyone who looks at it. All those faithful people who were gazing at the cross and its mutilated occupant must have suffered agony of mind that evening; for they must have felt that all their hopes and almost all their faith had been shattered at a blow. They must have separated in terror and dread that night, though each perhaps carried away with him one great thought, which was never eradicated from his mind forever afterwards. If this great Teacher of theirs could have seen Himself after the Crucifixion, how could He have consented to mount the Cross and to die as He did? This thought also comes into the mind of the man who gazes at this picture. (*The Idiot*, Book III, Chapter 6)

---

94 Holbein's *Christ in the Tomb* (1521): wood, 30.7 by 200 cm., in the Basle Museum. It is a terrible depiction, devoid of any spritual connotation: a rotting corpse, jaw dropped, the flesh spotted with a bluish decay, the eyes rolled upward in a grimace – the perfect image of the denial of immortality. Myshkin's comment on seeing it was Dostoevsky's own as reported by his wife, Anna Grigorievna.

This analogy is worth considering since Myshkin, like Holbein's Christ, is not only abandoned by his followers and friends, but also by the message itself. At the end of the book, when we see him silently sitting next to his rival/brother Rogozhin hopelessly trying to hold him back from the abyss he is about to fall into, he sounds like Christ on the cross when he cries in a moment of despair "Father, Father, why hast thou forsaken me?"[95] This is Christ as purely human since despair is not meant for deities. As Terry Eagleton points out, what makes the crucifixion genuinely tragic, is this moment of despair in which Jesus cannot conceive his suffering as something meaningful, something instrumental on the road that leads to redemption.

> If his death was a mere device for rising again in glory, a kind of *reculer pour mieux sauter*, then it was no more than a cheap conjuring trick. It was because his death seemed to him a cul-de-sac, as his despairing scriptural quotation on the cross would suggest, that it could be fruitful... Only by accepting this as the last word about the human condition can it cease to be the last word. Jesus was left only with a forlorn faith what he called his Father, despite the fact that his power seemed now to have abandoned him. (*Sweet Violence*, 37)

In Süleyman Kargı's notes to Selim's long autobiographical poem called "Yesterday, Today, Tomorrow," the idea of man's forsaken existence on earth manifests itself in Atay's uniquely ironical tone, through which he presents us with another carnivalized story, this time his own version of Christ's abandonment reflected in Selim's resentment towards God:

> *Stanza 193 and more: Dear God...*
>
> Dear God, why did you abandon him? Why did you let him feel lonely and make friends with boring people? Why did you make him pay the price of every single minute he lived? Why didn't you rip fear out of his breast? Why didn't you help him overcome the feeling of guilt? Why didn't you give him the courage to kiss Ayla when they were all alone in the basement while playing hide-and-seek? Yet, you are very generous with all your subjects, even the most insignificant ones, when it comes to such little braveries. [...] You kept knocking him about, pushing him around from one end to another. Where were you when his teacher said, "Don't lie to me! You did not draw this picture"? Why did you not help him to come up with an answer. He was the one who drew that picture. He was also not lying when Erdal slapped him on the face saying "Don't talk to my girl again!" He had nothing to do with that girl. Why didn't you see to it that he lose all the money at once when his father gave him 10 liras and asked him to bring back the change? Why did you allow it happen that he first lost 2,5 liras, and then dropped the remaining 4 liras while

95 "And at the ninth hour Jesus cried with a loud voice saying Eloi, eloi, lama sabachthani?, which is being interpreted 'My God, my God, why hast thou forsaken me?" (Mark, 15:34)

> he was searching for the money? Here I am, asking you: Why did you let it happen? Why did you not interfere when he went to the police to ask if someone found the money? Why did you make the police laugh at him, and why did you make him cry? Were the cops better people than Selim? I know what you're going to say. You will ask what this is compared to the suffering that Jesus had to face. You will say that he could not have gone into such detail. You know what I think? I think he should have gone into detail. He should have lived through everything. You should have sent him to the primary school Selim went to. [...] You think you can fix everything with the Second Coming of Christ. You'll see what happens if Selim also comes back for a second time. By the way, will you please see to it that their coming overlaps this time! Don't put thousands of years in between as you did last time. And finally, do not abandon them the way you did in their first coming. (173-175)

As one can see also in this manifesto against God, Selim's life has been a long struggle of not being laughed at. Laughter, however, like an inescapable fate, befalls on him. The cops laugh at him, his friends laugh at him. He trembles at the thought of women laughing at him. There are several different instances in the novel, where he mentions the strength that would make him call the waiter without hesitating, the courage to look the waiter in the eye, which makes him sound as if he were dreading the snicker of Prufrock's "eternal footman."

His naiveté is what makes him a laughing-stock, as it is the case in the Idiot, which Dostoevsky underlines by letting his Prince be compared to Don Quixote. The scene at Lebedyev's villa in Pavlovsk, Aglaya, the youngest daughter of the Yepanchin family who hates herself for having fallen in love with the Idiot, recites the poem, "The Poor Knight," to Myshkin and the others. In speaking of the poem, Aglaya remarks: "because the poem depicts a man who is capable of an ideal, and secondly, once having set up his ideal, capable of believing in it, and in that belief capable of devoting his whole life blindly to it." Although she later says that the "poor knight" is Don Quixote, and was intended to be a serious poem, everybody notices that she changes the initials in the poem to be Nastasya's initials, in order to mock the Prince's idiocy and simplemindedness.[96]

Both Myshkin and Selim display a quixotic oddity in their persistent saintliness and complete isolation. But what tells them apart is the prince's lack of self-consciousness. There are very few moments in *The Idiot*, when we can sense an understanding, on the side of Myshkin, of his own position among all these people surrounding him: the position of an abandoned Messiah. The prince never displays an awareness that could match Selim's self-consciousness. Alt-

96 In *The Idiot*, the constant reference to Quixote is not coincidental. Dostoevsky was a great admirer of *Don Quixote*, which he called "grandest and saddest book conceived by the genius of man," in awe and appreciation of Cervantes. *See* Fyodor Dostoevsky, *The Diary of a Writer*, trans. Boris Brasol (New York: Scribner's Sons, 1949), 260.

hough he is a developed character, in the sense that he exhibits a subjectivity that he expresses in his own unique manner, one can plausibly argue that Myshkin is one of the few monological characters Dostoevsky ever created. In fact, Holquist argues that this is as far as you can get in turning Jesus Christ into a character in a novel. Pointing out to the fact that the prince is a Christ-figure who is denied the "systematic time of *Heilsgeschichte*," he says we have to grant him his subjectivity, and hence his uniqueness:

> Jesus' meaning is contained in the *telos* built into his biography; his life is lived toward resurrection, back toward his extra human, supra-individualistic state. The problem, on the other hand, for Myshkin is that he is only a subjectivity: his task is precisely to find a *telos*, to *achieve* a universality that can endow his particularity with meaning. (*Dostoevsky*, 111, emphasis original)

It seems Dostoevsky truly suffered while trying to create his beautiful Idiot. It is obvious in the *Notebooks for the Idiot* that as late as the sixth plan, he does not know who or what the Idiot is. As the deadline for the novel approaches we see him writing repetitiously 'Who is he?' He started with the idea of a monstrous man who would finally discover love and forgiveness. As he did with many other novels, he was after a tragic phrase, which would be forgiven and transcended in the end, which, for instance, happens in *The Brothers Karamasov*, as Blackmur says:

> Tragic phrases should be forgiven, they must be... Without them sorrow would be too heavy for men to bear'. In a sense, the action of this whole novel is a tragic phrase; and in another sense, this moment of conversion in Alyosha's life is such a phrase *present and transcended.* (220)

The Idiot of the first six plans is a 'double' character. He was supposed to struggle with the baseness of his nature transcending it to a higher truth in the end. Dostoevsky talks of 'the dualism of a deep nature', of an Idiot who is capable of feeling hate and love for the very same people, and making others suffer while he himself suffers for them. However, it is also obvious that this time he was looking for the 'beautiful' in its absolute form in the character of the Idiot. He searches for him from the very first plan and in the seventh he finds him. In the last plan, we have the Myshkin of the pure heart, the beautiful soul who loves without cruelty, sacrifices without pride. Of him Dostoevsky says: "His way of looking at the world: he forgives everything, sees reasons for everything, does not recognize that any sin is unforgivable" (*Notebooks*, 165). Dostoevsky makes sure that Myshkin has the touch of the infinite, in his selfless love for the others, yet, he tragically fails to communicate it and remains purely human in his vulnerability to suffering. Hence, the "tragic phrase" remains untranscended.

Though granting him the subjectivity of a character in a novel, we can hardly claim that the Idiot possesses the divided interiority and a dialogized consciousness typical to Dostoevsky characters. What Atay achieves, in his dialogue with Dostoevsky is creating in Selim's person, a Myshkin who is endowed with the self-consciousness of the Underground Man. Selim's homelessness strikes us from the very beginning of the book. From the very first pages on, we see him seeking a 'home' in every single individual that he meets in the course of the novel. His friendship with Esat and his sister, his relationship with Metin, the way he is attached to Turgut: all this indicates how he desires to communicate with other people without any reserve. His readiness to open himself to others is remarkable.

Selim tries to open himself up to others several times in the novel, to Metin, to Süleyman, to Turgut, and finally to Günseli. The problem with Selim is that of the Underground Man, who, on the one hand, wants to be recognized, and on the other hand, is too proud to accept the judgment. Thus, what Bakhtin says for Stavrogin of *The Possessed* – "without recognition by another person, he is incapable of accepting himself, but he does not want to accept the others' judgment" (Bakhtin, *Problems*, 244) – applies with equal force to Selim. That is why, the only confession that carries him to the possibility of transcending his own being is the one that he makes to Günseli, since she recognizes him without any judgment. She is the only person in the novel who is capable of accepting Selim as he is: a man who is suffering an unendurable pain —the agony of being here. Like the Underground Man, who bows before Lisa, Selim bows before Günseli, opening himself to the other, or more precisely, to the suffering of the other —which only lasts for a moment.

Selim's desire for wholeness, for grasping the totality of existence is what characterizes Myshkin. According to Hesse, what makes him different from the others is this feeling of wholeness: "For a lightning moment he has felt the all-being, the all-feeling, the all-suffering, and the all-understanding. He has known all that is in the world. There lies the kernel of his magical being." The problem with this feeling of wholeness is that it is momentary, as Selim discovers later in the novel. Like Myshkin, he tries to hang on to this "meaning" but loses it because of being human rather than divine.

> Myshkin may succeed in experiencing at one given moment a sense of wholeness, but the next moment will rob him of it. His attempt to live a unified existence is constantly exposed by the novel's relentless insistence on the multiplicity of identities that are merely human, merely personal. (Holquist. *Dostoevsky*, 112)

One of the several episodes from *The Idiot* that get reenacted in *The Disconnected* is the party scene towards the end of the book. The social gathering at the

Yepanchins' to introduce the prince to high society as Aglaya's fiancé is duplicated in Selim's visit to Gunseli's aunt. In *The Idiot,* when the family discovers that Aglaya is in love with the Prince, they invite a group of aristocrats to their house in order to formally announce the engagement. They invite Princess Belonkonsky, an influential person from high society who is also Aglaya's godmother. Her approval of the prince is especially important. At the party, Myshkin's frankness is in such a sharp contrast with the hypocrisy of the aristocrats, that one cannot read this passage without feeling actual pain in one's chest. In this scene, Myshkin performs all the 'idiocies' that Aglaya has warned him against. He first gets into a heated discussion about Roman Catholicism with the guests present at the party, then gives a speech about how noble and good this high society is, and how good all the people are. Finally, he gets so excited that he knocks over a great vase, and falls into an epileptic fit. In the eyes of the Yepanchins – and what is even worse, of Aglaya's – the prince has disgraced them. Aglaya, revealing her real nature of a selfish and capricious girl busying herself with the romantic ideal of chivalric love, turns her back to the prince, and leaves him all alone when he most needs him. Although she will not denounce her love completely until she takes him to Nastasya for a final test, this is the moment when she actually abandons Myshkin.

Selim's visit to Gunseli's aunt bears similar motives of a search for approval and social acceptance on the side of Günseli, and what can be called an intellectual "epileptic fit" on the side of Selim.

> Gunseli was surprised to see me. Why do people get surprised when they see me? And then why do they pull themselves together after a while? At least, they could be sincere enough not to hide their amazement. Will I never be able to give you a continuous feeling? So, Gunseli pulled herself together. [...] I shook some hands, I heard some names: I forgot all of them the moment they were said. I cannot learn everything at once. It makes me dizzy. It occurred to me that I could pass out. Fainting in the house of strangers! I collapsed into an armchair. (572-73)

Selim's desire to rule out all phoniness out of his relationship with Gunseli is obvious here in this episode. What is it that makes him so nervous? What is it that makes him think he might faint like Myshkin? It is not only that he finds himself in the presence of complete strangers, but also that he recognizes that Gunseli is no different from her aunt in the sense that she wants to belong into the picture that her aunt has designed for her: a successful marriage with an eligible bachelor. This is Gunseli's failure, her silent betrayal, which Selim will not tolerate. Her desire for being accepted and her pretended indifference makes Selim nervous and too much self-conscious:

In order to seem relaxed, I crossed my legs and tried to smile. My leg was shaking: my leg in the air. I tried holding it with both my hands, but it did not help. Their legs were not shaking. I checked all the legs in the room with rage, and a little fear. Everybody was looking at me, at my quivering leg. They pretended as if nothing was happening – out of politeness, of course. Damn you! Damn your politeness! [...] Gunseli also behaved as if she did not care. Obviously, she did this in order to comfort me. Is this what it means? This makes me even more nervous. On one hand, she pretends she does not care, on the other hand, she fears something. She fears that I might do something bad. (573)

Selim, unlike Myshkin, is able to recognize the social mask worn by the bourgeois, and see through their pretentious politeness. While Myshkin, tragically, thinks that he is in the company of kind and loving people, Selim knows that he is surrounded by a group of cruel observers who are ready to put him in a "formulated phrase." The tragedy, of course, is that he discovers that Gunseli is no different from them.

Here, it is important to note that Selim attempts for reconciliation – and in a sense salvation – not through the several theoretical arguments he carries with his friends, but after he completely gives up his ego and accepts that he loves Günseli. Even if it lasts only for a moment, he sees the possibility of opening himself to another. Only after he admits to himself and to Günseli that he loves her, that is to say, only after he opens himself to the presence of another, he overcomes his particularity and grasps the universal, in the form of discovering in himself the 'other' in its full presence. The tragedy is that it lasts only for a moment. The possibility of transcendence is, then, lost forever.

Let us go from here, Gunseli. I am embarrassed because of all this sweat. My throat hurts, I have a fever. Gunseli kept looking at me. She loved me. She hoped that everything would be ok. She wanted our love to set everything right. I wanted that too. No, I don't have any strength. I only think I wish, I have to wish something like that. But I don't want it. What I want is to walk among these crowds with dreamy eyes and to find the exit no matter what it takes. (579)

The exit that Selim is searching for is not only a door that would lead him out of tedious lives of the bourgeois, such as Turgut or Gunseli's aunt. It is Selim's graceful exit from life altogether. His suicide is what marks the loss of the message, and the impossibility of Being-Selim.

With the portrait of his 'Godman' Selim committing suicide at the end of the novel, Atay provides us with a Jesus that is reduced to a layman who totally collapses. The most horrible truth that *The Disconnected* conveys is that there is no remedy for suffering, no place for Christ-like love on earth, as Ivan Karamasov says: "To my thinking, Christ-like love for men is a miracle impossible on earth. He was God. But we are not gods" (*The Brothers Karamasov*, Part II, Book V).

In his dialogue with Dostoevsky's writing, Atay questions issues like man's groundlessness and the impossibility of attributing any meaning to our existence, which come to be voiced in Selim's suicide. Somewhere in the novel, echoing Camus who says, "there is but one truly serious philosophical problem and that is suicide," Selim tells Turgut that he will be the first one to die because of an ontological problem. And this is what he does. All through the novel, we observe him in a useless effort to attribute some kind of a meaning to man's vulnerability to suffering which renders him incapable of finding any truth other than itself. His suicide, his plunge back into the darkness, tells us that there is no ground for man to rest and transcend his finitude. This is the death of man, which inescapably, is also the death of God, as Rilke says: "What will you do, God, if Death takes me? / I am your jug (if someone breaks me?) / I am your drink (if curdling cakes me?) / I am your trim, your trade, - it makes me / think, with me goes your meaning too."[97]

97 "*Was wirst du tun, Gott, wenn ich sterbe?/Ich bin dein Krug, (wenn ich zerscherbe?)/Ich bin dein Trank (wenn ich verderbe?)/Bin dein Gewand und dein Gewerbe, /mit mir verlierst du deinen Sinn.*" Rilke, Rainer Maria. *Prose and Poetry*, ed. Egon Schwarz. (New York: Continuum, 1984), 159.

# TALKING TO THE DEAD: JOYCE AND ATAY

> I want to travel in Europe, Alyosha, I shall set off from here. And yet I know that I am only going to a graveyard, but it's a most precious graveyard, that's what it is! Precious are the dead that lie there, every stone over them speaks of such burning life in the past, of such passionate faith in their work, their truth, their struggle and their science, that I know I shall fall on the ground and kiss those stones and weep over them; though I'm convinced in my heart that it's long been nothing but a graveyard.
>
> Dostoevsky, *The Brothers Karamasov*

As we have argued throughout this study, every attempt to write necessarily implies a dialogue with the past. As Booker nicely puts it in his analysis of Bakhtin, the author, in the process of writing, finds himself following the traces left by other, often long-dead, writers (1). Yet, for a novelist who lives in the East, writing is also a practice that demands a constant conversation with the West. Like Dostoevsky's frustrated intellectual Ivan, every modern artist in the East is torn between two poles; on one hand, he wants to be authentic, true to his subjective experience (and local material) in his artistic practice, and on the other hand, in his search of the best form to express this subjectivity, he feels obliged to remain within the realm of Western forms that offer the position of a detached onlooker. Therefore, the artistic work produced in the East, being aware of the tension between the material and form seeks a consensus between these two in terms of an open-ended dialogue.

This is probably one of the reasons that made Moretti conclude that the rise of the novel in the non-Western world is the outcome of a consensus between two conflicting elements. Drawing upon Jameson's observation that in the take-off of the modern Japanese novel, 'the raw material of Japanese social experience and the abstract formal patterns of Western novel construction cannot always be welded together seamlessly,' Moretti develops what he calls the law of formal compromise ("Conjectures" 54).[98] Relying on examples from all over the world, Morretti voices his conviction that the same configuration occurs in various cultures, as different as Japan and Turkey for instance, and confirms his "law" of literary evolution that "in cultures that belong to the periphery of the literary system (which means: almost all cultures, inside and outside Europe),

98 *See also* Fredric Jameson, 'In the Mirror of Alternate Modernities', in Karatani Kojin, *Origins of Modern Japanese Literature*, Durham–London 1993, p. xiii.

the modern novel first arises not as an autonomous development but as a compromise between a western formal influence (usually French or English) and local materials" (61). This observation makes Moretti contend that Jameson's "law" has completely reversed the historical explanation of the rise of the novel, because the Western European novel, though it comes first in the tradition, does not emerge as the typical form of the genre: "the 'typical' rise of the novel is Krasicki, Kemal, Rizal, Maran—not Defoe."[99]

One of the implications of Moretti's argument is that the form did not emerge as the natural result of the demands of the content in the third world countries. It was rather an artificial means imposed on the content. In short, it was "a borrowed jacket." Something that is too short or maybe too tight to wear. According to Moretti, this conflict between form and content is essential for the novel, because this is exactly what gave rise to the blooming of the typical examples of the genre.

Parla, however, departs from Jameson and Moretti regarding the application of the law of formal compromise. In "The Object of Comparison," she responds to Moretti's endeavor and argues that the rise of the novel necessitates a formal compromise everywhere. Parla maintains that one can "think of no novel or novelist that does not betray the uneasiness of a formal compromise." Pointing at the instability of the narrative voice in early examples such as Defoe's *Moll Flanders*, Parla says that Moretti's formal compromise "cannot be confined to the rise of the novel in the third world countries; it was very much there in the rise of the novel in England and France as well" (121).

Parla obviously contends that the novel as a genre is the product of such compromise. The content will always be more than the form. It will shape the form constantly challenging it into new ways of literary devices and techniques. Keeping Parla's objection in mind, it would be interesting to approach *The Disconnected* from the point of view of the law of formal compromise, and to study the source of compromise in Atay's novel – if there is any. Can the Turkish social experience be fused seamlessly with "the abstract formal patterns of West-

---

99 Having concluded saying that "the Western European novel is not a rule but an exception" when regarded as a system of variations, Moretti suggests a method of looking at things from a distance and seeing the whole picture rather than concentrating on a small portion of it and believing that it constitutes the whole. He calls the method "distant reading," – as opposed to close reading- "where distance [...] is a condition of knowledge: it allows you to focus on units that are much smaller or much larger than the text: devices, themes, tropes—or genres and systems." Since it is impossible for one person to read the "great unread" of world literature, Moretti proposes that we rely on the readings and assessments of those who have already studied the works with which the West is not familiar ("Conjectures" 54).

ern novel construction"? Or would it be possible to say that in its dialogue with the canon, the non-Western novel is capable of opening a new page and introduce new themes or techniques?

In this chapter, this is exactly what we will explore in reference to *The Disconnected.* Atay's novel is distinctly of his own, but on some level, it also seems to be a response to Joyce's *Ulysses*; a quite singular and a very Turkish response. Atay's writing is dominated with the desire of talking to the dead as it is the case in Joyce's *Ulysses*. As Irzık notes, *The Disconnected* is a novel that is "dominated by a voice from the grave," because Selim Isık, the protagonist, has already committed suicide when the novel begins ("Allegorical" 553). Therefore, it is worth noting that Joyce and Atay, like their protagonists, whose journeys have been marked by a conversation with the dead (Stephen with his mother, Bloom with his son Rudy, and Turgut with his friend Selim), find themselves talking to the literary tradition that existed before them, to their dead predecessors, whose voices we can hear throughout *Ulysses* and *The Disconnected.*

In the final chapter of this book, again drawing upon the work of Mikhail Bakhtin, we will compare the poetics of Joyce and Atay demonstrating how they cope with the authority of the past while building a new structure upon it. In addition to demonstrating that it is central to the work of both authors that they recognize the impossibility of a language untainted by others, this study will also aim at showing that the novel is always destined to be based on the tension either between past and present, or West and East, or individual and society.

## Atay and Joyce face their literary fathers

### Rabelais and grotesque realism: the employment of the carnivalesque

Joyce insists that "*Ulysses* is a fundamentally humorous work," and he is known to have regularly complained that critics failed to see the place that comedy occupies in his work (Power 89). Strangely enough, the same fate befell *The Disconnected* when it was published in 1971. The critics regarded it as a depressing book with melancholic and gloomy characters, which, obviously, added to the initial assessment that the book was practically "unreadable" —evidently, part of the fate that Atay's novel shares with Joyce's *Ulysses*, as we have discussed earlier.

However, there are also some critics who have noticed the importance of the employment of the "comic" in *Ulysses*, and they all seem to agree on the point that the novel's climactic chapter Circe provides the best example of how

Joyce's text is saturated with humor. Robert H. Bell, in his *Jocoserious Joyce*, draws the reader's attention to the "carnivalesque tendencies" in Circe (161-162), and Zack Bowen in his focused analysis *Ulysses as a Comic Novel* refers to Bakhtin's understanding of the carnival-grotesque and maintains that "Circe is the prime example of exactly that grotesquerie." He even goes further and states that "it is difficult to understand why this episode has not always been universally viewed as comedic" (19).

While acknowledging the employment of the grotesque and its "carnivalistic comic strain" in the Circe episode, Bowen also states that the emphasis on sex in that episode is typical to the carnival "more comforting than disconcerting because it underlies the comic regenerative force in a natural cycle that sees the grotesque as a part of a new and joyous beginning." (Bowen 19) The constant reference to body is the outcome of a typical carnivalistic gesture of turning things 'upside down,' a continuous reversal of the spiritual and the material (the upper and the lower) levels, which is an essential quality of grotesque realism. The ambivalence of the carnivalesque dominates this episode, and lifts the barriers between the binaries involving class, race, and gender.

This Rabelaisian quality, which introduces a continuous reversal to the text, becomes more obvious when Bloom says, referring to the Nighttown: "You call it a festivity. I call it a sacrament" (15: 1681), then takes a step back and claims that he is innocent: "I am guiltless as the unsunned snow. It was my brother Henry. He is my double" (15: 1769-1770). The theme of the double supports the ambiguity of the episode as a whole: "this is midsummer madness, some ghastly joke again" (15: 1768). In fact, as Bell shows in his analysis of "Circe," free play with the sacred turns out to be one of the essential qualities of the episode. Referring to the implicit comparison between Bloom and Christ, Bell points out to the fact that the mock-biblical picture that Joyce draws is "complete with revelations, miracles, calumny, passion, sacrifice, and resurrection" (164). Since the festive pattern of this episode is a reversal typical to the carnivalesque, the Christ-like quality of Bloom also is turned upside down, when he imagines himself as the Anti-Christ (15: 209) and eventually turns the ritual into Black Mass (15: 4711).

In a comparative study, one can suggest with confidence that the brothel scene in *The Disconnected* bears a strong resemblance to the "Circe" episode of *Ulysses* in that we observe in both passages the regeneration of the medieval synthesis of the spiritual and the material. What unites these two very comic scenes is that in each case, the bodily principle is not sacrificed for the sake of the mental; on the contrary, the process is always blended with a 'gay relativity,' through which the purely spiritual is transformed into the level of the material, and vice versa. Besides, while it inverts codes of proper behavior and communication and highlights the functions of the bodily lower stratum, the Circe episode questions the persistence of hierarchy, inequality, and oppression, as it is the case in the climax of Atay's novel.

Even the fact that Atay chooses a brothel for the climactic scene in his novel, like Joyce, who locates the critical crux of the novel in the night-town, tells us something about the authors' emphasis on the regeneration of the spiritual in the form of the bodily. The background of both scenes, therefore, appears to be indisputably carnivalesque being loaded with sexual and grotesque imagery and language, masks, inversions, verbal and physical abuse, images of birth and death, and multiple intersections of the fictive and the real. What makes it possible to compare these two scenes is what we can call the "the politics of the carnivalesque," which always involves a challenge with authority. While it is possible to read the brothel scene as Atay's criticism of the totalizing power of the State which clamps down on the individual, it is equally possible to assert that one of the dynamics in "Circe" is the hegemonic power exercised upon Ireland by the imperialist Britain. And we can conclude saying that both of these episodes are dominated with a desire to laugh in the face of authority, as is typical of the carnivalesque.

Bloom's first appearance in "Circe" is marked by the reflection of his image in representations of colonial figures, such as Nelson, Gladstone, and Wellington.

> Snakes of river fog creep slowly. From drains, clefts, cesspools, middens arise on all sides stagnant fumes. A glow leaps in the south beyond the seaward reaches of the river. The navvy staggering forward cleaves the crowd and lurches towards the tramsiding. On the farther side under the railway bridge Bloom appears flushed, panting, cramming bread and chocolate into a side pocket. From Gillens hairdressers window a composite portrait shows him gallant Nelson's image. A concave mirror at the side presents to him lovelorn longlost lugubru Booloohoom. Grave Gladstone sees him level Bloom for Bloom. He passes, struck by the stare of truculent Wellington but in the con vex mirror grin unstruck the bonham eyes and fatchuck cheekchops of Jollypoldy the rixdix doldy. (15: 138-150).

Nelson's pillar and Wellington's monument emerge as the most obvious landmarks of the British imperial presence in 1904 Dublin. The episode, like the rest of the novel, unfolds under the gaze of these imperial/colonial figures, as it is the case in *The Disconnected*, where the utopian understanding of freedom and equality accentuated by Selim's Christ-like portrait in the brothel scene is challenged by a number of monuments and buildings underlining the penetration of the authority to the remotest corners of everyday life in the capital city. The feeling of being followed by the panoptical gaze of authority is one of the motives that are common to both novels. In fact, this is exactly what Cheng means when he characterizes Ulysses as “a detailed and symptomatic portrayal of how cultural hegemony shapes the discourse of [...] everyday life” (170) Nelson’s pillar reappears several times throughout the Circe episode, especially in the scene where Bloom performs his miraculous act of imitating historical personages (15: 1842) and in Stephen’s “dance of death” (15: 4139).

One other element that underlines the theme of the panoptical gaze of the imperial power in “Circe” is the presence of Private Carr and Private Compton and the two watchmen. They are there from the very beginning of the episode as the representatives of British administration keeping an eye on the visitors of the Nighttown. Their presence becomes more meaningful when they get into a quarrel with Stephen at the end of the episode. The third and final part of “Circe” begins with Stephen’s dashing out of the bordello and commenting on the unwanted British military presence in Ireland. Stephen announces his own personal intent to mentally subvert both priest and king, and puts himself into trouble with Private Carr, “But in here it is I must kill the priest and the king” (15: 4437) Carr thinks that Stephen is threatening to assassinate Edward VII; he will not listen to Bloom’s entreaties that Stephen has been drinking absinthe.

> PRIVATE CARR (Pulls himself free and comes forward.) What's that you're saying about my king?
> *(Edward the Seventh appears in an archway. He wears a white jersey on which an image of the Sacred Heart is stitched, with the insignia of Garter and Thistle, Golden Fleece, Elephant of Denmark, Skinners' and Probyns' horse, Lincoln's Inn bencher and ancient and honourable artillery company of Massachusetts. He sucks a red jujube. He is robed as a grand elect perfect and sublime mason with trowel and apron, marked made in Germany. In his left hand he holds a plasterers bucket on which is printed: Défense d'uriner. A roar of welcome greets him.)*
>
> EDWARD THE SEVENTH (*Slowly, solemnly but indistinctly.*) Peace, perfect peace. For identification bucket in my hand. Cheerio, boys. (*He turns to his subjects.*) We have come here to witness a clean straight fight and we heartily wish both men the best of good luck. Mahak makar a bak.
> (*He shakes hands with Private Carr, Private Compton, Stephen, Bloom and Lynch. General applause. Edward the Seventh lifts the bucket graciously in acknowledgement.*)
>
> PRIVATE CARR (*To Stephen.*) Say it again.
>
> STEPHEN (*Nervous, friendly, pulls himself up.*) I understand your point of view, though I have no king myself for the moment. This is the age of patent medicine. A discussion is difficult down here. But this is the point. You die for your country, suppose. (*He places his arm on Private Carr's sleeve.*) Not that I wish it for you. But I say: Let my country die for me. Up to the present it has done so. I don't want it to die. Damn death. Long live life! (15: 4448-74)

Wollaeger, who is especially interested in the carnivalesque reversals of this episode, focuses on the elements of religious, imperial, and colonial power in the text that emerge as "lord mayor, king, and pope in the narrative of Bloom's empowerment" (143). Among these figures of power, Wollaeger specifically underlines the "interpellative role of the police" in this episode and associates it with the colonial administration in Dublin Castle. Therefore, in a sense, Dublin Castle enters the Nighttown, and hence the non-official public place of the carnival is marked by the presence of Private Carr and Private Compton, the instruments of the oppressive official ideology. The way Stephen faces authority in this scene is worth noting because it is one of those instances where the character adopts the language of the Fool challenging the authority seeking refuge in the power of laughter. With a typical carnivalesque reversal he evacuates the meaning out of the nationalist motto that one should be ready to die for one's country. This gesture of inversion with respect to the discourse of the privates exemplifies a potentially subversive response to authority, which is one of the main issues of this episode.

Similarly, the carnivalesque gesture of reversal enters also Bloom's world, as demonstrated in his fantasy of being backed by Irish and Zionists, and getting coronated as leader of the new "Bloomusalem." Since an uncrowning follows every crowning, the nationalist hallucination does not last long and soon gets spoilt when Bloom is accused of being a libertine. Yet, this scene is important in that it displays Bloom's parodic vision of a religious/colonial utopia, his Bloomusalem, and questions the nature of power politics, which remains the same be it imperialist or nationalist. This is a moment foreshadowing the chaotic ending of the episode, where the images of nationalist figures (O'Connell, Parnell, Tone and others) appear in the apocalyptic vision of "Dublin's burning," as a counterpart to the imperial/colonial monumental figures (15: 4660). The way Joyce devised this episode, therefore, does not allow the reader to seek refuge in one form of monological discourse while condemning another, and underlines the fact that the lives of the Dubliners are threatened not only by the colonialist, but also the nationalist ideology. Accordingly, Edna Duffy's study *Subaltern Ulysses* sees Joyce's novel as a work which:

> [...] relentlessly pinpoints the mechanism of colonial regimes of surveillance and the panoptic gaze, as well as the secrecy they generate: it exposes nationalism and other chauvinist ideologies of imagined community chiefly as inheritances of the colonist regime of power of knowledge they condemn; and it mocks imperial stereotypes of the native while it delineates their insidious interpellative power. (Duffy 3)

Serhat Uyurkulak's analysis of *Ulysses* in relation to Tanpınar's *Huzur* also provides an interesting approach in that it observes the difficulties involved in the construction of a cultural identity, and draws attention to the similarities between the Irish and Turkish cases as they are represented in these novels. Referring to the problem of constructing a cultural identity when the country is trapped between the two extremes of nationalism and colonialism, Uyurkulak draws attention to the perception of history in these two novels. He underlines the fact that it is impossible for characters like Stephen and Mumtaz to identify themselves with the history of their country, because they are cut off from their past, the former by facing colonial oppression as an everyday reality, the latter by failing to "overcome the identity crisis they [he] had after he modernization project had launched in the Ottoman Empire and reached its climax with the Republic" (116). According to Uyurkulak, that kind of an history is exactly the nightmare that Stephen is trying to wake up (41). Therefore, it does not strike us as a surprise when Selim, just like Stephen, refers to history as a bad dream (Atay, 201-202). We understand why he cannot relate to his past. This is a history that is dominated with the wish to legitimize the implementation of the modernization project, which has little to do with the authentic character of the nation.

## Two readings of Hamlet: the problem of patriarchal authority

Any analysis of Joyce's dialogue with Shakespeare and especially of his allusions to *Hamlet* would be to "plow well-tilled ground" as Osteen acknowledges in his review of Booker's book on Joyce (515), but it still might be interesting to compare the way Joyce and Atay read Shakespeare. The dialogue between these two authors and Shakespeare takes on a significant meaning, not only because it represents the encounter between two different genres, but also because it sheds new light on Shakespeare's text, which is the result of the clash between two different cultural moments in history. No wonder that Stephen's Hamlet is ambitious and bent on revenge (Booker 119), while Turgut's Hamlet is melancholic and paralyzed. As we have already argued in Chapter 4, while acknowledging that he is another Hamlet, Turgut focuses on this character's hesitation rather than his desire to take revenge: "Yet, instead of taking Selim's revenge, here I sit, between the legs of Ophelia-Magdalena." (255) Atay's reference to Hamlet here is one of the many instances, when he initiates a dialogue with Shakespeare, and helps us read the text and the character in unprecedented ways. Turgut's transformation of Hamlet/Christ into a character that is almost childishly lingering can be read as the portrayal of the Turkish intellectual, who envisions himself as a savior but prefers to spend his time engaging in a semi-philosophical brooding "between the legs of" a woman, as Sibel Irzık observes.[100]

100 Sibel Irzık. "*Tutunamayanlar*'da Çokseslilik ve Sınırları," *Varlık Dergisi*, Ekim 1995.

For Joyce, Shakespeare is also associated with the British forces and with the atrocities they committed against Ireland, which is probably why Stephen reads Hamlet as a rebellious character. For Atay, however, Shakespeare represents the western canon, and the cultural dominance of the West over the East. Hence, his Hamlet is a reflection of the Turkish intellectual vis-a-vis his western counterpart. In short, neither of the two authors approaches Shakespeare with absolute reverence. Instead, while acknowledging his stance as the symbolic 'father', they repeatedly question his authority.

There are allusions to Shakeaspeare and *Hamlet* all through *The Disconnected* and *Ulysses*, in the latter we even have an analysis of the play in the "Scylla and Carybdis" episode. In "Scylla and Charybdis," Stephen feels that in many ways Shakespeare was extremely narrow minded. He bordered what we would call racism today and always supported "conservative" causes, like anti-Semitism and imperialism. Besides, he was petty, penny-pinching, and vindictive.

> He drew Shylock out of his own long pocket. The son of a maltjobber and moneylender he was himself a cornjobber and moneylender, with ten tods of corn hoarded in the famine riots. His borrowers are no doubt those divers of worship mentioned by Chettle Falstaff who reported his uprightness of dealing. He sued a fellow player for the price of a few bags of malt and exacted his pound of flesh in interest for every money lent. How else could Aubrey's ostler and callboy get rich quick? All events brought grist to his mill. Shylock chimes with the jewbaiting that followed the hanging and quartering of the queen's leech Lopez, his jew's heart being plucked forth while the sheeny was yet alive: Hamlet and Macbeth with the coming to the throne of a Scotch philosophaster with a turn for witchroasting. The lost armada is his jeer in Love's Labour Lost. His pageants, the histories, sail fullbellied on a tide of Mafeking enthusiasm. Warwickshire jesuits are tried and we have a porter's theory of equivocation. The Sea Venture comes home from Bermudas and the play Renan admired is written with Patsy Caliban, our American cousin. The sugared sonnets follow Sidney's. As for fay Elizabeth, otherwise carrotty Bess, the gross virgin who inspired The Merry Wives of Windsor, let some meinherr from Almany grope his life long for deephid meanings in the depths of the buckbasket. (9: 740-760)

Stephen, obsessed with the ghosts of his own past, including that of his mother, believes that Shakespeare himself was very much like King Hamlet of Denmark, who appears as a ghost to his son. Stephen's summary statement about Hamlet is that Shakespeare is both Prince Hamlet and King Hamlet, the ghost. Firmly believing in his account of Shakespeare as the ghost, Stephen also emphasizes the analogy between God the creator and the artist as creator. The artist, therefore, being the author of his own text, is the God/father of his creation:

> He goes back, weary of the creation he has piled up to hide him from himself, an old dog licking an old sore. But, because loss is his gain, he passes on towards eternity

in undiminished personality, untaught by the wisdom he has written or by the laws he has revealed. His beaver is up. He is a ghost, a shadow now, the wind by Elsinore's rocks or what you will, the sea's voice, a voice heard only in the heart of him who is the substance of his shadow, the son consubstantial with the father. (9: 475-81)

Shakespeare is the "ghost" in many different senses: He is present as the ghost of the author in his own text; he is the ghost of the father that mourns for his dead child and attempts to immortalize his name in his best play, but what interests us even more is that he is also the ghost that haunts Stephen, the ghost of the fellow poet that is the metaphorical father to all the poets that will be.

It is no coincidence that Stephen deals especially with *Hamlet*, a play centrally concerned with patriarchal authority. The father-son theme is, evidently, one of the leitmotifs of Joyce's novel, where the father and the son are supposed to get reunited in line with the Homeric parallel. In reference to the relationship between Odysseus and Telemachus, this theme keeps coming back to the surface all through the novel, especially in the episode called "Oxen of the Sun," where Joyce recreates the process of human evolution: "Bloom is the spermatozoon, the hospital the womb, the nurse the ovum, Stephen the embryo" (Ellmann 475). Bloom's own son Rudy died soon after childbirth, and so upon meeting Stephen at the hospital, he adopts him as his own son. However, the father-son theme gains another perspective in the "Scylla and Charybdis" episode, as the paternity issue is also translated into a literary problem, which is part of the portrayal of how Stephen deals with patriarchal authority. Simon, his biological father, and Shakespeare, his literary father, in the end come to represent two equally strict and monological discourses that we have already mentioned above, the national and the imperial/colonial. Apparently, Stephen's struggle with his father, and his desire to create a space untainted by the father's language, stretches far beyond the realm of Simon Dedalus and his bitter nationalism. As the novel unfolds, it gets transposed into the struggle with the authority of God, the authority of the British empire, and especially in "Scylla and Charybdis," the authority of Shakespeare, which becomes a tool in the hands of Stephen to express his ideas about paternity.

-- A father, Stephen said, battling against hopelessness, is a necessary evil. He wrote the play in the months that followed his father's death. If you hold that he, a greying man with two marriageable daughters, with thirtyfive years of life, nel mezzo del cammin di nostra vita, with fifty of experience, is the beardless undergraduate from Wittenberg then you must hold that his seventyyear old mother is the lustful queen. No. The corpse of John Shakespeare does not walk the night. From hour to hour it rots and rots. He rests, disarmed of fatherhood, having devised that mystical estate upon his son. Boccaccio's Calandrino was the first and last man who felt himself with child. Fatherhood, in the sense of conscious begetting, is unknown to man. It is

> a mystical estate, an apostolic succession, from only begetter to only begotten. On that mystery and not on the madonna which the cunning Italian intellect flung to the mob of Europe the church is founded and founded irremovably because founded, like the world, macro- and microcosm, upon the void. Upon incertitude, upon unlikelihood. Amor matris, subjective and objective genitive, may be the only true thing in life. Paternity may be a legal fiction. Who is the father of any son that any son should love him or he any son? (9: 828-46)

Joyce's struggle with Shakespeare's authority and the related question of "literary paternity" continues also in "Circe" — particularly in the scene when Shakespeare himself appears as a character. In fact, the appearance of Shakespeare is one of the strangest transformations of the Circe episode. The scene depicts a moment when Stephen and Bloom look into a mirror and see their images merge to form that of Shakespeare: "*Stephen and Bloom gaze into the mirror. The face of William Shakespeare, beardless, appears there, rigid in facial paralysis, crowned by the reflection of the reindeer antlered hatrack in the hall.*" (15: 3820-3824, italics original) Daniel Ferrer talks about this moment in the Circe episode, and says that the image of Shakespeare with horns in the mirror is a reference back to Stephen's argument in Scylla and Charybdis where he claimed that Shakespeare was being cuckolded. Similarly, this brings us back to one of the themes of Ulysses, Bloom's unfaithful wife Molly.

> This leads to the following results: Bloom, as a cuckold, replaced in his wife's bed by a more manly man, symbolically castrated and soon, perhaps syphilitic, sees himself as Shakespeare, a horned paralysed Shakespeare, capon-voiced and beardless; Stephen, in so far as he resembles Shakespeare (i.e. his father) sees himself cuckolded, castrated, and syphilitic. [...] Every reader must continue to unfold for himself the picture of Shakespeare with horns. His own discoveries will take him closer either to Stephen or to Bloom. (130)

One can not help but agree with these very apt observations of Ferrer. But this is not all. What we see in that scene is much more than that: Shakespeare might not be "literally" cuckolded, as Stephen claims it to be, but it is for sure that he is "literarily" cuckolded in this scene by Joyce himself. From the very beginning of the novel, we observe that Shakespearean discourse enters the thoughts, the daily musings of both characters. The voices of Stephen and Bloom are tainted with a Shakespearean discourse. They talk not only about him, as Stephen does in Scylla and Charybdis, but also like him all over the novel. No wonder that Joyce can not resist the desire of portraying him as a cuckold in his climactic scene, because it is Shakespeare's language that he takes control of and uses against him. The echoes of Shakespeare's play are heard all through "Circe," where Hamlet's bedroom scene remark about the King "look you how pale he glares!", is repeated by Florry the whore, who points to the ghost-enthralled Stephen and says, "Look! He's white" (15: 4209). When she tragically says "Hamlet, I am thy father's gimlet!" (15: 3655) Zoe reverses the meaning of the ghost scene all together, as it happens again in the same episode when Paddy Dignam appears and says, “Bloom, I am Paddy Dignam's spirit. List, list, O list!” (15: 1119) As Bloom says, “All insanity. Patriotism, sorrow for the dead, music, future of the race. To be or not to be” (15: 1065), and Stephen adds “To have or not to have, that is the question” (15: 3521)

The problem about the clash of two discourses reaches its peak, when Joyce finally portrays Shakespeare as a babbling freak hopelessly trying to recite lines from Hamlet: “Weda seca whokilla farst” (15: 3853).[101] As the poet loses his divine voice, so does the father lose his authority over the son. In a sense, Joyce enters the domain of the highest literary authority, and topples his reign, because, as Ferrer reminds us, “Shakespeare is the father of all poets.” (130) Thus, we can state with confidence that Stephen’s initial announcement of “we have shrewridden Shakespeare,” turns into a self-fulfilling prophecy in the Circe episode (15: 111).

Although this should probably be the subject of another analysis, there are also structural references to Shakespeare’s plays in this episode. Similar to the clowning scenes in Shakespeare’s plays,[102] Joyce introduces carnivalesque moments into the text through Mulligan. Mulligan, especially in the Scylla and Charybdis episode, emerges as a cheerful counterpoint to Stephen’s sober voice. In fact, Bell claims in *Jocoserious Joyce,* Mulligan is another fool in the Rabelaisian manner, but while Bloom is the picture of the holy fool, Mulligan appears as the clown more like in the Shakespearean tradition (16). Mulligan’s sacrilegious humor not only resembles the combination of the sacred and the profane found in medieval carnivals, but also brings to mind the type of humor employed in the gravediggers’ scene in *Hamlet.* Nothing escapes Mulligan’s scorn in Scylla and Charybdis; for Shakespeare he says “I seem to know the name” (9: 508) and then “the chap that writes like Synge;” Synge gets also burlesqued when Mulligan starts a talk mimicking the dialogues in his plays: “The tramper Synge is looking for you, he said, to murder you” (9: 569); Stephen gets his share because of his biographical interpretation of all reality; “the aunt is going to call on your unsubstantial father,” a parody of Stephen’s musings

101 In "The Murder of Gonzago," the play within *Hamlet*, Baptista, the Queen says: "In second husband let me be accurst! / None wed the [weda] second [seca] but who kill'd [whokilla] the first [farst]” (Act III, scene ii).

102 For a detailed discussion of the significance and the carnivalesque quality of clowning scenes in Shakespeare’s plays, see *Chapter 3*.

about consubstantial fatherhood, which Mulligan overheard as he was entering the discussion room (9: 553).

Interestingly enough, Mulligan is also named among the characters that would possibly complete the list of "metaphorical" fathers whom Stephen is addressing all through this episode. Joseph Campbell, who wrote *Mythic Worlds, Modern Words*, provides an analysis of the father/son relationship in the novel regarding the Homeric parallels. While admitting like many other critics that Leopold Bloom is Stephen Dedalus' spiritual father, he surprisingly claims that Buck Mulligan, should be regarded as Stephen's false father (57). One feels obliged to give Campbell credit for his acute observation of male rivalry between these two characters. Drawing upon the parallels between the *Odyssey* and *Ulysses* Campbell writes, "The two works are similarly structured and use the same mythic motifs, and the central concern of both is male initiation into a world different from that of brutal masculine assertion" (49).

"Brutal masculine assertion"? This is actually what defines Mulligan *per se*. He is the embodiment of a cruel humor that is usually hanging in the air like a gun pointed at Stephen. His down-to-earthness and practicality tells us that he is neither the fool nor the clown, but the rogue in this scene. According to Bakhtin, the rogue, the clown and the fool were similar in that they "create around themselves their own little world, their own chronotope" (Bakhtin, Dialogic 159). Yet, while the rogue "still has some ties that bind him to real life," the clown and the fool are "not of this world" (159)

In line with the role of the rogue, Mulligan is interested in the mundane as opposed to the highly intellectual and spiritual Stephen. When Stephen ends his reading of Hamlet with the assertion that "in the economy of heaven, foretold by Hamlet, there are no more marriages, glorified man, an androgynous angel, being a wife unto himself" (9: 1051-52), Mulligan cries "Eureka!" and suddenly starts scribbling on a piece of paper announcing that the Lord has spoken to the messenger. This is what he comes up with a few pages later:

> -- *Everyman His Own Wife*
> *or*
> *A Honeymoon in the Hand*
> *(a national immorality in three orgasms)*
> *by*
> *Ballocky Mulligan*
> (9:1171-77, italics original)

Mulligan is obviously mocking Stephen's intellectualism and his obsession with proving himself in the eyes of knowledgeable men, such as Eglinton and A.E., who he is trying to persuade to publish his Hamlet theory, and in his own talent in general. In doing this, Mulligan uses "the language of the merry rogue," which is capable of "re-processing any pathos but always in such a way as to rob it of its harm, `distance it from the mouth,' as it were, by means of a smile or a deception, mock its falsity and turn what was a lie into gay deception." (Bakhtin, *Dialogic* 401-02)

Mulligan's relationship with Stephen is a tense one, a friendship tainted with masculine rivalry and hegemony. Thus, Mulligan like Shakespeare and Simon Dedalus represents a failed relationship for Stephen. No wonder that he calls him his enemy: "Hast thou found me, O mine enemy?" (9: 481) Thus we do not get surprised when the episode closes with the full development of Stephen's ideas concerning Shakespeare, which does not only end by making men their own wives, but also puts an end to the problem of paternity and announces all men to be their own fathers.

> Well: if the father who has not a son be not a father can the son who has not a father be a son? When Rutlandbaconsouthamptonshakespeare or another poet of the same name in the comedy of errors wrote Hamlet he was not the father of his own son merely but, being no more a son, he was and felt himself the father of all his race, the father of his own grandfather, the father of his unborn grandson who, by the same token, never was born for nature, as Mr. Magee understands her, abhors perfection. (9: 863-71)

As Stephen denounces his father (both his biological father Simon and his literary father Shakespeare) and assumes that every artist is self-begotten, he also takes us back to one of the Dostoevskian problems of Joyce's text: a subjectivity that wants to be his own ground. Therefore, Atay's Selim and Joyce's Stephen are also similar in that they emerge as the literary reincarnations of the Underground Man.

The subject and his individuality is very much at the heart of Joyce's work, which is, after all, one of the reasons for his continuous allusions to *Hamlet*, the first modern play depicting an individual facing a particular decision. Booker draws our attention to Virginia Woolf's views on the subjectivism of Joyce's fiction and her remark that his works run the risk of getting ruined by the excessive emphasis on "the damned egotistical self" (Booker 171). The same criticism hit Atay in the 70's, because *The Disconnected* dares to talk about the individual at a time when the whole country was dominated by a wave of populism. Ecevit repeatedly draws our attention to this particular quality of Atay's novel:

> At a time, when Turkish literature mostly depicted protagonists coming from a rural background, and attributed to them a social mission while ignoring the spiritual/individual aspect of their personalities, *The Disconnected* emerged as a novel which introduced into the literary scene a completely new character: the urban intellectual stripped of his social responsibilities and indulging in his individuality (Ecevit 281).

In this sense, we can assert that Atay and Joyce borrow from Dostoevsky their specific focus on the character as an individual while problematizing subjectivity as the central issue of their novels. Both Selim and Stephen can be read as elaborations of Dostoevsky's Underground Man, in that they both display consciousnesses that are constituted by literary discourses. What we observe in the Scylla and Charybdis episode, is that Stephen employs narrative as a central strategy in his attempt to formulate a coherent and continuous sense of selfhood. He wants to ground himself in his own art, and to detach himself from his literary father, Shakespeare. And as he finds out that his language is tainted by the discourse of the father, he comes face to face with his literary belatedness.

Like Selim and the Underground Man, Stephen is suffering because he discovers that he can never be one and the same with himself. And hence, he can never ground himself in himself. His acute sense of literary belatedness in addition to his contempt of modernity, equips him with a strong sense of difference from others, which leads to a radical isolation and alienation. Stephen's desire to awaken from the nightmare of history, therefore, like Selim's battle against official history, is an echo of the far cry that belongs to the Underground Man, who underlines the individual's right to his particularity while questioning modernity and its claim for universality.

Therefore, we can say that Atay and Joyce owe to Dostoevsky, as much as they do to Shakespeare, not only the issue of a problematic subjectivity, and an awareness of belatedness in the literary tradition, but also a contempt for modernity which views history as an oppression.

## Middle class entanglements in Atay and Joyce: the portrait of Odysseus as a bourgeois

*Ulysses* has its own quixotic elements, and as Zack Bowen argues in *Ulysses as a Comic Book*, the hero and the sidekick are given their usual task of pushing the novel forward. While attributing a Sanchoesque quality to Bloom, Bowen suggests that Stephen is the Quixote of Joyce's text, and argues that the source of his problems is his canonization of E.C. which might be compared to the Don's principal delusion, that is to say, the one regarding Dulcinea.[103] In addi-

103 Stephen has fixed his romantic yearnings since childhood upon the insubstantial "E. C." in *The Portrait*. In *Stephen Hero* she appears more vigorously as Emma Clery, with whom Stephen is cautiously involved. A friend of Stephen's observes that he could marry her, but Stephen considers that price too high; and he feels that the institution of marriage is an unwarranted intrusion of State and Church into private relationships.

tion to these, he also claims that Stephen gets engaged in "a quixotic battle" for "the Irish Literary Revival." (85-86)

Stephen Dedalus, like his counterpart Quixote, is rather abstract or maybe even deluded if compared to the practical and mundane Leopold Bloom. Although Joyce reserves more space to the sidekick rather than the hero, he sticks to the modern distinction between the ideal and material, or as Bakhtin would say it, in the fashion of Cervantes, he puts a distance between the upper and the lower levels being represented by Stephen and Bloom, respectively. In fact, this sharp distinction between the two characters is the source of comedy in Cervantes's novel, as Bowen reminds us: at the heart of Don Quixote there lies the comic effect deriving from "the interaction of a deluded character, living intellectually in a bygone area, with a group of mundane, occasionally idiosyncratic, but also very realistic characters and events contemporaneous to the narrative present." (87) Though he does not always use it as a source of comedy, Joyce also relies on this contrast between his characters: the highly idealistic Stephen is juxtaposed to the down-to-earth Bloom.

Atay's characters, on the other hand, are much more ambiguous as we have discussed before. Although they can be compared with Joyce's double protagonists in *Ulysses* — where Stephen corresponds to the melancholic Selim and Bloom overlaps with Turgut, especially when we consider his middle class entanglements at the beginning of the novel —they can never be said to possess this sharp distinction that is typical to Quixote and Sancho. It is true that both Turgut and Bloom are portrayed as individuals within the "anti-tragic modality of modern experience," as Moretti would say, the unheroic heroes embodying a new subjectivity, that of the everyday, worldly, "normal," as opposed to Selim and Stephen who refuse to accept this social reconciliation. But the similarity ends there. While it is possible to read the novel as Turgut's journey from the material to the spiritual, which is probably the source of many interpretations of *The Disconnected* as a *Bildungsroman*,[104] a more interesting reading would be

104 If we are to read *The Disconnected* as a *Bildungsroman*, we have to rely on Turgut's experience. In the case of Selim, on the other hand, there can be no talk of *Bildung*. Yet it is interesting and therefore worth noting that Selim, like his counterpart Stephen, has gone through a transformation, has completed his movement towards a *Bildung* sometime earlier, somewhere outside the boundaries of this novel. This becomes especially obvious when Turgut conveys us bits and pieces of information about Selim's youth. In his notes about his depression, Selim portrays himself as having a chat with Jesus "about the beauty of spirit and all" Then he feels guilty thinking that he has not told him everything about himself. Feeling sad and a little bit angry, he goes to a bar together with some of his friends, where they tell obscene jokes about priests, and decide that Jesus should rather exercise some control on his own flock in the first place. They decide

approaching both characters from the perspective of grotesque realism, which renders them unique in that they possess the unity of the ideal and the material, that is to say, the Quixotic and the Sanchoesque.

However, even if we feel obliged to admit that there is a journey in both *Ulysses* and *The Disconnected*, which leads the protagonists to some form of self-knowledge, then we have to acknowledge that it is not the same journey because it does not offer same *telos* at the end. In fact, I seriously doubt whether we can talk about the presence of *telos* in *The Disconnected*: the last time we hear of Turgut, he is in the middle of nowhere with no map for his life, no plot to follow, and no final destination. When viewed from a more idealistic perspective, we can say that he is liberated from the dull routine of his daily life, from the claustrophobic atmosphere of his middle class home, from everything that is humdrum. Therefore, in a sense, the book remains unfinished. We leave our main character on the road going God-knows-where. In the case of Bloom, however, the journey ends —in line with the Homeric parallel— in the Bloom household, i.e., the temple of the middle class enjoyments. If Turgut gets liberated, then what happens to Bloom? He goes back to the warm and familiar tediousness of his bourgeois life —the life of half-truths. While Turgut gets completely "disconnected," Bloom ends up more connected as ever looking for a shelter in Molly's bosom – or in the infinite irony of Joyce's novel, in her bottom.

The second half of "Ithaca," which, in line with the structural parallelism to the Homeric text where Odysseus returns to his court and wife, details Bloom's return to his house and his preparation for bed. As the journey comes to and end, Bloom is portrayed stuck in the web of his bourgeois desires and habits. Bloom's fantasy as the dark wanderer is tempered by the ambition of owning a well-furnished suburban bungalow.

---

to be really bad since it is obvious that they failed to be good. Selim's dialogue with Jesus has already started at this point, and he rather sounds like a young Stephen questioning his Catholicism in *The Portrait*: "You should have told your father not to create a guy like Freud, they said. You both are Jewish, you should be ashamed of yourselves, they said. Honey, what's your name? Is it Hulya, they said. You've got a gorgeous pair of legs, they said. Does anyone work here with the name of Maria Magdalena, they asked. When the woman did not get it, they howled with laughter. They danced until they got soaked with sweat. They drank until dawn. They fought on the way back home. Selim fell down, and twisted his ankle." (132)

Following this instance of losing control over his life, Selim is completely repentant. He lies in bed for one week because he can not step on his injured foot. He gives up drinking, keeps reading the Bible. Finally, he sits down and writes a letter to Christ asking him to come down, so that they can chat. The chapter ends with a single sad line informing the reader: "Jesus did not come."

In what ultimate ambition had all concurrent and consecutive ambitions now coalesced?

Not to inherit by right of primogeniture, gavelkind or borough English, or possess in perpetuity an extensive demesne of a sufficient number of acres, roods and perches, statute land measure (valuation #42), of grazing turbary surrounding a baronial hall with gatelodge and carriage drive nor, on the other hand, a terracehouse or semidetached villa, described as Rus in Urbe or Qui si Sana, but to purchase by private treaty in fee simple a thatched bungalowshaped 2 storey dwellinghouse of southerly aspect, surmounted by vane and lightning conductor, connected with the earth, with porch covered by parasitic plants (ivy or Virginia creeper), halldoor, olive green, with smart carriage finish and neat doorbrasses, stucco front with gilt tracery at eaves and gable, rising, if possible, upon a gentle eminence with agreeable prospect from balcony with stone pillar parapet over unoccupied and unoccupyable interjacent pastures and standing in 5 or 6 acres of its own ground, at such a distance from the nearest public thoroughfare as to render its houselights visible at night above and through a quickset hornbeam hedge of topiary cutting, situate at a given point not less than 1 statute mile from the periphery of the metropolis, within a time limit of not more than 5 minutes from tram or train line (e.g., Dundrum, south, or Sutton, north, both localities equally reported by trial to resemble the terrestrial poles in being favourable climates for phthisical subjects), the premises to be held under feefarmgrant, lease 999 years, the message to consist of 1 drawingroom with baywindow (2 lancets), thermometer affixed, 1 sittingroom, 4 bedrooms, 2 servants rooms, tiled kitchen with close range and scullery, lounge hall fitted with linen wallpresses, fumed oak sectional bookcase containing the Encyclopaedia Britannica and New century Dictionary, transverse obsolete medieval and oriental weapons, dinner gong, alabaster lamp, bowl pendant, vulcanite automatic telephone receiver with adjacent directory, handtufted Axminster carpet with cream ground and trellis border, loo table with pillar and claw legs, hearth with massive firebrasses and ormolu mantel chronometer clock, guaranteed timekeeper with cathedral chime, barometer with hygrographic chart, comfortable lounge settees and corner fitments, upholstered in ruby plush with good springing and sunk centre, three banner Japanese screen and cuspidors (club style, rich wine-coloured leather, gloss renewable with a minimum of labour by use of linseed oil and vinegar) and pyramidically prismatic central chandelier lustre, bentwood perch with a fingertame parrot (expurgated language), embossed mural paper at 10/-per dozen with transverse swags of carmine floral design and top crown frieze, staircase, three continuous flights at successive right angles, of varnished cleargrained oak, treads and risers, newel, balusters and handrail, with stepped-up panel dado, dressed with camphorated wax, bathroom, hot and cold supply, reclining and shower: water closet on mezzanine provided with opaque singlepane oblong window, tipup seat, bracket lamp, brass tierod brace, armrests, footstool and artistic oleograph on inner face of door: ditto, plain: servant's apartments with separate sanitary and hygienic necessaries for cook, general and betweenmaid (salary, rising by biennial unearned increments of #2, with comprehensive fidelity insurance annual bonus (#1), and retiring allowance (based on the 65 system) after 30 years service), pantry, buttery, larder, refrigerator, outoffices, coal and wood cellarage with winebin (still and sparkling vintages) for distinguished guests, if entertained to dinner (evening dress), carbon monoxide gas supply throughout. (17: 1498-1550)

"Ithaca" is an episode dominated by objects and reminds us of the first chapters of *The Disconnected*, where Turgut seems to be haunted by the furniture in his apartment. He almost compulsively describes the details of tea tables, couches, lamps, ashtrays and other objects.[105] Bloom's journey, as opposed to Turgut's, is not marked with an escape from whatever that is bourgeois. On the contrary, he returns to his petty life, which is signified with his immediate interest in objects in this episode, where the desire to control gets translated into the desire to possess. Every single detail, every specific aspect, every particular constituent of the middle class home is carefully depicted and meticulously listed one after the other. One cannot help but wonder whether this is a suburban house or an intensive care unit. What can reflect the truth about the middle class better than the desire to control the world of objects? With the pathological behavior of a collector, Bloom the everyman, Bloom the bourgeois, imagines getting the control of his life by putting together these objects and constructing a life out of them. Obviously, this is the only way that he organizes his life and keeps himself intact.

As Levitt points out, Bloom, being a "false Messiah" cannot keep his promises (41). He fails as a businessman, fails as a husband and father, "fails even as a Jew to understand his sole heritage" (44). However, he obviously lacks the power to come face to face with his failure, or as Moretti observes in *Modern Epic*, he is too lethargic to do that. Moretti maintains the epic of the twentieth century is a story with no real hero. "We were seeking a hero, but have found a spectator," he adds pointing out to the fact that a feeling of lethargy is a distinguishing quality of the new epic (147). The epic hero of the modern age, "the universal individual of mankind," can only be sought in passivity. In this new scenario, the grand world of the epic no longer takes shape in transformative action, but in imagination.

Bloom perceives, Turgut analyses. Therefore, Moretti's diagnosis of Bloom, "the Oblomov of the twentieth century" (147), holds for Turgut, maybe even more than it does for Bloom. What determines both of the characters is a passivity that makes them comparable to Oblomov. But there are two different types of lethargy that we are talking about here. Bloom's day comes to an end, quiet and heavy with languor, which is definitely not comparable to Turgut's idleness at the end of the novel that emanates a sense of freedom. Bloom's tragedy is not that he did not adopt the right means to put things right and make it work with

105 See *Chapter 4*.

Molly, but that he can think of no place to return to other than the convenience of his habits. When viewed from this perspective, *Ulysses* reads as the story of a man put into the house. And in this sense, Joyce's Bloom is no different from Goethe's Wilhelm.

At the first sight, Goethe's novel is hardly comparable to Joyce's because of numerous differences in their approach to subjectivity and their employment of point of view and style. As we already remarked in Chapter 5, Goethe's work is strictly monological allowing no space to any characters that can challenge the omniscient point of view of the author/narrator, whereas Joyce's *Ulysses* is a textbook example of a polyphonic novel, where several voices are juxtaposed against each other.

However, in terms of the central theme of the novels, it is possible to talk about parallelisms between *Wilhelm Meister* and *Ulysses* in terms of their protagonists' loyalties to the class they belong to. In his analysis of modernist literature, Gerald Gillespie refers to Stephen's reference to Goethe's employment of *Hamlet* in *Wilhelm Meister*, and says that the moment Goethe's Wilhelm detaches himself from the Hamletic experiment, he is ready to become a useful bourgeois, and adds that this feels as if "he foreshadows the crossing over from being a Stephen to being a Bloom" (161). I think this is a very valuable insight in determining the flow and the destination of Joyce's novel. Ulysses starts with Stephen and his wandering thoughts, through which we catch a glimpse of his disconnectedness as an artist, a son, and a citizen (especially in the Proteus episode), and ends with Bloom, the portrait of the conformist as a frustrated man. The only difference between Wilhelm and Bloom is that the former embraces his fate more willingly.

Interestingly enough, what distinguishes Atay's novel from both Goethe and Joyce is that Turgut's Hamletic experience detaches him from his middle class life rather than resulting in reconciliation. In fact, it becomes the absolute manifestation of his madness and "disconnection," as we argued in Chapter 4. Therefore, we should add as a final note to this comparative analysis, the point that as opposed to the feeling of reconciliation we get from Joyce's novel, we are faced with a complete rupture in Atay's book: as the plot flows from Stephen to Bloom in *Ulysses*, the movement in *The Disconnected* is the other way round, i.e., from Bloom to Stephen.

## Stream of consciousness: the limits of personal identity

Any discussion of Joyce's modernism inevitably boils down to an exploration of his employment of stream of consciousness. The technique is not unique to Joyce, but he is unarguably one of the authors who brought a new perspective to its application, and helped to give it its ultimate name. Stream of consciousness is usually treated as a specific form of interior monologue, or what Auerbach calls "*erlebte Rede*," (535) and, as it is widely agreed upon, it is different from the latter in that it presents the interiority of the character in a flow of thoughts and feelings without regard to any rational or logical framework. As a new narrative technique, therefore, stream of consciousness demanded considerable amount of freedom on the side of the character, which necessitated a new understanding of point of view, challenging the traditional position of the author as the omniscient narrator —which we have discussed in detail in the fifth chapter of this study in relation to Goethe's *Wilhelm Meister*.

According to Ronald Bush, Flaubert was the first modernist author to recognize the need to part with the omniscient narrator if one really wants to represent the interiority of one's character. By rejecting the employment of an all-seeing narrator in *Madame Bovary*, Bush says, Flaubert came up with a fundamental decision that marks the end of realist writing. The refusal of an omniscient narrator not only stripped the discourses of Flaubert's characters (primarily, that of Emma) "of an implied moral authority," but also helped to shape the outline of modern thought based on "a self-conscious or 'aestheticized' acknowledgment of contingency" (18). This decision opened the way for Flaubert and his successors to portray truth in a fragmented way as opposed to an absolutized subjectivity represented by an all-knowing point of view. In a sense, we can say that it made a novel like *Ulysses* possible.

Hugh Kenner also refers to this shift in point of view while pointing to the lack of a storyteller in Joyce's writing. While illustrating Joyce's uniqueness, Kenner compares him to Charles Dickens and Joseph Conrad, arguing that both use the convention of the storyteller. Dickens' novels are "scripts to be brought to life in oral delivery" and Conrad's are studies of a "spoken narrative discharged into a reflexive silence." While *Ulysses* is Joyce's *Odyssey*, it lacks all evidence of storytelling. Unlike the narratives of Dickens, which require a storyteller, or those of Conrad, which feature narrators who reflect in silence, or those of Homer, which are "organized in memory and unfolded in time," Joyce's novels have no speaker and unfold on the printed page, a "technological space" (34-35).

The emphasis on space, here, is related to the modernist understanding of time, which Michael Hollington discusses in his short but insightful article on Joyce and Svevo, where he claims that the perception of time in modernist writing is inspired by Bergson's refusal of an understanding of absolute time. According to Hollington, this valuable observation that consciousness can never be in a state is what gave rise to the emergence of stream of consciousness as a narrative technique, which appears to be the perfect tool for modernist writing in that it represents the mind as in a flow, that is to say, a constantly changing picture due to present impressions integrating with past experiences (431). Hence, Hollington concludes, nothing really happens in modernist literature. Referring this quality of "non-events" in the masterpieces of modernist literature, such as *The Trial*, *Magic Mountain* and *The Man Without Qualities*, he maintains that the main feature of modernist writing in general is that it "uses our normal temporal expectations, and then frustrates or complicates them" (430).

Erich Auerbach, in his influential essay "The Brown Stocking," comments on Virginia Woolf's employment of stream of consciousness, and observes a similar problematization of the perception of time. According to Auerbach, Woolf's uniqueness begins with an "attempt to render the flow and the play of consciousness adrift in the current of changing impressions." What is important in this modern technique, according to Auerbach, is that it approaches reality "by means of numerous subjective impressions received by various individuals (and at various times)" (536). And this "multipersonal representation of consciousness" in combination with her "elaboration of the contrast between 'exterior' and 'interior' time" is what makes Woolf's technique unique (538). As Auerbach voices it, in Virginia Woolf's texts, "the external events have lost their hegemony, they serve to release and interpret inner events, whereas before her time [...] inner movements preponderantly function to prepare and motivate significant external happenings" (538). In short, by emphasizing the character's interiority in terms of a private temporality as opposed to the outside reality, Woolf problematizes the absolutized conception of time.

Although he approaches the issue from a different perspective, Joyce shares with Woolf an "ironic distrust of all absolutes, including those of temporal or spatial form" (Hollington 432). It is true that most of what we see in Ulysses also gets filtered through the consciousness of the character owing to the way Joyce employs stream of consciousness. However, Joyce's elaboration of this narrative technique, as Moretti reads it, is one of the artistic outcomes of the excess of stimulation produced by the modern capitalist metropolis: "A different style is required, in order to find one's way in the city of words; a weaker grammar than that of consciousness; an edgy, discontinuous syntax: a cubism of language, as it were. And the stream of consciousness offers precisely that: simple, fragmented sentences, where the subject withdraws to make room for the invasion of things; paratactical paragraphs, with the doors flung wide, and always enough room for one more sentence, and one more stimulus" (135). Moretti insists that, in the hands of Joyce, stream of consciousness emerged as a technique "of the *meaningless*: of banal everydayness," which accepts this banality, and does not "try to be poetry" (180).

Marjorie Perloff, however, in her review of *Modern Epic*, asks the question whether what we see getting filtered through the consciousness of Bloom in Ulysses, is really as random as Moretti claims. In other words, Perloff questions whether Joyce's stream of consciousness really has the freedom Moretti attributes to it, that is, whether it is not a great deal more organized and subordinated to narrative requirements. According to Perloff, Moretti fails in his effort to show us that Leopold Bloom's language is characterized by its passivity and absent-mindedness, the replacement of action by consumption, "because this mechanism does not work at the macrolevel, though it allows some freedom to such a fragmentary existence at the microlevel." Giving examples from the passages cited from "Lotus Eaters" and "Hades," Perloff argues that "even Bloom's stream of consciousness is highly controlled." [106]

In my comparison of "Penelope" with Günseli's monologue in *The Disconnected*, I will adopt an attitude similar to that of Perloff, and ask whether Molly's soliloquy fits into the framework that Moretti describes: the representation of "non-selective" details that are not rationally organized. The general tendency is to regard Molly's long interior monologue as the typical example of stream of consciousness where we enter the "flow" of Molly's thoughts. Molly's thoughts are contradictory, yet orderly, flowing between many topics from Leopold Bloom and Boylan to her fantasies about young Stephen, and the death of her son Rudy. As she moves from one thought to another, we witness her conflicting emotions. For example, she is aroused thinking about her next meeting with Boylan, while feeling affection for Leopold at the same time. Though Molly's eight sentences are uttered without regard to any grammatical rule, which suggests a sense of freedom, it does not mean that this episode represents a mind that operates unsystematically.

The lack of proper punctuation in this episode is usually considered to be representative of the female consciousness in general, and Molly's personality in particular. Katie Wales, in *The Language of James Joyce*, draws attention to the difference between Leopold's and Molly's voices, and claims that the latter sounds effortless and easy. She compares Bloom's inner voice to Molly's and says unlike the staccato structure of Bloom's inner monologue, Molly's stream of consciousness flows without any interruption. She points to the "excessive frequency of punctuation" in Bloom's voice, as opposed to the complete lack of

---

106 The full text is available at http://www.altx.com/ebr/ebr4/perlott/ htm.

punctuation in Molly's discourse, which gives it a reading pace unequalled else where in Joyce's text (91-92). Blamires compares Molly's thoughts to a "flowing river" while also noting that she was born on the Rock of Gibraltar (246) – Molly is both flowing river and steady rock, her consciousness one that is dynamic and constantly in motion, yet simultaneously grounded and centered by its ability to encompass the opposites she vacillates between.

Alyssa J. O'Brien, on the other hand, is not comfortable with the common acknowledgment of Molly's consciousness as a "flowing river" exhibiting the interiority of one single character. O'Brien suggests in an article called "The Molly Blooms of 'Penelope': Reading Joyce Archivally" that although the final episode of the book creates the illusion of a flowing monologue "emanating from a single female consciousness" (O'Brien 7), it is more like a linguistic experiment than what Karen Lawrence calls "the sound of one mind thinking" (Lawrence 204). As the name of her article indicates, O'Brien reviews this episode going through the archives, and reminds us that fifty-four percent of Penelope was added through insertions that Joyce made across nine proof stages, as Card has already shown (Card 16). "As a result," she insists, "Penelope is a less flowing monologue than it is what James Van Dyck Card calls 'the art of the mosaic': a carefully constructed text that did not spring whole from Joyce's head but rather was skillfully woven into its final form with linguistic treads" (O'Brien 9).

Though from another perspective, Derek Attridge also argues against the way critics have used the metaphor of "flow" to denote the style of Molly Bloom's interior monologue. He lists several critics, female and male, who use this metaphor and related ones (rivers, streams, liquids), such as Blamires, Burgess, French, Hayman, Card, and many others, and shows that characterizing Molly's language as "flowing" occurs in "almost every attempt to determine the style" of "Penelope" ("Molly's Flow" 544). According to Attridge, the metaphor of "flow" is highly questionable as a tool to describe Molly's language, and it is even more questionable to associate this flow, this "emblematically signaled continuity" with the "female mind" (549).

In what follows, we will compare Molly's and Günseli's monologues in *Ulysses* and *The Disconnected* while arguing that the representation of consciousness in the former is more authentic in that we observe almost a "styleless style" in Atay's text as opposed to Joyce's highly engineered style in "Penelope." As Molly Bloom's monologue is more or less rationally ordered, Günseli's has the quality of a compilation of fragments rather than a consistent whole. It is the stream of a consciousness that sounds unedited and unstructured. In addition to the lack of a consistent structure, what begins like Günseli's monologue develops into a more complicated text where the voices of Günseli, Selim and Turgut merge and become inextricable from each other.

## Günseli's soliloquy and limits of dialogue

Upon first encounter, Günseli's monologue seems very similar to the "Penelope" episode in *Ulysses*: the absence of third-person narration, the unpunctuated, unbroken "utterances," and the representation of thought in the form of continuous speech distinguish it from the earlier chapters, where we have seen Turgut's and Selim's monologues. At the beginning of her monologue, Günseli's consciousness is represented —like that of Molly Bloom— as a combination of stream of consciousness, free association, and, mostly, narration of events. One thing that we should remember, however, is while Molly's thoughts are silent as she lies awake next to Leopold, Günseli is actually voicing hers. The similarity in the tone stems from the fact that she is talking as if in a trance, and telling Turgut about the way she remembers Selim:

> [...] he would say Günseli I wish you knew me when I was eighteen no I am taking it back I dont wish you knew me then I really do not want to go back to those days to my foolishness to my clumsiness to my hands that used to break everything they touched to my hands that would never find the right doors to my absentmindedness that would lead me to wrong doors to my stupidity which would make me apologize when I actually wanted to express my gratitude and my hands again I don't want to go back to my sweaty hands [...] (430)

The language that Molly uses when she remembers Ben Howth and confesses that she needed to hear Poldy admit his love of her, is very rhythmical and is interrupted with several "yes"es towards the end of this passage. Adding to the intensity of emotion, one of the rare moments in this episode, this stylistic device helps the reader to follow Molly's thoughts and adjust himself to the continuous rise of tension towards the end of the episode:

> [...] he said the day we were lying among the rhododendrons on Howth head in the grey tweed suit and his straw hat the day I got him to propose to me yes first I gave him the bit of seedcake out of my mouth and it was leapyear like now yes 16 years ago my God after that long kiss I near lost my breath yes he said was a flower of the mountain yes so we are flowers all a womans body yes that was one true thing he said in his life and the sun shines for you today yes that was why I liked him because I saw he understood or felt what a woman is and I knew I could always get round him and I gave him all the pleasure I could leading him on till he asked me to say yes [...] (Ulysses, 18: 1571-81)

We observe a similar stylistic quality in Günseli's monologue interrupted by a set of "yeses" uttered by Selim. As it increases sexual tension in the previous passage, here this repetition serves the purpose of demonstrating Selim's desire to capture all the missed moments of his life in one single call. Almost in the fashion of Prufrock, he uses an elaborate language to declare his affection to Günseli, while regarding himself as an emotional cripple incapable of voicing his feelings:

> [...] I have to remove the word to know from the dictionary I have to find the pleasures I have missed when I used to live in between the lines and when I was out of love yes I have to hold myself accountable for all these yes for the things that I could not enjoy by myself no for the things that I did not know how I could enjoy no maybe for the things that I knew how to enjoy but could not bring myself to express yes these I should weld together with your beauty yes they had some meaning they are not outside your realm although they were lived at a time when you were absent I have to grasp the magic of all things suddenly being loaded with meaning [...] (424)

One striking similarity between the two monologues is that they can be used as strong evidence to suggest that there is a sharp contrast between the male and female voices in both *Ulysses* and *The Disconnected.* Arguing that Joyce never gives Molly Bloom the scope or the diversity that he attributes to his male characters, Suzette A. Henke draws our attention to the restrained portrayal of female characters in *Ulysses*. According to Henke, Molly's monologue is limited, because it is reduced to the "libidinous preoccupations that men have traditionally projected onto women" (235). In order to support her thesis, she compares Molly with Stephen:

> Molly Bloom is such an anti-Stephen—so much a corrective to literary erudition—that her formal knowledge is limited to the emanations of popular culture. Like Gerty MacDowell and Leopold Bloom, she has been fed a steady diet of pornography and penny papers. She interprets even the classics in terms of kinetic sensation. Molly believes, for instance, that Aristotle was the author of an obscene picture book on embryology; that Daniel Defoe created a lascivious namesake quite unlike our present Moll; and that Rabelais was a French hack writer who specialized in grotesque accounts of gestation. She paradoxically sits in moral judgment of these scandalous authors who offend her sense of decency (Henke 235).

Although it is a highly controversial issue whether Molly's discourse is tainted with the voice of patriarchy,[107] or whether it is an "extended protest of the tales

107 Following the writings of Cixous, Irigaray, Kristeva, feminist theorists Gilbert and Gubar, for instance, say that Joyce wrestles "patriarchal power from the mother tongue" (535). (See Sandra Gilbert, and Susan Gubar. "Sexual Linguistics: Gender, Language, Sexuality." *NLH* 16.3, Spring 1985. 515-544.) Suzette Henke, on the other hand, asks the question whether Joyce can be reclaimed for feminism. Offering a psychoanalytical reassessment of the Joycean canon "in the wake of Freud, Lacan, and Kristeva," Henke

made up by all these bearers of assumptions about women" (Harper 249), it is obvious that Joyce intends to draw a contrast between male and female principles in his novel. While this contrast is maintained mostly on an intellectual basis in *Ulysses*, it emerges as an emotional difference in *The Disconnected.* Berna Moran draws attention to the dramatic change in the tone when the narrative shifts into Günscli's voicc, and draws our attention to the intensity of emotions in this passage as opposed to the glittering logic of the male mind, which manifests itself as the sharp sense of humor that dominates the novel up to that point.

> The dominant tone in *The Disconnected* is the sarcastic tone of a provocative mind, because this is inherent in the voices of both Selim and Turgut. However, in the second half of the book, in the fifteenth chapter where Günseli becomes the narrator, this bitter voice is at times replaced with a sensitive and sentimental tone. In fact, what we hear is actually Selim's voice. It is Günseli who is talking but she is telling Turgut what Selim told her. This sincere declaration of love, through which Selim opens his heart and soul to Günseli in a way that he never did before, constitutes a striking contrast with the other discourses in the book saturated with irony. (Moran 278)

One feels obliged to agree with Moran. Throughout this monologue, we are able to see the reflections of Selim in Günseli's mind. We see him through her eyes, we hear him through her voice. The result is striking: what we observe in this episode is a Selim that we have not seen before anywhere in the book. This Selim is able to give himself completely to another person; he is capable of opening himself up to the other. The choice of a female voice, therefore, assumes a meaning different from that of Joyce's last episode in *Ulysses*, where Molly's voice seals up the whole book with the language of, what we might call, "the mother-earth". Here in *The Disconnected,* Günseli emerges not as a character that reveals the flow of the female mind, but rather a device that shows us the feminine quality in our main character. Seen through the eyes of a woman, our protagonist, who has been suffering because of his abstract bookish existence, finally abandons his literariness and becomes human. Although he still thinks that "people become real as long as they resemble the characters in the novels" (423), although he is scared thinking that he became "ordinary, like everybody else" (428) , he admits having fallen in love: "I am ruined he said there is no

---

discusses Molly's monologue as "steeped" in the languages of Edwardian pornography and "Victorian sentimental fiction" (i). (See Suzette Henke, *James Joyce and Politics of Desire.* New York and London: Routledge, 1990.) Mahaffey, however, positions Molly's "collective" and "largely unconscious" discourse as opposed to the patriarchal authority. (7-8). (See Mahaffey, Vicki. *Reauthorizing Joyce.* Gainesville: UP of Florida, 1995.)

cure for romanticism here I am now a laughing-stock after all these years of solitude" (427).

Günseli's voice is sincere, moving, and tender. It sounds natural and not worked upon. Like the moment below where she in a very simple language tells us why she could not let Selim go. The passage is expressive of the magnetic power of love between them, which, unlike Molly's very explicit account of the sensuous love scene at the end of "Penelope," has only a subtle reference to sexuality.

> [...] that summer he was working at a construction site he used to get so grubby during the day that he practically became unrecognizable in the evening under all that mud and dirt one day I stopped by to say hello he was embarrassed by my presence because of the workers his lips looked white with all that dirt on his face there was something that made him look disarming under all the dust that I got really excited I was supposed to leave but I couldnt leave I didnt want to leave the workers were staring at us he was tired embarrassed sweaty happy I could not stand the idea of letting him go [...] (427)

The expression of love, in the case of Selim, takes the form of a manic sermon from time to time. Günseli's short remarks interrupt his long sentences, and her calm and tender voice counterbalances his intoxicated tone. Through the eyes of Günseli we observe how the two got closer and closer, and how Selim blew the relationship not being able to handle such intensity. He is full of worries and cannot tolerate being in such an intimate relationship; as he beautifully and simply puts it, he does not know how to protect himself:

> [...] oh my God I have so many things to do I have to go home now I have to go home and start loving you now if you don't mind she would look into my eyes inquiringly I failed to make you smile how can I make you smile do you want me to tell you a joke about the color of your hair do you want me to say that one day a man was walking down the street only to see you smile with your eyes do you want me go like this ok one day this man way going down the street and he met this woman called Günseli [...] where were you until now why did you encourage me to talk to you why did you let your long face be so inviting why did you not smile if you smiled you would be less troubled finally I would smile good that's it that's fine now I can relax he would never tire of talking he could never gauge the limits of his power I'm not like my citizens I don't know how to protect myself I keep squeezing myself like a lemon you will dispose of me and you will call the waiter to ask for a new slice of lemon waiter one more vodka please I know I shouldnt drink I know that Im embarrassing you everybody is staring at us if there is anything you want to say if you can interrupt me I mean you can say it Im all ears Im listening to you with all my heart and all my ears please have mercy on me Ive said everything I know I used to tell him to stop talking I used to say Selim relax a little bit when I am relaxing you should talk he would say please tell me how come you are so beautiful I

> cannot find the right words as you do I would stutter opening my hands in a gesture of helplessness you are the tall Selim with the untidy hair no tell me about you he would say I have to start from you my dear Selim only in your shadow do my lines shine [...] (424-425)

What we observe here is a dialogue between Selim and Günseli that is being narrated to Turgut. Here it is still possible to observe the differences between Günseli's and Selim's voices, which will gradually disappear toward the end of the monologue, where the contours of their unique voices get blurred and their discourses melt into each other's. Turgut's voice is also separate from the voices of Selim and Günseli at this point of the episode, where things are still under control, and characters keep their individuality.

> [...] Selim was lucky to be able to talk about this he was lucky to have his Günseli how about the people that do not have a Günseli to talk this is what I have been thinking for the last couple of months what are they going to do Selim showed me a few ways told me a few things about what can be done to save these people but I don't know what measures can be taken to help them I cannot think of any party that is going to defend their rights [...] Turgut would say exactly the same things finally would say they cannot stand these jokes Günseli you do not know them they are very fragile who are they Selim the disconnected did he also tell you about them of course he did why shouldn't he you have no idea Günseli he used to say if life were a test that one should take every day again and again nobody could endure it this used to break my heart I would stretch and caress his hair my poor sweetheart I would say please dont be upset I would say but he would be upset [...] (430-431)

What looks like a braided structure composed of two different dialogues (the dialogue between Selim and Günseli in the past, and that of Turgut and Günseli in the present) assumes a different quality as the text unfolds. Gradually, we witness the consciousnesses of Turgut, Selim and Günseli blend in one single monologue. Atay seamlessly moves from one voice to another while representing the consciousnesses of all three characters, and forges them up to a point where it becomes difficult to identify who is speaking. An additional complication is, although most of the time we feel that we are listening to Günseli and Turgut talking about Selim, there are moments in the text when we cannot decide whether they are really uttering these words, or just talking to themselves without voicing them:

> [...] I wish you had invited me to that dinner Günseli I had never seen him like that and now its too late how am I supposed to know the way he acted [...] I feel like I can see him standing next to you now no I dont think I can see him how am I going to deal with so much pain how are we supposed to get used to this [...] youre crying Günseli I wish I could cry too a long forgotten habit will you teach me how to cry how to mourn for a lost friend [...] (428)

Turgut sounds more like he is thinking here. While this passage has the meditative quality of an interior monologue, the following part from the same episode demonstrates a moment where the voices of all three characters completely merge. It is also interesting that this technique enables Turgut to talk to his friend again as if they were face to face. The lack of punctuation allows the author to create a lapse in the conventional understanding of time, a literary space that is not limited by any laws of neither nature nor grammar. As a result, the words that the characters utter merge regardless of the time that they were pronounced.

> [...] at least I have hands I have feet and I have Günseli who loves me this is not much you are saying but it is good enough for me Günseli who has humbly accepted to be among the audience is going to watch us perform tonight yes Günseli now that you are here in this world youve got to get used to this dream of mine let me join Turgut thought well why not welcome to the company its cool you were supposed to wipe your shoes on the doormat you fool nice to see you Selim nice to see you bro dont you think the stage is way too empty though [...] (453)

The two friends easily shift back to their old and familiar jargon of college days, when they used to talk in rhymes. We do not know whether this encounter takes place privately in Turgut's mind, or whether he reports this to Günseli returning the favor of her long account of her relationship with Selim. In fact, it does not matter at this point of the text, because such boundaries have already been crossed, limits exceeded, and promises broken. Following a typical gesture, the text takes another wild turn, and assumes a game-like quality, where anything goes as long as it allows the author to question the limits of the text. In one such moment, Atay introduces a parodic device and lets Selim imitate the language of the street vendors in any Istanbul ferry. The playful voice of the street vendor is familiar to the natives of the city, and signals the beginning of the show:

> [...] I am not talking Günseli there are hundreds of people everybody knows them but I am not talking I am judging Im Im looking down upon them Im not crawling like them I am on my feet Im Im Im you look tired Günseli lets take a break lets have an entracte and taking advantage of the fifteen minute break dear passengers I will ask for another five minute of your precious time and tell you exemplary stories about the exciting lives of the celebrities of our country take it as a portable cinema and enjoy the show while you are peacefully sailing towards your destination [...] (436)

A similar gesture can be observed towards the end of the text when we arrive the point no return, that is to say, when the text completely gets out of control and approaches the limits of total chaos. This is what Günseli remembers from last couple of days before Selim's suicide. Here the monologue turns into a suicide note, which starts with Selim's soliloquy addressed to his father:

> [...] father I don't want to live in this house anymore you have been killing our spirit for all those years you have never read a single novel you were never excited watching a movie you have been keeping me and my mother captive here in this house amongst this ugly furniture your only concern was what your next meal was going to be whatever I know as feelings has developed as a reaction to your insensitivity you ruined us with your stale logic I am ashamed of my physical resemblance to you I hate my hands and feet because they look like yours I am utterly scared of becoming like you when I get old no you were not evil because you lacked the imagination for being evil but you kept an exact account of everything you did for us the first man's suit you bought for me the first pocket money you gave me even the sleepless nights you spent at my bed when I was sick you did not let me fill this house with music with books you did not care that everything beautiful died in this house in fact I wonder how anything beautiful got into our house in the first place [...] (457)

However, what begins like Selim's suicide note addressed to the ghost of his father suddenly turns into the report of a football game on the radio. As opposed to Selim' desire for some light, some music, something beautiful in the house, the only sound that emerges from the radio is the voice football commentator talking about the game. The breathless voice of the commentator merges with the gasps Selim's dying father:

> [...] you were nothing but a fault-finding bore dont leave the lights on close the windows turn off the radio it gives me headache dont ruin your eyes reading novels [...] shut the window Im cold open the window Im burning only death gives me pangs Im scared of dying [...] turn on the radio maybe there is some nice music since youve been to the military service yes for a long time we havent seen such a goal on the fields it was carefully prepared and nicely scored but what is happening over there our hero our striker is lying on the ground the first aid teams is rushing towards him lift me up son I can not breathe they lift him up they give him the kiss of life he faints he faints for good the whole audience is clapping madly [...] (458)

This part of the episode is genuinely interesting because of several reasons. Technically, it is taking advantage of the lack of punctuation and pushing the limits of language by merging the two scenes together and adding the voices seamlessly to each other. When the images of the suffocating father and the injured footballer overlap ("our striker is lying on the ground the first aid teams is rushing towards him lift me up son I can not breathe they lift him up"), we also notice the similarity in the voices of the announcer and the father. So, in addition to the visual symmetry, the two voices also coincide. Another point is the artificiality of the father's voice: the way he keeps staging little dramas trying to manipulate his sons feelings is reflected in the whole idea of a football game (we must not forget that in this little piece Turgut is acting as Selim's father). The uninterrupted flow, which is the defining quality of this episode, also fits the radio commentator's voice as he talks about the game: no punctuation, no staccato, and the unmistakable distance of the observer.

And finally, what is definitely to be noted is the joke that Atay plays on us. He is fully aware of the challenge that this episode poses to the reader. If the book is hard to read in general, this is the least readable part. It is not difficult to assume that a number of readers will give up on the novel precisely at this point – if they ever managed to come this far in the first place. Being fully aware of this, Atay resorts to an old student joke about the teacher who would never really read assignments tempting students to write anything so that the whole page looks neatly filled with words. Of course, the joke ends with a street smart student filling the pages with the comments on a recent football game and getting an A in return. Atay deliberately draws on this idea, he pushes on the limits of "meaning" in this part of the episode. He seems to be saying that it does not have to make any sense, because no one is going to read it anyway. Is this what Moretti means when he talks about the "technique of the *meaningless*"? I doubt it.

This takes us back to Moretti's discussion of Joyce's employment of stream of consciousness in *Ulysses,* and now that we are there again, I should add the following detail: In *Modern Epic*, Moretti draws a line between interior monologue and stream of consciousness by offering a comparison of the Joyce's style with that of Tolstoy and Faulkner, categorizing Anna's or Benjy's monologues as "selective" (168-173). It is true that they have come very close to the limits of stream of consciousness, but their particular intake of stimuli is momentary, because both novelists employ the technique to increase the dramatic effect at certain moments of narrative crisis. Anna's interior monologue at the end of the novel, for instance, shows the reader her thoughts leading up to her suicide (170). The stream of consciousness in *Ulysses*, on the other hand, is "non-selective;" it presents the protagonist being bombarded by images regardless of their relevance to the particular psychological state that he finds himself in. [108]

108 I doubt whether this would apply to any Woolf character, whose personality and psychology would definitely determine the flow of thoughts and feelings, as in the case of Mrs Dalloway, for instance, who is highly selective in what she sees and what she ignores. Besides, every image that gets filtered through Clarissa's mind gets tied up to the general framework of the novel and adds to the mood. For instance, the effect of Big Ben's bells are described as, "The leaden circles dissolve in the air," which contributes to a previous image of a plunging bird. This image reminds one of water after a body has plunged into it. Once water is disturbed, a ring of circular ripples emanates outward

Therefore, according to Moretti, Tolstoy presents Anna's thoughts flow regardless of a rational structure, because he portrays a moment of crisis in her consciousness. Her mind opens itself to outside stimuli, and becomes "non-selective," because she is about to commit suicide. Can we say the same thing for Selim? Do we owe this unleashed flow of thoughts simply to the fact Selim is about to commit suicide? Not really. Selim is challenging rationality in this episode, not because he is mad in the conventional sense of the word, or not because he knows he is going to commit suicide, but because, being a "disconnected," he has always lived on the verge of reason.

As opposed to the highly realistic nature of Tolstoy's text, what we have here in the final part of this episode is a narrative style that pushes the limits of rationality as a whole – a gesture that is completely in line with the main theme of the novel. What Atay has been arguing theoretically up to this moment in the book is being put into practice here. He demonstrates the disintegration of rationality in the discourse of his main character taking advantage of the freedom that the lack of punctuation offers to him. If Joyce's is "a cubism of language," then Atay's language here in this episode is surrealism *par excellence*. This is a surrealism that is not intended to entertain the reader, but to detach him from anything that is conventional – and, therefore, convenient. Hence, the motto of the disconnected resurfaces: Dread the establishment, fear the ordinary!

The episode nears the end on a sad note. The story of Selim's relationship with his father, his loneliness, his "out-of-placeness" which finally drives him away from Günseli – and eventually drives him mad – is being told through a very intricate, complicated structure, which sounds like live broadcast from a stage play, a concert, and a football game – all at the same time.

> [...] we are proud to present you the inauguration speech that Turgut Özben wrote especially for this opening concert at the moment you are listening to your announcer Özdinç Erkaplan the author of this play you are about to listen is called Selim Işık he is born in the small town N in 1936 and now they are pressing him they are pressing hard to get the ball they are flooding towards the goal keeper from the side of the Bosphorus and corner his father was Numan Bey the head of the finance office he noticed his sons talents at a very early age a brilliant pass from the left winger and goal yes dear listeners it is a goal goal goal all the members of the orchestra are giving the striker a standing ovation wait there is an objection no the referee is not going to change his mind he looks resolute it is a goal let me repeat for the ones who have just turned their radios on the prime minister has just entered the hall and be-

---

from the central point. This image provides an insight into Mrs. Dalloway's personality, as well as the approaching fate of Septimus, who later commits suicide by throwing himself out of the window.

> cause he has noticed his sons talents at a very early age he bought him a piano a football a typewriter and a one act play so that Selim could act in it [...] (455)

Let us compare this to the closing lines of "Penelope," which despite Moretti's insistence in the lack of poetry, presents one of the most lyrical endings in the history of literature:

> I was a Flower of the mountain yes when I put the rose in my hair like the Andalusian girls used or shall I wear a red yes and how he kissed me under the Moorish wall and I thought well as well him as another and then I asked him with my eyes to ask again yes and then he asked me would I yes to say yes my mountain flower and first I put my arms around him yes and drew him down Jo me so he could feel my breasts all perfume yes and his heart was going like mad and yes I said yes I will Yes. (Ulysses 18: 1602-09)

It is hard to argue against critics who suggest that "Penelope" has a "privileged position" in the novel. Its location at the end of the book and the specific style that Joyce reserves for Molly's voice support the idea that it is a form of closure he intended for the novel. After the succession of several styles competing for attention —and probably erasing each other's impact on the reader— Molly's soliloquy emerges as the last, and arguably the least forgettable, voice of the text, which possesses some kind of an authority over the other voices. As Kenner says, it is as if we finally hear the solitary voice of the Muse (*Voices* 98). Joyce's resolution to end the monologue with "the female word Yes" further enhances this authority, and Molly truly has the last word: "The last word (human, all too human) is left to Penelope. This is the indispensable countersign to Bloom's passport to eternity. I mean the last episode Penelope" (Joyce, *Letters*, February 28th 1921). And later in another letter, he repeats the emphasis on the female consciousness embracing the whole of the book and the world, or better as Marilyn French puts it, "the book as world":

> Penelope is the *clou* [star-turn] of the book. The first sentence contains 2500 words. There are eight sentences in the episode. It begins and ends with the female word yes. It turns like the huge earth ball slowly surely and evenly round and round spinning, its four cardinal points being the female breasts, arse, womb and cunt expressed by the words because, bottom (in all senses bottom button, bottom of the class, bottom of the sea, bottom of his heart), woman, yes. Though probably more obscene than any preceding episode it seems to me to be perfectly sane full amoral fertilisable untrustworthy engaging shrewd limited prudent indifferent *Weib. Ich bin der Fleisch der stets bejaht* [Woman. I am the flesh that always affirms]. (Joyce, *Letters*, August 16th 1921)

However, if the book is going to end with a final word in the end, are we not supposed to question the author's promise of open-endedness? This is a question that Karen Lawrence asks:

> Because my own reading of the book depends upon the notion that Ulysses presents possibilities instead of conclusions, the "Penelope" chapter seems to me to be regressive, to present something denied by the nest of the book. If Molly's monologue contains the truth or resolution, hasn't the book implicitly suggested that we cannot trust messages or any version of the truth? All along it has played with and subverted its own momentary climaxes and seeming resolutions. As a result, it has sharpened our suspicion of any "last word." (Lawrence 206)

*The Disconnected* shares with *Ulysses*, what Michael Hollington calls in regard to Joyce's book, "a radically skeptical attitude towards all absolutes" (438). However, Atay's novel distinguishes itself in the articulation of this attitude towards rationalism, which seems to know no boundaries. In fact, Atay is fully aware that he is writing from the borders of irrationality, disorder, and chaos. We hear him questioning himself in the process of writing. While leading us into the labyrinthine mind of his main character Selim, he conveys an anxiety of losing touch with the subject and the reader. On the one hand, he looks for the best way to give a voice to the uproar that spreads from Selim's mind, on the other hand, he searches for a form that would suit the sentiment of the novel, i.e., a consistent contempt for any kind of limitation, regularity, and rationalization. Atay projects this pursuit to his character: "He thought the best way to express the confusion in his mind would be to write in a free style. But the free style looked like a deformation, a disorder of style, a lack of style." (134)

# CONCLUSION

Matei Calinescu talks about modernity's constant strife with itself and quotes Octavio Paz, who characterizes modernity as "A Tradition Against Itself." According to Calinescu, whenever we talk of the modern tradition, we are using a phrase that is paradoxical in itself, since "modernity always implies the sense of an 'antitraditional tradition,' and this accounts for, among other things, modernism's renewed capability of denying itself – its various historical 'traditions' – without losing its identity" (78).

On the one hand, there is the bourgeois modernity which is deeply rooted in the idea of progress, what Calinescu calls "the cult of action and success," and on the other hand, there is the other modernity, the one that is "disgusted with middle class scale of values," and is "inclined toward radical anti-bourgeois attitudes"(41-42). By defining these "two distinct and bitterly conflicting modernities," Calinescu draws attention to the split between "modernity as a stage in the history of Western Civilization —a product of scientific and technological progress, of the industrial revolution, of the sweeping economic and social changes brought about by capitalism— and modernity as an aesthetic concept," and suggests what defines the latter is its contempt of the former: "what defines cultural modernity is its outright rejection of bourgeois modernity, its consuming negative passion" (5-42).

Our reading of *The Disconnected* as a modernist novel owes a great deal to Calinescu's approach to cultural modernity as a hearty refusal of middle class values. Atay's novel starts within the realm of the "cult of success and action" portraying Turgut in the convenience of his middle class environment. However, as the plot unfolds, the story gradually moves towards "anarchy" and "aristocratic self-exile," which, according to Calinescu, are signaling the presence of the "other" modernity. This negative passion towards the cult of reason is what constitutes the backbone of Atay's novel. This is not a random or momentary sentiment, but a solid stance that has penetrated every single line of *The Disconnected*, as well as the rest of Atay's work. In *Dangerous Games* for instance, we hear Hikmet Benol,[109] the main character of the novel, saying: "Ergo sum, but no Cogito, dear Colonel, no Cogito!" (120)

In this study, I have tried to demonstrate the radical attitude that Atay takes against the totalitarian and pragmatic aspect of Turkey's project of modernization. He voices his argument from a standpoint that can be called, in the manner

109 One should note here that Hikmet Benol's name translates roughly into Descartes's dictum, since "hikmet" means "reason," and "benol" is a conglomerate of the pronoun "I" and the verb "to be."

of Calinescu, “the other modernity.” In this sense, he is no different from the modernist authors in the West who have questioned the uniformity that modernity imposed upon the lives of people. Therefore, it is possible to claim that Atay shares with other modernist novelists a skeptical attitude towards all absolutes as well as a “subjectivism” that has been the essential quality of modernist art from Dostoevsky through to Joyce and Kafka.

*The Disconnected* bases its central issues on the question of “totality,” and unfolds its story focusing on the relationship between authority that tends to totalize all meaning, and that which situates itself against this authority. The novel elaborates this question on several different levels. The central problem, however, remains the same: how would it be possible for the ones who can not find their place in the system, in the narrative of modernity, i.e. the disconnected, to stand against the “truth” fabricated by authority? And if they do, how are they going to articulate their own position?

One way of answering the question is reading *The Disconnected* as a “national allegory,” as Jameson would have it. It can be read as a book that challenges the totalizing attitude of political authority, and the illusion that the country is on its way towards a more Western and modern state; i.e., the Occidentalist fantasy. However, for me, what is even more interesting than Atay’s criticism of the pragmatism that lies beneath Turkey’s project of modernism is the way he challenges the cult of reason as a whole. Rationality, for Atay, is the ultimate form of totality in that it claims to stand for all that there is. So, in the rhetoric of Atay’s book, reason turns out to be a serious problem, which gets called into question at every single opportunity.

As we have argued in Chapter 1, the excess of meaning generated by Atay’s text, which seems to be reminding us that there will always be something that lies beyond the limits of reason, mocks the rigid totality of the epic. In Chapter 4, which mainly deals with the “Hamlet metaphor,” however, Turgut’s madness emerges as the only way out of the boundaries of analytical thinking, which sets the book free from the syntax of the West, giving it a unique characteristic and underlining its particularity as opposed to what claims to be universal. Chapter 5 is about Atay’s dialogue with Goethe in particular and Bildungsroman in general. It approaches the problem of totality from another angle, and demonstrates the disintegration of the relationship not only between author and character, but also individual and society. As the chapter about Dostoevsky focuses on the fragmentation of the subject as regards the modern world, the last chapter deals predominantly with language, and centralizes around the question on the stream of consciousness as a technique verging on the limits of rationality. In short, all sections of this study deal with the same problem approaching it from various angles, and hopefully establishing the value of *The Disconnected* as one of the texts of "the other modernity."

This also makes it clear why Bakhtin's work constitutes the theoretical axis of, and emerges as the ultimate inspiration for this study. Being one of the first philosophers to talk about the totalizing nature of rationality, Bakhtin gave the voice of authority its well-deserved name, and baptized it as the "monological discourse." The "other modernity," however, is by definition, what wages war against this monolithically solid entity that speaks in one voice. The perspective that Bakhtin brings to the argument is the anarchic strain that puts much emphasis on the power of laughter as the only tool to challenge authority. In the Bakhtinian universe, therefore, the carnivalesque emerges unarguably the unique gesture of "the other modernity." Its voice, however, proves to be polyphony.

Atay shares Bakhtin's derisive attitude towards rationalist theories of language, which tend to totalize communication suggesting the attainment of an abstract and frozen "meaning," an origin of some kind. This makes it very interesting to read Atay's novel from a Bakhtinian perspective, because it is possible to observe how elaborately Atay avoids all implications of authority in his characterization of voice. *The Disconnected* is a novel of voices —especially those that are in conflict: Turgut's long monologues of grief are set against Nermin's small talk; the meanderings of the young Selim are presented against the background of the calm and soothing voice of Esat, Süleyman's grave and sincere voice is contrasted with the pseudo-romanticism and banality of Metin's tangos. Similarly, different discourses are also set against each other. Being fully aware of the fact that language is an ideological construct, Atay juxtaposes these discourses in a manner that they constantly clash with each other, and are never able to establish themselves as the absolute. The passages concerning the language reform prove to be a case in point, as we have demonstrated in Chapter 1.

The dialogical relation between the voices of characters has been one of the concerns of this study. However, more important to this study is the dialogue that Atay establishes with his "literary fathers," that is to say, the canonical authors of the West. The dialogue between Atay and authors of the canon takes on a significant meaning, not only because it represents the encounter between different genres, but also because it provides us with new readings of these familiar texts, which is the result of the clash between different cultural moments in history. Besides, in starting a dialogue with these authors, Atay does not simply borrow from them or pay them homage, but mainly questions the possibility of writing in the East, where the voice of the canon sounds as the revelation of the absolute truth, its words read as a sacred text, and its authority remains unchallenged. The voice of the western canon becomes the voice of the cult of reason, as we hear it in Jameson's declaration that condemns all third world texts not only to a collectivity that robs them from their individuality, but also to a world that is devoid of metaphysics. The third world is not privileged enough to think about man's relation to the rest of the universe.

In this study, I have tried to demonstrate that the opposite holds true for Atay's novel. *The Disconnected*, apart from being a novel that gives considerable thought to the collectivity that Jameson mentions, is also a novel about the aperture modernity opens in the way the individual conceives itself as regards to the rest of the world. Atay's dialogue with the authors of the western canon emerges as one of the ways of problematizing this situation: the individual positioning himself against his other calls the absolute into question, challenging it through laughter, which emerges like a cosmic weapon capable of shattering the ground of anything that has manifested itself as authority - - rationality being the first item on the list.

In its battle against reason, the language of *The Disconnected* assumes the quality of madness, and grants Turgut the opportunity to speak of what is essentially unspeakable: the anguish he feels in the face of death. What is more, it equips Atay with an authentic language, the voice that he has been seeking from the beginning of the novel. The most important aspect of madness is the anarchic element involved in it, as Parla emphasizes in her analysis of *Don Quixote*: "an artistic language that identifies itself with madness is capable of shattering all systems" (222). By acquiring the language of madness, Turgut voices a militantly anti-authoritarian attitude characteristic of the carnivalesque and celebrates the anarchic elements contained within the otherness of the disconnected. Atay's language, which finds its best expression in carnival laughter, is capable of posing universal problems and is thereby just as admissible in great literature as the seriousness of rationality.

# REFERENCES


Ahıska, Meltem. "Occidentalism: The Historical Fantasy of the Modern." *South Atlantic Quarterly 102*, no. 2/3 (2003): 351-379. Print.

Ahmad, Aijaz. "Jameson's Rhetoric of Otherness and the 'National Allegory,'" *Social Text*, No. 17. (Autumn, 1987): 3-25. Print.

Atay, Oğuz. *Günlük*. Istanbul: İletişim Yayınları, 1987.

_________. *Korkuyu Beklerken*. Istanbul: İletişim Yayınları, 1988.

_________. *Tehlikeli Oyunlar*. Istanbul: İletişim Yayınları, 1987.

_________. *Tutunamayanlar*. Istanbul: İletişim Yayınları, 1984.

Attridge, Derek. *The Cambridge Companion to James Joyce*. Cambridge UP, 1990.

_________. "Molly's Flow: The Writing of 'Penelope' and the Question of Woman's Language." *MFS* 35, 1989: 543-565. Print.

Auerbach, Erich. *Mimesis: The Representation of Reality in Western Literature*. Princeton and Oxford: Princeton UP, 1953/2003.

Bakhtin, Mikhail M. *Art and Answerability: Early Philosophical Essays*. Austin: U of Texas P, 1990.

_________. *The Dialogic Imagination: Four Essays,* trans. by Caryl Emerson and Michael Holquist. Austin: U of Texas P, 1981.

_________. *Problems of Dostoevsky's Poetics*. Ed. and trans. Caryl Emerson. Minneapolis: U of Minnesota P, 1984.

_________. *Rabelais and His World*. Trans. Helene Iswolsky. 1968; repr. Bloomington: Indiana UP, 1984.

_________. *Speech Genres and Other Late Essays*. Trans. by Vern W. McGee. Ed. by Caryl Emerson and Michael Holquist. Austin: U of Texas P, 1986.

Barrie, Robert. "Telmahs: Carnival Laughter in Hamlet." *New Essays on Hamlet*. Ed. Mark Thornton Burnett and John Manning. Hamlet Collection 1. New York: AMS, 1994: 83-100. Print.

Barthes, Roland. *Image, Music Text*, trans. Stephen Heath. Glasgow: Fontana Press, 1977.

Belge, Murat. "Tutunamayanlar" *Yeni Dergi*, Sayı 99, Aralık 1972, 278-285.

Bell, Robert H., *Jocoserious Joyce: The Fate of Folly in Ulysses*. Ithaca and London: Cornell UP, 1991.

Berdyaev, Nicholas, *Dostoevsky*. New York: Meridian, 1957.

Blackmur, R.P., *Eleven Essays in the European Novel*. Harcourt: Brace & World, 1964.

Blamires, Harry. *The New Bloomsday Book: A Guide through Joyce's Ulysses*. London and New York: Methuen, 1986.

Booker, M. Keith. *Joyce, Bakhtin, and the Literary Tradition: Toward a Comparative Cultural Poetics.* Ann Arbor: U of Michigan P, 1995.

Bowen Zack, *Ulysses As a Comic Novel* Syracuse, NY: Syracuse UP, 1989.

Boyle, Fr. Robert, S.J. "Penelope." *James Joyce's Ulysses.* Ed. Clive Hart and David Hayman. Berkeley: U of California P, 1974.

Bozdoğan, Sibel and Reşat Kasaba, eds., *Rethinking modernity and national identity in Turkey.* Seattle: U of Washington P, 1997.

Bristol, Michael D. "'Funeral bak'd-meats': Carnival and the Carnivalesque in Hamlet." *William Shakespeare, Hamlet.* Ed. Susanne L. Wofford. Case Studies in Contemporary Criticism. Boston: St. Martin's, 1994. 348-67. [Reprinted in *Shakespeare's Tragedies*, ed. Susan Zimmerman (1998).]

_________ . *Carnival and Theatre: Plebeian Culture and the Structure of Authority in Renaissance England.* New York and London: Routledge, 1989.

Burnett, Mark Thornton. "'For they are actions that a man might play': Hamlet as Trickster." Hamlet. Ed. Peter J. Smith and Nigel Wood. *Theory in Practice.* Buckingham: Open UP, 1996. 24-54. Print.

Bush, Ronald. "Joyce's Modernisms" *Palgrave Advances in James Joyce Studies*, ed. Jean-Michel Rabate. New York: Palgrave McMillan, 2004 (10-38).

Calinescu, Matei. *Five Faces of Modernity.* Durham: Duke University Press, 1987.

Campbell, Joseph. *Mythic Worlds, Modern Words: Joseph Campbell on the Art of James Joyce.* Novato, California: New World Library. 2003. 47-191. Print.

Card, James Van Dyck. *An Anatomy of "Penelope".* Rutherford: Fairleigh Dickinson UP, 1984.

Chekhov, Anton. *Letters on the Short Story, the Drama and other Literary Topics*, Ed. Louis S. Friedland. 1924. New York: Dover, 1966.

Cheng, Vincent John. *Joyce, Race, and Empire.* Cambridge: Cambridge UP, 1995.

Clark, Katerina and Michael Holquist. *Mikhail Bakhtin.* Cambridge: Harvard UP, 1984.

Cowan, Louise. *The Epic Cosmos.* Ed. Larry Allums. The Dallas Institute of Humanities and Culture Publications, 1992.

Culwell, Lori M. "The Role of the Clown in Shakespeare's Theatre", from http://extra.shu.ac.uk/emls/iemls/shaksper/files/ROLE%20CLOWN.txt.

Derrida, Jacques. "Structure, Sign and Play in the Discourse of the Human Sciences" *Critical Theory Since 1965*, Ed. Adams, H. and Searle, L. Florida State Univ. Press, Tallahassee: 1986: 83-94. Print.

_________. *Of Grammatology*. Trans. Gayatri Chakravorty Spivak. Baltimore & London: Johns Hopkins University Press, 1976.
_________. *Positions*. Trans. Alan Bass. Chicago: U of Chicago P, 1981.
_________. *Writing and Difference*, trans. Alan Bass, Chicago: U of Chicago P, 1978.
De Quincey, Thomas. "On the Knocking at the Gate in *Macbeth*," from http://www.4literature.net/Thomas_De_Quincey/On_the_Knocking_at_the_Gate_in_Macbeth/
Dostoevsky, Fyodor. *The Brothers Karamasov*, The Penguin Classics. Trans. David Magarshack. Middlesex, 1958.
__________. *Crime and Punishment*. Barnes and Noble Edition. New York: Barnes and Noble Books, 1994.
__________. *The Diary of a Writer*. Trans. Boris Brasol. New York: Scribner's Sons, 1949.
__________. *The Grand Inquisitor: with related Chapters from The Brothers Karamasov*, ed. with an introduction by Charles B. Guignon (Cambridge: Hackett Publishing Comp., 1993)
__________. *The Idiot*. Trans. Alan Myers. New York: Oxford UP, 1992.
__________. *Notes from the Underground*. New York: Dover Publications Inc., 1992.
__________. *The Notebooks for The Idiot*, ed. Edward Wasiolek, trans. Katherine Strelsky. Chicago: U of Chicago P, 1967.
Duffy, Edna. *The Subaltern Ulysses*. Minneapolis: U of Minneapolis P, 1994.

Eagleton, Terry. "I Contain Multitudes" LRB | Vol. 29 No. 12, 21 June 2007.
__________. *Sweet Violence: The Idea of the Tragic*. Oxford: Blackwell Publishing, 2003.
Ecevit, Yıldız. *Ben Buradayım: Oğuz Atay'ın Biyografik ve Kurmaca Dünyası* Istanbul: İletişim Yayınları, 2005.
Eco, Umberto. *The Limits of Interpretation*. Indianapolis: Indiana UP, 1994.
Eliot, T. S. "Ulysses, Order and Myth." *Selected Prose of T. S. Eliot*. London: Harvest, 1975.
Ellmann, Richard, *Ulysses on the Liffey*. London: Faber and Faber, 1972.
___________. *James Joyce*. Oxford: Oxford UP, 1982.
Ellmann, Richard and Charles Feidelson, Jr, eds. *Modern Tradition, Backgrounds of Modern Literature*. New York: Oxford UP, 1965.
Epstein, Norrie. *The Friendly Shakespeare*. New York: The Penguin Group, 1993.

Ertuğrul, Suna. "Belated Modernity and Modernity as Belatedness in Tutunamayanlar." *The South Atlantic Quarterly* 102, no. 2/3 (2003) 639-644. Print.

Evin, Ahmet 0. , *Origins and Development of the Turkish Novel*, Minneapolis, 1983.

Fairhill, James. *James Joyce and the Question of History*. Cambridge: Cambridge UP, 1993.

Fanger, Donald, *Dostoevsky and Romantic Realism, a Study of Dostoevsky in Relation to Balzac, Dickens and Gogol* (Cambridge, Massachusetts: Harvard UP, 1965)

Fargnoli, N., M.P. Gillespie, *James Joyce A-Z*. London: Bloomsbury, 1995.

Ferrer, Daniel. "Circe, Regret, and Regression," in *Poststructuralist Joyce: Essays from the French*. Ed. Derek Attridge and Daniel Ferrer. Cambridge: Cambridge UP, 1984.

Fister, Barbara. "On the Threshold of Representation: The Function of the Holbein Christ in The Idiot" (presented at the Kentucky Foreign Language Conference, University of Kentucky, April 1996) from http://homepages.gac.edu/~fister/ThresholdofRepresentation.html

Forster, E. M. *Aspects of the Novel*, Abinger Edition. London: Edwin Arnold, 1974.

Foucault, Michel. *Madness and Civilization*. London: Tavistock, 1961.

__________. "What is an Author?" *The Foucault Reader*. Ed. Paul Rabinow. New York: Pantheon Books, 1984.

French, Marilyn. *The Book as World*: *James Joyce's Ulysses* London: Harvard UP, 1976.

Frye, Northrop. *Anatomy of Criticism*. Princeton: Princeton UP, 1957.

*Fyodor Dostoevsky*, ed. with an introduction by Harold Bloom. New York: Chelsea House, 1988.

Gilbert, Sandra, and Susan Gubar. "Sexual Linguistics: Gender, Language, Sexuality." *NLH* 16.3, Spring 1985. 515-544. Print.

Gillespie, Gerald Ernest Paul: *Proust, Mann, Joyce in the Modernist Context*, Washington, D.C.: Catholic University of America Press, 2003.

Girard, René. *Deceit, Desire, and the Novel: Self and Other in Literary Structure*. Translated by Yvonne Freccero. Baltimore: Johns Hopkins UP, 1965.

Goethe, Johann Wolfgang von. "Ueber epische und dramatische Dichtung von Goethe und Schiller," in *Saemtliche Werke*. Munich: Hanser, 1986.

_________. *Wilhelm Meister's Apprenticeship*. Eliot, Charles William, ed. The Harvard Classics Shelf of Fiction. New York: P.F. Collier & Son, 1917; Bartleby.com, 2000.

Gorfain, Phyllis. "Toward a Theory of Play and the Carnivalesque in Hamlet." *Hamlet Studies* 13 (1991): 25-49. [Reprinted in Donald Keesey's Contexts for Criticism (1994) and in Ronald Knowles' *Shakespeare and Carnival: After Bakhtin* (1998).]

Graves, Michael. "Hamlet as Fool," *Hamlet Studies*, 4 (1982), 72-88.

Gürbilek, Nurdan. "Dandies and Originals: Authenticity, Belatedness, and the Turkish Novel," *South Atlantic Quarterly*. 102, no. 2/3, 2003: 599-628.

_________. *Ev Ödevi*. Istanbul: Metis Yayınları, 1998.

_________. *Kötü Çocuk Türk*. Istanbul: Metis Yayınları, 2001.

_________. *Kör Ayna, Kayıp Şark*. Istanbul: Metis Yayınları, 2004.

_________. *Yer Değiştiren Gölge*. Istanbul: Metis Yayınları, 1995.

Gürle, Meltem. "'Cinema Grande'and the Rhetoric of Illusion in Uyurkulak's *Har*," *New Perspectives on Turkey*, No. 36, Spring 2007: 125-144. Print.

**H**ainsworth, J.B. *The Idea of Epic*. Berkeley: U of California P, 1991.

Harper, Margaret M. "'Taken in Drapery': Dressing the Narrative in the *Odyssey* and 'Penelope'" *Molly Blooms: A Polylogue on "Penelope" and Cultural Studies*. Ed. Richard Pearce. Wisconsin: The U of Wisconsin P, 1994 (237-263).

Hart, Clive, and Leo Knuth, *A Topographical Guide to James Joyce's Ulysses* Colchester: A Wake Newslitter Press, 1976, 1981.

Hegel, G.W.F. *Aesthetics: Lectures on Fine Art*, trans. T. M. Knox, Oxford: Oxford UP, 1975.

_________. *Lectures on The History of Philosophy*, trans. E. S. Haldane Routledge & Kegan Paul, 1955.

_________. *Philosophy of Right*, trans. T. M. Knox, Oxford: Oxford UP, 1967.

_________. *The Phenomenology of Mind.* Trans. by J. B. Baillie. London: George Allen & Unwin LTD, 1910.

Henke, Suzette A. *Joyce's Moraculous Sindbook: A Study of Ulysses*. Ohio State UP: Columbus, 1978.

_________. *James Joyce and Politics of Desire*. New York and London: Routledge, 1990.

Hesse, Hermann. "Thoughts on the Idiot of Dostoevsky" Trans. Stephen Hudson http://world.std.com/~raparker/exploring/books/hesse_hudson_idiot.html

Holderness, Graham. *Hamlet*. Philadelphia: Open UP, 1987.

Hollington, Michael. “Svevo, Joyce and Modernist Time,” *Modernism: A Guide to European Literature.* Malcolm Bradbury and James McFarlane (eds.), London: Penguin, 1976 (430-442).

Holquist, Michael. *Dialogism: Bakhtin and His World.* London: Routledge, 1990.

__________. *Dostoevsky and the Novel.* Princeton: Princeton UP, 1977.

Horkheimer, Max and Theodor Adorno. *Dialectic of Enlightenment.* California: Stanford UP, 2002.

Hyppolite, Jean, *Genesis and Structure of Hegel's Phenomenology of Spirit.* Trans. Samuel Cherniak and John Heckman. Evanston: Northwestern UP, 1974.

Irzık, Sibel. “Allegorical Lives: The Public and the Private in the Modern Turkish Novel,” The South Atlantic Quarterly 102.2/3, 2003: 551-567. Print.

_________. “Tutunamayanlar’da Çokseslilik ve Sınırları,” *Varlık* 1057, 1995: 44-47. Print.

İnci, Handan. Ed. *Oğuz Atay’a Armağan: Türk Edebiyatının Oyun/Bozanı.* Istanbul: İletişim Yayınları, 2007.

Jameson, Fredric. “Cultural Logic of Late Capitalism,” *The Jameson Reader*, ed. Michael Hardt and Kathi Weeks, Massachusetts: Blackwell Publishers, 2000.

__________. "Postmodernism and Consumer Society." *The Anti-Aesthetic.* Ed. Hal Foster. Port Townsend: Bay Press, 1983: 111-125. Print.

__________. ‘Third-World Literature in the Era of Multinational Capitalism’, *Social Text 15*, 1986: 65-88. Print.

Jeffers, Thomas L. "Goethe's Classical Bildungsroman: Mastering the Art of Living." *Apprenticeships: The Bildungsroman from Goethe to Santayana.* New York: Palgrave Macmillan, 2005: 9-34. Print.

Johnson, Carroll B. “Beyond Metaphysics: Semiotics and Character in *Don Quijote*, I” *Cervantes: Bulletin of the Cervantes Society of America* 5.1, 1985: 3-17. Print.

Joyce, James. *Selected Letters of James Joyce.* Ed. Richard Ellmann. London: Faber and Faber, 1975.

___________. *Ulysses.* London: Penquin Modern Classics, 1986.

___________. *A Portrait of the Artist as a Young Man.* Dover Publications, 1994.

Kabat, Geoffrey C. *Ideology and Imagination: The Image of Society in Dostoevsky.* New York: Columbia UP, 1978.

Kamuf, Peggy, ed. *Between the Blinds: A Derrida Reader*. New York: Columbia UP, 1991.
Kellen, Christopher. "The Great Wall of China and Kafka's Limitless Tropology." *Queen: A Journal of Rhetoric and Power,* Vol. 2.1. from http://ars-rhetorica.net/Queen/Volume21/Articles/Kelen.htm
Kenner, Hugh. *Flaubert, Joyce, and Beckett: The Stoic Comedians*. London: Dalkey Archive Press, 2005.
__________. *Joyce's Voices*. Berkeley: U of California P, 1978.
Kierkegaard, Soren. *Fear and Trembling*, trans. Walter Lawrie. New York: Doubleday Anchor Books, 1955.
Killeen, Terence. *Ulysses Unbound: A Reader's Companion to James Joyce's Ulysses* Bray: Wordwell Ltd, in association with the National Library of Ireland, 2004.
Kinser, Samuel. *Rabelais's Carnival: Text, Context, Metatext* (Berkeley: U of California P, 1990.
Knowles, Roland. "Hamlet and Counter-Humanism," *Renaissance Quarterly*, Vol. 52, No. 4. 1999: 1046-1069. Print.
Krieger, Murray. "Dostoevsky's Idiot: The Curse of Saintliness," *Dostoevsky: A Collection of Critical Essays*, ed. René Wellek. Englewood Cliffs, NJ: Prentice-Hall, 1962: 39-52. Print.

Larsen, Neil. "Imperialism, Colonialism, Postcolonialism," in *A Companion to Postcolonial Studies*, ed. Henry Schwartz and Sangeeta Ray, Oxford: Blackwell, 2000: 38–39.
Lawrence, Karen. *The Odyssey of Style in Ulysses*. Princeton, New Jersey: Princeton UP, 1981.
Levin, Harry. *The Question of Hamlet*. New York: Oxford UP, 1959.
Levinas, Emmanuel. *Totality and Infinity: An Essay on Exteriority*. Translated by Alphonso Lingis. Pittsburgh: Duquesne UP, 1969.
Lukacs, Georg. *The Theory of the Novel: A Historico-Philosophical Essay on the Forms of Great Epic Literature*. Trans. Anna Bostock. London: Merlin, 1971.

Mahaffey, Vicki. *Reauthorizing Joyce*. Gainesville: UP of Florida, 1995.
Mann, Thomas. "Die Kunst des Romans," in *Altes und Neues*: *Kleine Prosa aus fünf Jahrzehnten*, Frankfurt: Fischer Verlag, 1961: 363-377.
McGee, Arthur. *The Elizabethan Hamlet*. New Haven: Yale UP, 1987.
Mendelson, Edward. "Encyclopedic Narrative: From Dante to Pynchon," *MLN*, Vol.91, No. 6, Comparative Literature, 1976: 1267-1275. Print.
Moran, Berna. *Türk Romanına Eleştirel Bir Bakış (2)*, Istanbul: İletişim Yayınları, 1990.

Moretti, Franco. *Atlas of the European Novel: 1800-1900*. London: Verso, 1998.

_________. 'A useless longing for myself': The Crisis of the European Bildungsroman, 1898-1914." *The Way of the World: The Bildungsroman in European Culture*. Trans. Albert Sbragia. London: Verso, 2000. 229-45.

_________. *The Modern Epic: The World-System from Goethe to García Márquez*, London: Verso, 1996.

_________. *The Way of the World: The* Bildungsroman *in European Culture*. London: Verso, 1987.

_________. *Signs Taken for Wonders*. 2nd rev. ed. London: Verso, 1988.

Morris, Pam. "Introduction." *The Bakhtin Reader*, ed. Pam Morris. London: Edward Arnold, 1994.

Nabokov, Vladimir. *Lectures on Literature*. Ed. Fredson Bowers. New York: Harcourt Brace Jovanovich/ Broccoli Clark, 1980.

_________. *Pale Fire*. New York: Random House, Inc., 1962.

_________. *The Real Life of Sebastian Knight*. New York: Vintage. International. 1992.

Neubauer, John. "Bakhtin versus Lukács: Inscriptions of Homelessness in Theories of the Novel," *Poetics Today*, Vol. 17, No. 4, Creativity and Exile: European/American Perspectives II, 1996: 531-546. Print.

Nietzsche, Friedrich. *The Gay Science: With a Prelude in Rhymes and an Appendix of Songs*, Ed. Walter Kaufmann. New York: Random House, 1974.

O'Brien, Alyssa J. "The Molly Blooms of 'Penelope': Reading Joyce Archivally," *Journal of Modern Literature*, 24.1 (Fall 2000): 7-24.

Osteen, Mark "Book review: Joyce, Bakhtin, and the Literary Tradition: Toward a Comparative Cultural Poetics" *MFS Modern Fiction Studies* - Volume 43, Number 2, 1997: 515-517. Print.

Parla, Jale. *Babalar ve Oğullar: Tanzimat Romanının Epistemolojik Temelleri*. Istanbul: İletişim Yayınları, 1990.

_________. *Don Kişot'tan Bugüne Roman*, Istanbul: İletişim Yayınları, 2000.

_________ . "From Allegory to Parable: Inscriptions of Anatolia in the Turkish novel," *New Perspectives on Turkey*, no. 36, 2007: 11-26. Print.

_________. "The Object of Comparison," *Comparative Literature Studies* 41.1, 2004: 116-125. Print.

Patterson, David. "Dostoevsky's Poetics of Spirit: Bakhtin and Berdyaev" *Dostoevsky Studies*, Volume 8, 1987: 220-231. Print.

Peake, Charles H. *James Joyce: The Citizen and the Artist*. Stanford: Stanford UP, 1977.

Perloff, Marjorie. Rev. of *Modern Epic: The World System from Goethe to Garcia Marquez,* by Franco Moretti, *ebr* 4 (1997). http://www.electronicbookreview.com/thread/internetnation/encyclopedic
Pierce, David. *James Joyce's Ireland.* New Haven and London: Yale UP, 1992.
Power, Arthur. *Conversations with James Joyce.* Ed. Clive Hart. Chicago: U of Chicago P, 1982.

Rabelais, Francois. *Gargantua and Pantagruel.* Trans. with an introduction by J.M. Cohen, London: Penquin, 1955.
Reed, Walter L. "The Problem of Cervantes in Bakhtin's Poetics," *Cervantes: Bulletin of the Cervantes Society of America* 7.2, 1987: 29-37. Print.
Rilke, Rainer Maria. *Prose and Poetry*, ed. Egon Schwarz. New York: Continuum, 1984.

Shklovsky, Victor. "The Making of *Don Quixote." Theory of Prose.* Trans. Benjamin
Somay, Bülent. "Hamlet Kuşağı, in *Defter 37*, 1999: 50-67. Print.
Spender, Stephen. *The Struggle of the Modern.* London: Hamilton, 1963.
Sterne, Laurence. *The Life and Opinions of Tristram Shandy.* London: Penguin Books, 1967.
Steppe, W., H.W. Gabler, *A Handlist to James Joyce's Ulysses.* New York: Garland, 1985.
*Studies in Historical Change.* Ed. and intro. Ralph Cohen. Charlottesville: UP of Virginia, 1992.
Süreya, Cemal. "Oteller Hanlar Hamamlar için Sürekli Şiir," *Sevda Sözleri,* Istanbul: Can Yayınları, 1984.

Tanpınar, Ahmet Hamdi. *The Time Regulation Institute.* Trans. Ender Gürol. Madison: Turko-Tatar Press, 2002.
Todorov, Tzvetan. *Mikhail Bakhtin: The Dialogical Principle*, Minneapolis: U of Minnesota P, 1998.

Urgan, Mina. *Shakespeare ve Hamlet.* Istanbul: Altın Kitaplar, 1984.
Uyurkulak, Murat. *Har.* Istanbul: Metis Yayınları, 2006.
Uyurkulak, Serhat. *Imagining the Nation: Two Failed National Imaginings in Ulysses and Huzur.* Unpublished M.A. Thesis, Boğaziçi University, 2003.

Wales, Katie. *The Language of James Joyce.* New York: St. Martin's Press, 1992.
Watt, Ian. *The Rise of the Novel: Studies in Defoe, Richardson and Fielding,* University of California Press, 2001.

Wiles, David. *Shakespeare's Clown: Actor and Text in the Elizabethan Playhouse* Cambridge: Cambridge University Press, 1987.

Willeford, William. *The Fool and His Scepter: A Study in Clowns and Jesters and Their Audience.* Northwestern UP, 1969.

Wilson, J. Dover. *What happens in 'Hamlet.'* Cambridge: Cambridge UP, 1935.

Winthrop-Young, Geoffrey. "How the Mule Got Its Tale: Moretti's Darwinian Bricolage," *Diacritics*, Vol. 29, No. 2, 1999: 18-40. Print.

Wollaeger, Mark A. "Reading Ulysses: Agency, Ideology, and the Novel." James Joyce's Ulysses: A Casebook. Ed. Derek Attridge. Oxford: Oxford UP, 2004: 129-54.

Woolf, Virginia. *Mrs Dalloway.* Penguin Books Ltd., 1992.